Writing and Reading
DIFFERENTLY

NANCY R. COMLEY

SHARON CROWLEY

ANDREW P. DEBICKI

GEOFFREY H. HARTMAN

BARBARA JOHNSON

DAVID KAUFER

VINCENT B. LEITCH

J. HILLIS MILLER

JASPER NEEL

PAUL NORTHAM

GAYATRI CHAKRAVORTY SPIVAK

GREGORY L. ULMER

GARY WALLER

Writing and Reading
DIFFERENTLY

DECONSTRUCTION
AND THE TEACHING OF
COMPOSITION AND LITERATURE

Edited and with an Introduction by

G. DOUGLAS ATKINS & MICHAEL L. JOHNSON

UNIVERSITY PRESS OF KANSAS

"The Two Rhetorics: George Eliot's Bestiary." © 1985 by J. Hillis Miller.

"Deconstruction and Pedagogy," by Vincent B. Leitch, is from *Theory in the Classroom*, edited by Cary Nelson, forthcoming in 1986 from the University of Illinois Press. © 1984 by the Board of Trustees of the University of Illinois.

"Reading the World: Literary Studies in the 1980s," by Gayatri Chakravorty Spivak, is reprinted from *College English*. Copyright © 1981 by the National Council of Teachers of English. Reprinted by permission of the publisher and the author.

"Understanding Criticism," by Geoffrey Hartman, is reprinted from *Criticism in the Wilderness: The Study of Literature Today* (New Haven, Conn.: Yale University Press, 1980) by permission of Yale University Press.

Published by the University Press of Kansas (Lawrence, Kansas 66045), which was organized by the Kansas Board of Regents and is operated and funded by Emporia State University, Fort Hays State University, Kansas State University, Pittsburg State University, the University of Kansas, and Wichita State University

Library of Congress Cataloging in Publication Data

Main entry under title:

Writing and reading differently.

Includes bibliographies and index.
1. English philology—Study and teaching—Addresses, essays, lectures. 2. Deconstruction—Addresses, essays, lectures. I. Atkins, G. Douglas (George Douglas), 1943–   . II. Johnson, Michael L.
QE66.W74   1985   807   85-13464
ISBN 0-7000-0282-8
ISBN 0-7000-0283-6 (pbk.)

Printed in the United States of America

Contents

Preface

G. Douglas Atkins

This is a book about relations: between writing and reading, literature and composition, and the teaching of the one and the other. In a number of areas, including literary theory, philosophy, and religion, deconstruction has already proven productive if not exemplary in revealing that relations exist where only differences were seen before. But until now the powerful resources of deconstruction have not been trained, in any sustained fashion, on pedagogy and some of the most pressing questions confronting those of us engaged in the teaching of composition and literature. This volume signals our belief that deconstruction points to the relations, rather than simply the differences, between reading and writing and that it has immense practical value in the classroom.

The essays assembled here, most of them written expressly for this volume, do not pretend to cover all aspects of "writing and reading differently." Nor do they pretend to resolve all issues concerning the so-called literacy crisis, the "crisis in the humanities," or the many and complex problems involved in the attempt to relate (the teaching of) composition and (the teaching of) literature. What these essays do is to open questions and suggest, explore, and develop certain alternatives to more or less traditional ways of considering reading and writing. The essays follow no "party line" on deconstruction; indeed, several different "approaches" to deconstruction appear in these pages, attesting to the variety that currently marches under its banner.

The book itself results from a collaboration. It grew out of a graduate course that Michael L. Johnson and I "team-taught" in the fall of 1982, when he was director of Freshman-Sophomore English and I was coordinator of Graduate Studies in English (as well as a devotee of deconstruction hoping to open eighteenth-century studies to its insights and strategies). I admit that I had not always been sympathetic to either composition theory or the need to deconstruct its marginal status in the curriculum and in the profession at large. The course treated the relations between contemporary criticism and composition theory, and teaching it with Mike Johnson, I learned a great deal, about many things. The course was a symbolic and political act (not unlike this volume), one that, not surprisingly, generated suspicion among some of our colleagues. But it worked—thanks to the interest and assiduity of the students involved, the sheer attraction of the subject, and the professional and personal respect, trust, and friendship that developed between the teachers. Relations are, as I remarked above, what this volume is all about—and I am grateful for the relationship that led to this book and for the truly collaborative effort that it represents.

Both of us wish to thank our contributors: for their essays above all, but also for their patience and cooperation. We also wish to acknowledge the great debt owed to the superb word-processing skills, patience, and cooperation of Sandee Kennedy. She was ably and cheerfully assisted by Pam Lerow. They worked together to enter several hundred pages on the ATMS in an unbelievably short time. We thank, too, Ann Shaw for meticulously preparing the index. Finally, we express our gratitude to the staff of the University Press of Kansas, which was supportive from the day we broached the idea.

Writing and Reading
DIFFERENTLY

ἣ δ' οὔτ ἀρνεῖται στυγερὸν γάμον οὔτε τελευτὴν
ποιῆσαι δύναται . . .
(And she neither refuses the hateful marriage nor can
Make an end. . . .)

—Homer, *The Odyssey*, I: 249–50

No, this is not a disentanglement from, but a progressive *knotting into*.
. . .

—Thomas Pynchon, *Gravity's Rainbow*

Each word would close an epitaph,
but no last word is last to laugh;
its self-division hosts a third,
the trace forever first deferred.

From that chiasmic difference
ghosts writing, not a presence heard:
reference of self-reference,
an echo in a cenotaph.

Placed in abysmal discontent,
Penelope, to play the rent,
aberrantly undoes the text,
stories performance (not mimesis
but wavering allegoresis)
always already till the next. . . .

—Michael L. Johnson, ''Deconstruction''

Introduction

G. Douglas Atkins and Michael L. Johnson

> Parce que nous commençons à écrire, à écrire autrement, nous devons relire autrement.
> (Because we are beginning to write, to write differently, we must reread differently.)
>
> —Jacques Derrida, *De la grammatologie*

The nervous pluralism that presently characterizes critical and rhetorical theory has in large part stemmed from and been sustained by controversies surrounding deconstruction. Those controversies, however disagreeable, impertinent, or dismissible they may seem to some, have served to invigorate the intellectual life of the humanities, especially that of departments of English, as nothing has since New Criticism in the 1930s and 1940s and transformational grammar in the 1960s. Nonetheless, probably because of those controversies—and the ignorance, misunderstanding, and spleen associated with them—the full implications of deconstruction for the teaching of writing and reading are just now being explored.[1] While we do not pretend to be able to "resolve" those controversies simply by the publication of this collection of essays, we are interested in exploring the pedagogical implications of deconstruction for teachers of composition and literature.

As a term, *deconstruction* derives from the work of the contemporary French philosopher Jacques Derrida (where it denominates more a radical philosophical strategy than a coherent and unified position or "school" of thought) as interpreted by critics he has influenced such as

1

J. Hillis Miller, Geoffrey Hartman, Barbara Johnson, and Gayatri Chakravorty Spivak, all of whom are contributors to this collection. These theorists and practitioners define deconstruction in a variety of ways. All their definitions implicitly or explicitly agree that deconstruction refutes the conventional idea of the straightforward referentiality of language as it accepts the complex and finally equivocal play of signifiers that constitutes language. Among the most helpful and useful definitions are that of Hillis Miller, who asserts, against the charge that deconstruction is "nihilism or the denial of meaning in literary texts," that it is "an attempt to interpret as exactly as possible the oscillations in meaning produced by the irreducibly figurative nature of language,"[2] and that of Barbara Johnson, who characterizes it as "the careful teasing out of warring forces of signification within the text."[3] These definitions are consonant with Jonathan Culler's: "To deconstruct a discourse is to show how it undermines the philosophy it asserts, or the hierarchical oppositions on which it relies, by identifying in the text the rhetorical operations that produce the supposed ground of argument, the key concept or premise." Thus, "deconstruction appeals to no higher logical principle or superior reason but uses the very principle it deconstructs," so that "the practitioner of deconstruction works within the terms of the system but in order to breach it."[4] Impossible to freeze conceptually, deconstruction is above all an enacted strategy, an interpretive praxis that must be "seen in action," as one may in the essays assembled here, before it can be understood and adopted.[5]

Writing and reading differently. What would it mean to write and read differently? What difference would it make? Any such difference would entail refiguring the relationships between reading and writing, reader and writer, literature and composition—differences traditionally regarded (and arrested) as oppositions. What difference would it make to consider writing and reading, not in opposition, but in a relationship involving *différance*?[6] To begin to understand what might be involved in the question, we need to look, albeit briefly, at the term *difference*. Since the pioneering structuralism of Ferdinand de Saussure, difference has figured prominently in linguistic, critical, and theoretical discourse. It is a crucial concern of the various modes of poststructuralism and, especially, deconstruction. Accepting Saussure's demonstration that in language there are no positive terms, only differences, Derrida has shown how meaning derives not so much from the differences *between* terms as from the differences *within* each term. Coining the word *différance* (the *a* indicating both "difference" and "deferral," spatial as well as temporal movement), he argues that "without a retention in the minimal unit of temporal experience, without a trace retaining the other as other in the same, no difference would do its work and no meaning would appear. It is not the question of a constituted difference here, but rather, before all determination of the content, of the *pure* movement which produces difference. *The (pure) trace is differance.*"[7] What is at stake here is, as Barbara Johnson has insightfully written, "nothing less than a revolution in the very logic of meaning. . . . Instead of 'A is opposed to B' we have 'B is both added to and replaces A.' A and B are no longer opposed, nor are they equivalent. Indeed, they are no longer even equivalent to themselves. They are their own differance from themselves."[8] At work in reading and writing, as in other polarities, *différance* effects a complex and interanimating relationship, not an opposition or a simple difference—or an identity, either. Each containing within itself a trace of the other, reading and writing now emerge as supplements of each other (*supplément*, signifying both "addition" and "substitution" or "replacement"). The essays assembled here work out, in their respective ways, aspects of this relationship between writing and reading, affirmatively seeking to make a difference.

Deconstruction may, then, prove useful in assisting students not only as readers but also as writers and in illuminating for them the interrelationships of reading and writing. Behind our efforts in assembling this collection—and behind the efforts of its contributors—operates the desire to bring together composition and literature, writing and reading, and the teaching of them, thereby "bridging the gap" between them and displacing the either/or thinking that has too long dominated the pedagogy, especially of English, in secondary and postsecondary education. Some attempts at such bridging are now appearing, and in the remaining pages of this Introduction we want to suggest some current contexts for situating the essays that follow.

Among others, Mariolina Salvatori has recently argued against "an artificial separation between the activities of reading and those of writing," a separation that is more a product of professional territorial imperatives than of any careful pedagogical rationale. Salvatori contends that the two activities must be understood and taught as interrelated processes. Furthermore, her own research indicates that even such understanding of their interrelatedness as now exists should be interpreted deconstructively because that research "suggests that the improvement in writers' ability to manipulate syntactic structures—their maturity as writers—is the result, rather than the cause, of their increased ability to engage in, and to be reflexive about, the reading of

3

highly complex texts.'' The development of this latter ability may have profound implications for the development of the former, especially in regard to invention:

> The reading process . . . is an extremely complicated activity in which the mind is at one and the same time relaxed and alert, expanding meanings as it selects and modifies them, confronting the blanks and filling them with constantly modifiable projections produced by inter-textual and intra-textual connections. Because of the nature of the reading process, each reading remains as ''indeterminate'' as the text that it is a response to. But this is precisely the kind of activity—demanding, challenging, constantly structuring them as they structure it—that our students are either reluctant or have not been trained to see as reading. Specifically, it is with the indeterminacy of the text that they have their major difficulties. In their responses to a literary text most students do perform that one action, consistency building, that is central to the reading activity, and they identify what they consider the main idea. They fail, however, to realize that the identification of one idea among many others is only one step toward a more complete and dynamic reading. They perform one synthesis rather than various syntheses and tend to settle too soon, too quickly, for a kind of incomplete, ''blocked'' reading. Interestingly, the same kind of ''blocked'' pattern has a tendency to characterize their writing as well; they lift various segments out of the text and then combine them through arbitrary sequential connections (usually coordinate conjunctions)—a composing mode that is marked by a consistent restriction of options to explore and develop ideas. . . . It is then plausible to suggest that by enabling students to tolerate and confront ambiguities and uncertainties in the reading process, we can help them eventually to learn to deal with the uncertainties and ambiguities that they themselves generate in the process of writing their own texts.[9]

With its emphasis on a radically heuristic interpretive attitude, a playful grappling with figurality, and a generative rhetoric of doubleness and equivocation (whereby, in Derridean terms, authorial ''declaration'' gives rise to textual ''description''), deconstruction may prove fruitful in helping students to learn to ''deal with'' (etymologically, ''divide'') the rhetorical potentialities of the texts they read and write. A deconstructively based pedagogy might at least help to do away with that insipid, padded, and inauthentic language that Ken Macrorie has epitomized in the term *Engfish*, which is nothing if not writing ''blocked'' by the closure of simplistic and unexplored consistency, usually motivated by a desire to please a teacher who is perceived as expecting the same.

4

Salvatori argues cogently for the need to overcome the "artificial separation" that troubles the relationship between the teaching of writing and the teaching of reading, a need that seems self-evident to deconstruction. That important argument is echoed by Richard A. Lanham, who, in his recent and important book *Literacy and the Survival of Humanism*, directly addresses the issue of the relationship between the teaching of composition and the teaching of literature. In so doing, he eloquently describes the situation in which deconstruction intervenes:

> The history of twentieth-century English studies . . . chronicles the search for a literary theory which would legitimate English studies as an independent discipline. The resulting theory argued that literature should constitute an independent inquiry because its pseudo-statements present an independent order of truth. This legitimating departmental premise has surfaced in several guises since its synthesis from Renaissance golden poetics and its rebirth in Coleridgian thinking.
>
> If this theory is true, or assumed to be, no English department can bear an intrinsic relation to composition teaching. However the latter may go about its business, it deals with communication in the "real" world—"out there." It deals with nonprivileged texts, with "prose" rather than "poetry." To define literature as privileged by implication defines composition in an opposite way. Composition becomes the study of communication in a world that is posited as the very opposite of literature's "imaginative reality". . . .
>
> In such a polarized orchestration English departments will occupy themselves with the visionary moral order that literature is thought to present. The Composition Section will teach "effective communication" tailored to context. This division of labor represents pretty much where we are now—*or at least where we think we are*. For if this conception of literature is incomplete and misguided, then the state of affairs it implies can never fully come about. Literature can never absent itself from the "real" world nor composition do without literature and literary criticism.[10]

Even if we do not endorse all of Lanham's points and emphases, we believe that he has, on the whole, accurately described the present situation.

In his discussion of the theoretical reasons for bringing together the teaching of literature and the teaching of composition, Lanham explores an alternative:

> The definition of literature which legitimates English studies as an independent discipline—its departmental license—must be discarded if composition is to share more than a Xerox machine with literary

study. Strong reasons, even aside from the composition problem, suggest that this required theoretical change might be good for English studies. They suggest, too, a new kind of departmental franchise.

To conceive of literary texts as constituting a separate reality is also to conceive of a positivistic social reality just "out there" and a self just "in here," halfway between the ears. Both concepts have been discarded by almost every other discipline that deals with human behavior. . . . Literary critics who still think this way thus find themselves at war with the rest of the curriculum: with the sociologist who examines role-theory; with the cultural anthropologist who finds "ordinary" communication astoundingly full of literary ingredients; with the perception psychologist who stresses the active, participating, integrative role of perception . . . ; and, above all, with those who study the social behavior of animals and who are finding the sources of literature's mythic energy not in a mystic visionary imagination but in the deeply layered, fundamentally nonintelligent depths of the limbic system. If the composition problem were to force a paradigm change in English studies, one that enabled it to join this new consensus, such a change alone would make the composition crisis worth facing.[11]

We have quoted Lanham at such length not only because of the general relevance of his comments to our concern with integrating the teaching of composition and the teaching of literature but also because of their implicit consonance with the particular ways in which deconstruction is applicable in making that integration possible.

To illustrate that consonance, we need only juxtapose deconstruction with Lanham's "Post-Darwinian" model of motive, a model articulated through ideas concerning play, game, competition, and purpose drawn from several disciplines. Humanism, according to him, must be conceived stylistically, in the sophisticated and dynamic manner—to follow his Renaissance analogy—of Castiglione and not in the more naïve and static manner of Sir Thomas More. It follows from such a conception that "social reality . . . possesses no independent ontological security guaranteed by God," that it is in fact a drama, whose means are rhetorical and through which the self is constructed. Rhetoric, the self-conscious use of language, is, like Derrida's écriture, not separate from "reality" but constitutive of it, as Lanham demonstrates in what amounts to a deconstruction—or at least a revisionist reading—of Aristotle. Thus, what Lanham calls the "Clarity-Brevity-Sincerity, or C-B-S, theory of composition" is an "Edenic" one that generally "will not work," no matter how many "epicycles" are added to it.[12] That theory, incidentally, derives from the same notion of the transparency of language that, from an explicitly deconstructive point of view, Sharon

6

Crowley criticizes. Attributing the "poverty of current-traditional rhetoric" to the dominance in rhetorical theory of the "metaphysics of presence," which "postulates a reality, a truth, which exists outside the perceiving consciousness of man and which is unmoved, essentially unchanged, by his perception of it," she claims that too frequently "students are taught to use writing in good metaphysical style: don't let the written words get between the idea and the reader; words should be transparent, like glass. The result? Good, utilitarian, dull prose."[13]

Having displaced the C-B-S theory, along with Crowley's "good metaphysical style," Lanham sketches a radically different one. Starting with some meditations from Kenneth Burke concerning the nature of the truth embodied in the language of John Lyly's *Euphues*, he wonders if Sir Philip Sidney, like Lyly, was not "trying to glimpse a world where verbal ornament is as essential as essence, as serious as serious purpose, and as needful for man." He then spins out a "stylistic matrix" for the kind of "self-conscious rhetoric" involved in what he calls the "opaque style."[14] In this matrix, verbal ornament is not ancillary to otherwise transparent language (just as writing is not merely ancillary to speech, a metaphysical idea whose deconstruction Derrida elaborates)[15] but defines verbal language in general. Lanham finds suggestive analogues for this insight in painting (he cites the well-known anecdote in which Matisse, "when asked why his picture of a woman did not look like a woman, replied that it was not a woman but a picture") and poetry (he cites Wallace Stevens's dictum that "poetry is the subject of the poem"). And he argues that under its aegis, "style, instead of creating the decorative surface of reality, may be reality's major constituent element," an element that—in a phrase that recalls Miller's earlier one and that Lanham uses explicitly in reference to critical and rhetorical terminology—is conditioned by an "endemic metaphoricality."[16]

According to Lanham, "Either we notice an opaque style *as a style* (i.e., we look *at* it) or we do not (i.e., we look *through* it to a fictive reality beyond)," the former kind of attention involving "the sudden transformation of words when we look at them self-consciously." Such "*At/ Through*" styles, "whenever they return in force, signify not decadence but its opposite. They show a life and vigor in the oscillation that constitutes reality." And they "work to return us to play." Thus, treating language in terms of the rhetoric of opaque styles may contribute to a transcendence of the "worship of clarity" (which Lanham labels "a leftover positivist prejudice") and to the development of an effective alternative to the C-B-S theory: "A mature and sensible theory of clarity, when it comes, will, I think, chart a process which oscillates between looking *at* the surface and looking *through* it." Such a theory, by which the quality of prose (including its "clarity") is directly proportional to the frequency of this oscillation, *supplements* (both "adds to" and "replaces" or "substitutes for") the C-B-S theory because the former is concerned with "a symbiotic exchange in which a prose surface both creates the reality beneath and in turn is affected by it." One of the great advantages of this supplementary theory of clarity is that it implies spectra of attentional patterns (from dominant *Through* vision to dominant *At* vision, "Pure 'Life'" to "Pure 'Literature,'" etc.) and thus allows an "alternative conception of literature and of composition" in which "*the problematic relationship between the two simply disappears*. They represent different points on the same series of spectra. There is no difference *in kind* between them. Teaching literature and teaching composition form different parts of the same activity."[17]

Lanham's privileging of rhetoric, his questioning of conventional concepts of referentiality, his concern with the limits of the writer's control of the text—all suggest his affinity with deconstruction, though he is not regarded as a deconstructionist. Nonetheless, his conclusions seem to derive from considerations not radically different from those of Hillis Miller: "Learning to write well cannot be separated from learning to read well. . . . I view the development of integrated programs in reading well and writing well as the major challenge to our profession at the present time." Such an integration should bring together, Miller adds, "expository writing and the study of literature."[18]

Miller is hopeful about the possibility of this integration and is encouraged that the profession includes many teachers "for whom the paradigm shift from a mimetic to a performative view of language has occurred." Though he suspects that "the theory and practice of the teaching of expository writing—as sophisticated as they are—are still inhabited and inhibited to some degree by the mirage of straightforward referential language," he notes also that "at many of the colleges and universities" he has visited, the pedagogical and curricular implications of deconstruction are being explored and that he has found "young teachers who have been deeply influenced by this form of criticism."[19] Thus, he argues, "even those rarefied debates about literary theory [especially deconstruction] have practical implications for the teaching not just of reading but of writing. Such debates have their correlates in the day-to-day practices of writing and the teaching of writing." Thus he anticipates and helps to rationalize our collection here by suggesting that "much might be gained by trying to bring these correlations into the open."[20]

For Miller, those correlations—the kind brought "into the open" by the essays in this collection—have to do largely with the attitude toward and understanding of the processes of reading and writing that deconstruction affords. Reading, as Miller interprets it, "is itself a kind of writing, or writing is a trope for the act of reading. Every act of writing is an act of reading, an interpretation of some part of the totality of what is." But reading and writing are also complementarily antithetical processes (though not simply inversions of each other), as Miller notes in making his case more directly relevant to pedagogy:

> Reading is not rhetoric as putting together, composition, but rhetoric as taking apart, the study of tropes, decomposition. It is easy to see, however, that no skillful composition is possible without that prior act of decomposition practiced through reading models of composition by others. I learn to make a chair by studying the way another man has made a chair, and this probably means taking his handiwork apart to see in detail how he did it. There is no learning to write well without a concomitant learning to read well. There is no help for it. Those involved in programs in writing either must make sure that reading is being well taught by their colleagues in literature or must teach reading themselves. Of what would good teaching of reading consist?
>
> Among the most powerful and challenging techniques of reading today is the one called "deconstruction." . . . [D]econstruction is a currently fashionable or notorious name for good reading as such. All good readers are and always have been deconstructionists.

Miller is somewhat uncertain as to exactly what "a 'deconstructive' textbook of freshman writing would be like," but he openly assails textbooks to which New Criticism and the so-called current-traditional paradigm of composition have given rise and leaves no doubt that deconstruction has important lessons to teach:

> Insofar as the teaching of composition suggests that the student should write a literal version first and perhaps add metaphors later; insofar as it still assumes that figures are adventitious adornment; insofar as it assumes that the writer has the ideas before he or she writes them down and that revision is a matter of achieving closer and closer approximation to some preexistent model, whether in the mind of the writer or in some preliminary outline; insofar as it assumes that a good piece of writing should be or can be univocal, wholly unified, it still has much to learn from that form of the rhetoric of reading called at the moment, for better or worse, deconstruction.[21]

For Miller, the teaching of reading and writing deconstructively entails a process-oriented pedagogy, one that "supplements" the kind being elaborated through the more positivistic and empirically based theories of researchers such as Linda Flower, John R. Hayes, and Sandra Perl.[22]

Miller claims a great deal for the pedagogical possibilities of deconstruction; yet what he claims seems improbable if we are to judge by currently popular misconceptions about deconstruction, to some of which we alluded earlier. But these misconceptions to a great extent have been demonstrated to be *mis*conceptions. Miller and others have effectively refuted the charge that deconstruction is nihilistic. If that charge is now less frequently heard, there are still others to the effect that deconstruction is inherently perverse, dadaistic, and even terroristic. And anxieties concerning its difficulty need to be addressed. Deconstruction *is* difficult. No mistake about that. But despite the assertions of its enemies, who would oversimplify and dismiss it, or even of its allies, who occasionally indemnify it with additional complexities, the assumption of the essays collected here is that the strategic principles of deconstruction are accessible, that one need not be grounded in Continental philosophy in order to comprehend them.[23] What *is* necessary is explicitly discussed, and it is not as formidable as might be expected.

By means of this collection, we hope to show that—contrary to charges of its elitist, esoteric, or ethereal impracticality—deconstruction has immense practical value for teachers of English as well as of other languages. In proclaiming the usefulness of deconstruction, we (and the authors of the essays assembled here) may seem to run the risk of dulling and weakening what deconstructionists sometimes regard almost as a finely honed intellectual and even political weapon. Perhaps we do run such a risk. However, we question the assumption that a univocal and "proper" deconstruction exists. Deconstruction itself problematizes such an assumption, and Derrida has long been committed to denying univocity and various forms of the "proper." Certainly one can make valid distinctions about what deconstruction does and does not do; but by now there are many aspects to the strategy of deconstruction, as Barbara Johnson, for example, indicates in her essay in this collection. Other aspects surely will emerge as the implications of deconstruction are considered and reconsidered and as its effects are extended. Just as there are many Romanticisms, there are, in effect, many deconstructions. If deconstruction could be neatly defined and if the boundaries of its activities could be clearly demarcated, it would hardly be different from the tradition it challenges. Whatever else deconstruction is, it is certainly iconoclastic, shattering even the idol it is sometimes in danger of becoming and resisting or breaking through attempts to circumscribe and contain it. We see no reason why it should not be exploited (etymologically, "unfolded") for the teaching of writing and reading.

Furthermore, as Vincent B. Leitch argues in his essay included below, deconstruction is and has all along been concerned with pedagogy. Derrida himself has insisted repeatedly that deconstruction *is* teaching as well as an interventionist strategy. Its practical value inheres in its capacity to effect change—in institutions, in disciplines, in individuals. Moreover, if one works with deconstruction, within the classroom or without—using it, say, in the teaching of composition and literature— that act does not in itself constitute any diminution of its force. In fact, one might argue that any desire to keep deconstruction from being so used is precisely another form of the idealism that deconstruction calls into question. It seems to us that deconstruction is principally characterized by its orientation toward pedagogical use, practice, praxis.

As a practical strategy, deconstruction inevitably involves a certain *attitude*, a word that bears the etymological inscription of "action" and that, like *strategy*, is relatively free of the logocentric baggage of words such as *method*, *technique*, and *approach*. As an attitude, one that is simultaneously both skeptical and tolerant, both questioning and affirmative, it motivates and participates in our strategy in assembling these essays. We have divided the twelve essays into three groups: those in Part 1 consider the general pedagogical implications of deconstruction; those in Part 2, its implications for the teaching of composition; and those in Part 3, its implications for the teaching of literature. But these divisions—and the differences on which they are based—are fluid and shifting; thus, to take the most obvious and important example, the essays in Part 2 are concerned also with literature, and those in Part 3 also with composition. This situation accords with our premise that no absolute distinction can be made between composition and literature, writing and reading.

NOTES

1. These controversies seem generally to have afflicted teachers of literature more than teachers of composition—just one aspect of the split between their two camps, one that is, however, easy to exaggerate and in need of further assessment. Nonetheless, it is surely true that the latter have responded to recent innovations in literary theory—deconstruction in particular—more mildly, even more acceptingly and productively in some instances, than have the former. This situation may be partially explained by the fact that composition theory has blossomed only within the last decade or so and therefore has been more open to innovations, of many kinds from many disciplines, than has literary study, which was experiencing a "hardening of the categories" long before that. The difference, in any case, is not simply indifference to deconstruction on the part of, say, members of the National Council of Teachers of English as opposed to members of the Modern Language Association. Edward M. White

has some arguably apposite thoughts on the subject: "I want to suggest . . . that the general hospitality writing teachers and researchers have shown toward post-structural literary theory is the result of a basic correspondence between these theories and the practice of the best writing teachers. . . . It thus strikes me as no accident that the proponents of writing as process began articulating their views and pursuing their valuable research at about the same time that post-structural literary critics began arguing that reading was a process, a creative (rather than passive) interaction between reader and text. . . . [Deconstructionists] argue that, at best, the text offers only a guide to the reader, as if it were a musical score which must be performed or (to use the favorite term of these theorists) 'played' in order to become real. . . . [T]his theory of reading brings reading and writing together as parallel acts, both of them consisting of the making of meaning: the writer seeks to make meaning out of experience, while the reader seeks to make meaning out of a text" ("Post-Structural Literary Criticism and the Response to Student Writing," *College Composition and Communication* 35 [1984]: 187, 189, 190, 191).

2. J. Hillis Miller, "The Function of Rhetorical Study at the Present Time," in *The State of the Discipline*, a special issue of the *ADE Bulletin*, no. 62 (Sept.–Nov. 1979): 13.

3. Barbara Johnson, *The Critical Difference: Essays in the Contemporary Rhetoric of Reading* (Baltimore, Md.: Johns Hopkins University Press, 1980), p. 5.

4. Jonathan Culler, *On Deconstruction: Theory and Criticism after Structuralism* (Ithaca, N.Y.: Cornell University Press, 1982), pp. 86, 87, 96. It probably should be noted that although his definition here seems to be consonant with Miller's, Culler does distinguish his position from Miller's; see Culler, pp. 22–24, 27–29, 219, 249, 251, 269–70.

5. For other examples of deconstruction "in action" see G. Douglas Atkins, *Reading Deconstruction/Deconstructive Reading* (Lexington: University Press of Kentucky, 1983).

6. On the relationship of writer and reader see, for example, Paul de Man, *Allegories of Reading: Figural Language in Rousseau, Nietzsche, Rilke, and Proust* (New Haven, Conn.: Yale University Press, 1979), p. 17.

7. Jacques Derrida, *Of Grammatology*, trans. Gayatri Chakravorty Spivak (Baltimore, Md.: Johns Hopkins University Press, 1976), p. 62.

8. Barbara Johnson, Translator's Introduction, *Dissemination*, by Jacques Derrida (Chicago: University of Chicago Press, 1981), p. xiii.

9. Mariolina Salvatori, "Reading and Writing a Text: Correlations between Reading and Writing Patterns," *College English* 45 (1983): 657, 659, 661–62. The interrelationships of reading and writing, which are far from being well understood and are of paramount concern to deconstruction, recently have become a subject of interest to theorists and researchers of various persuasions. Roger W. Shuy, for example, argues that "the productive work of literacy, writing, should be concurrent with the receptive work of reading. . . . To write is to read" ("Finding a Sense of Wonder in Language and Literacy," *College Reading: Responses to the CUNY Reading Seminars*, a special issue of *Resource*, Fall 1983, pp. 30, 33). Nancy R. Comley and Robert Scholes, who wish "to deconstruct the system of oppositions that supports the split between literature and composition," contend that "the writer is always reading and the reader is always writing" ("Literature, Composition, and the Structure of English," in *Composition and Literature: Bridging the Gap*, ed. Winifred Bryan Horner [Chicago:

University of Chicago Press, 1983], pp. 101, 99). And Walter J. Ong, though no friend of deconstruction, writes that "there is no way to write unless you read, and read a lot" ("Literacy and Orality in Our Times," in Horner, ed., *Composition*, p. 32).

10. Richard A. Lanham, *Literacy and the Survival of Humanism* (New Haven, Conn.: Yale University Press, 1983), pp. 110–11.

11. Ibid., pp. 113–14.

12. Ibid., pp. 15, 10, 20.

13. Sharon Crowley, "Of Gorgias and Grammatology," *College Composition and Communication* 30 (1979): 279, 284. The alternative pedagogy that Crowley proposes she derives from a less "official" and historically less continuous philosophical tradition stretching from Gorgias of Leontini through Nietzsche to Derrida and beyond. For a cognate (if somewhat questionable) proposal for such a pedagogy see William A. Covino, "Making a Difference in the Composition Class: A Philosophy of Invention," *Freshman English News* 10, no. 1 (1981): 1–4, 13.

14. Lanham, *Literacy*, p. 58.

15. See Derrida, *Of Grammatology*, pp. 97–316, esp. pp. 269–316.

16. Lanham, *Literacy*, pp. 62, 67, 77, 78. Lanham also observes that because of the dialectic of "looking *at* a style or *through* it," the problematic referentiality of written language, "a single consistent position, *any* single consistent position, leads to inconsistencies" (p. 73).

17. Ibid., pp. 58, 83, 85, 95, 97, 111, 112. It is worthwhile to note that Lanham's elevation of the opaque-style theory over the C-B-S theory, with its simplistic notion of referentiality, parallels somewhat chiastically Derrida's argument that the "lived reduction of the opacity of the signifier" is "the origin of what is called presence" (*Of Grammatology*, p. 166), a parallelism that certainly could be pursued further but one that is beyond our scope here.

18. Miller, "Function of Rhetorical Study," pp. 12, 13. Though Miller is concerned specifically with writing as expository writing, much of what he says, like much of what is said in this Introduction and in the essays by our contributors, applies as well to what is unfortunately called (in its many forms) creative writing.

19. Ibid., p. 13. For a different approach to the use of Derrida, one that distinguishes between deconstruction and grammatology, see Gregory L. Ulmer, *Applied Grammatology: Post(e)-Pedagogy from Jacques Derrida to Joseph Beuys* (Baltimore, Md.: Johns Hopkins University Press, 1985). Ulmer, incidentally, stresses the contribution of grammatology to invention, a topic that is treated somewhat differently in the essays assembled here.

20. J. Hillis Miller, "Composition and Decomposition," in Horner, ed., *Composition*, p. 40.

21. Miller, "Composition and Decomposition," pp. 41, 42, 43, 55, 56.

22. Empirically based research itself sometimes involves methods that certainly ought to be supplemented (supplanted). See, for example, J. D. Williams, "Covert Language Behavior during Writing," *Research in the Teaching of English* 17 (1983): 301–12. Williams recounts (to the point of parody) experiments in which the faces and throats of student writers are wired up with a dozen electrodes connected to electromyographs connected to a computer. The conclusion drawn from the data obtained by such Frankensteinian gadgetry is merely an obvious one: that better writers think more than their counterparts during pauses in the writing process.

23. An extended consideration of the validity of this assumption may be found in Suzanne Gearhart, "Philosophy *before* Literature: Deconstruction, Historicity, and the Work of Paul de Man," *Diacritics* 13 (Winter 1983): 63–81.

1

DECONSTRUCTION AND TEACHING

Deconstruction and Pedagogy

Vincent B. Leitch

Within the domain of present-day deconstructionist studies, reflections on pedagogy typically focus on the historical and contemporary roles of power, authority, and language. Teaching happens in the school and in the university—in a cultural institution situated amidst a network of financial, political, and intellectual interests and concerns. That the university *serves* culture and society becomes, in deconstructive thinking, the grounds for a critique and positive transformation of educational institutions and pedagogical practices.

TAKING POSITIONS ON INSTITUTIONAL STRUCTURES

Let us first consider Jacques Derrida's writings on the scene of pedagogy, particularly in relation to his work with the Group for Research on Philosophic Teaching (GREPH), an organization that was established in Paris in 1974 and was spearheaded by Derrida. GREPH has sought, among other things, to resist the preemptive intrusions that the state has made over the past decade into the teaching of philosophy. Briefly, GREPH saw that a proposed government "reform," introduced in the early 1970s, would have shrunk the teaching of philosophy in the French secondary schools, cut drastically the number of future teaching positions, and reduced the ranks of philosophy majors in the universities. In short, GREPH foresaw the diminution and eventual death of philosophy as an academic discipline. Almost immediately, large numbers of people—six hundred professors and students and twenty work groups—began to inquire into the economic and political links between various social and pedagogical institutions—that is, into the nature and history of modern education. Derrida himself wrote half a dozen critical essays during the 1970s on the scene of pedagogy—all stemming from his work with GREPH.

In an essay of 1975 Derrida states that "deconstruction . . . has, then, always had a bearing in principle on the apparatus and the function of teaching in general."[1] In Derrida's view, deconstruction is, and has been, "inherently" related to and concerned with pedagogical theory and practice—despite what some narrow-minded American "readers" of Derrida may believe. Derrida goes on in the essay to suggest three general strategies for concerned academics: (1) don't abandon the "old" university, (2) create a critique of it, and (3) develop a positive and extensive transformation of it (pp. 66–67). Speaking generally, Derrida is less interested in protecting the university from the play of powers than in taking positions in regard to such power plays. In matters pedagogical, neutrality is unacceptable and activism is essential (p. 74). Basically, Derrida recommends that every constituted hierarchy and criterion, of any sort, be investigated as a prelude to any transformation.[2]

The approach of GREPH is characteristic of deconstructive inquiry: it starts with a local issue and quickly expands its critical investigation into the system of hierarchical relations underlying the institutions that are involved in the issue. Thus, in the GREPH statutes of 1975, we read: "We don't think that reflection on the teaching of philosophy can be separated from the analysis of the historical and political conditions and functions of the system of teaching in general."[3] And in the document that takes a position against the government "reform," GREPH seeks "a veritable recasting of the teaching of philosophy—and of school in general. . . ."[4]

What distinguishes Derrida's work with GREPH is not only a broadened set of concerns but also a special tone. Where we would expect, finally, apocalyptic and angry accusations and prognostications, we discover here and there an intractable gaiety—reminiscent of a certain radical strand in Nietzsche. This tone follows from several deconstructive fundamentals: (1) every field is a site of contending, differential forces; (2) every such site is historically constituted as a set of hierarchical values and apparatuses—an institutionalized axiomatics; (3) there is no outside to such a systematics—only a transformation from within; and (4) apocalypse and revolution, sometimes tempting and irresistible, tend to reconstitute more firmly the preexisting forms and practices. To catch a glimpse of Derrida's distinctive tone, we can turn to his opening remarks to the Estates General of Philosophy, a convention of twelve hundred people who met at the Sorbonne in June 1979 in order to combat the deteriorating situation of the teaching of philosophy in France. Noting a certain tranquilizing complicity between academia and officialdom, Derrida urges:

> It is this complementarity, this configuration—everywhere that it appears—that we must, it seems to me, combat. Combat simultaneously, and joyously, without accusation, without trial, without nostalgia, with an intractable gaiety. Without nostalgia for more discreet forms, sometimes (sometimes only) more distinguished, less noisy, which *in large part* will yesterday have prepared what we inherit today.[5]

The necessity for struggle, for vigilance, for noisy assertion—as opposed to discretion and nostalgia—override accusations and recriminations in favor of intractable gaiety in joyous combat. It's almost as though Derrida appreciated a threat, which fosters inquiry and transformation, not simply on a local but on a systemic level.

By the time Derrida in 1980 delivered "The Conflict of Faculties," an address at Columbia University in honor of the founding of the Graduate School, he could describe the project of deconstruction as avowedly activist: "what is somewhat hastily called deconstruction is not, if it is of any consequence, a specialized set of discursive procedures, still less the rules of a new hermeneutic method, working on texts or utterances in the shelter of a given and stable institution. It is also, at the very least, a way of taking a position, in the work of analysis, concerning the political and institutional structures that make possible and govern our practice, our competencies, our performances."[6] Between the founding of GREPH in 1974 and the establishment of the new International College of Philosophy in 1984, which Derrida directs[7]— that is, following the publication of *Glas* (1974)—Derrida has increasingly turned deconstruction toward sociopolitical and pedagogical inquiry and critique while maintaining and furthering its work of "narrowly" textual analysis. Or rather, he has situated institutions as well as texts more fully within their political and historical networks—grids that create and control our activities.

Given Derrida's progressive elaboration or broadening of the deconstructive project, we should not be surprised to hear his call to arms and tone of gaiety in the 1980 address delivered at Columbia, where he ties the work of deconstruction firmly to the critique of academic institutional structures: "But I *do* say that today, for anyone who belongs to an institution of teaching and research, the minimal responsibility, and also the newest, most powerful, and most interesting, is to make as clear and thematically explicit as possible such political implications, their system and its aporias" (pp. 54–55).

THE DEPROPRIATION OF PEDAGOGICAL DISCOURSE

The focus on pedagogy in Derrida's work has the broadening effect of bringing into the foreground the potential of deconstruction to become activist *cultural* criticism. In the work of Roland Barthes, on the other hand, reflections on pedagogy often lead to a narrowing and an intensifying of normally broad cultural concerns into a concentrated attention to and focus on the powers of classroom language. Where Derrida gazes more and more at the array of cultural institutions, Barthes focuses more and more on a limited range of effective teaching strategies that are available to the professor in the classroom. Let us consider Barthes's reflections on pedagogy as expressed during his decade of deconstructive work.

When asked at the close of an interview published in 1971 about what would constitute a valid teaching of literature, Barthes responded:

> The job of teaching would be to make the literary text explode as fully as possible. The pedagogical problem would be to throw the notion of the literary text into disorder and to succeed in making adolescents realize that there is text everywhere, but that all is no longer text; I mean that there is text everywhere, and everywhere at the same time there is repetition, stereotype, *doxa*. The goal is: arbitration between this text which is not only within literature and the neurotic activity of repetition of society. . . . Here would be an ensemble of tasks which would be in large part the tasks of *depropriation of the text*.[8]

Here, in the early stages of his involvement with deconstruction, Barthes transforms the task of critical work into a pedagogical goal. We should free the ubiquitous text from stereotype, repetition, and opinion—formations of a neurotic society. And we should, through such *depropriation*, unleash or explode the text: textuality (linguistic determinism) should spread across everything. In the process, "literature" undergoes decomposition and is replaced by the "text." The general movement here is from text as frozen form, stereotype, or "literature" to text as licentious play of signifiers. The general activity involves exploding, throwing into disorder, and depropriating. These, of course, are fundamental practices of deconstruction.

The pedagogical scene that Barthes characteristically describes includes two elements: neurotic society in the background and the subversive professor in the foreground of the classroom. With Derrida we typically glimpse, not the individual professor in the classroom, but the teaching corps and the university in their relations to the state and to society. Because the classroom is always a problematic arena, Barthes early grappled with the difficulties of teaching deconstructively. Almost all such difficulties for Barthes have to do with language—its powers, its writing, its speaking.

In the well-known essay "Writers, Intellectuals, Teachers," published in *Tel Quel* in the fall of 1971, Barthes observes that "language is always a matter of force, to speak is to exercise a will for power; in the realm of speech there is no innocence, no safety."[9] In effect, "*all speech is on the side of the Law*" (p. 191), and "the Law appears *not in what is said but in the very fact of speech*" (p. 192). That speech, the teacher's medium, is inherently violent and authoritarian means that the depropriation demanded by deconstructive teaching is difficult, if not impossible, to attain in the classroom. Barthes considers four options available to the classroom teacher. First, he can capitulate and accept the role of authority and *speak* "well." Second, he can remain mute and fall prey to the stereotype either of the "great silent mind" or of the "recalcitrant militant" who dismisses discourse as useless. Third, he can alter delivery, pace, and rhythm or add copious corrections and capricious revisions as a way to nudge speech toward writing (textuality), but then he courts the stereotype of the "fumbling, weak and ineffective speaker." Fourth, he can practice "peaceable speech," which for Barthes is the closest he can come to deconstructive teaching. Trying to *suspend* the violence and authority of speech, the "peaceable speaker" is never "the actor of a judgement, a subjection, an intimidation, the advocate of a Cause" (p. 214). As in a drugged state or in an ascetic posture, the speaker generalizes himself, "tracing out a pure form, that of a *floating* (the very form of the signifier); a floating which would not destroy anything but would be content simply to disorientate the Law" (p. 215).

Whether or not "floating discourse" can be effected, Barthes, we see, is working toward a classroom practice of deconstruction. In doing so, he shifts from throwing the (literary) text into disorder to exploding professorial speech itself. The critic-turned-professor is pressed to depropriate pedagogical discourse. Society fades into the background and then returns embodied in a violent and authoritarian language, which must undergo decomposition and pacification.

When he assumed the first Chair of Literary Semiology at the Collège de France in January of 1977, Barthes delivered the traditional *leçon*, ending with a peroration on pedagogy. Here we encounter a further elaboration of deconstructive teaching:

> What I hope to be able to renew, each of the years it is given me to teach here, is the manner of presentation of the course or seminar, in short, of "presenting" a discourse without imposing it. . . . For what

can be oppressive in our teaching is not, finally, the knowledge or the culture it conveys, but the discursive forms through which we propose them. Since . . . this teaching has as its object discourse taken in the inevitability of its power, method can really bear only on the means of loosening, baffling, or at the very least, of lightening this power. And I am increasingly convinced, both in writing and in teaching, that the fundamental operation of this loosening method is, if one writes, fragmentation, and, if one teaches, digression, or . . . *excursion.*[10]

Again, Barthes affirms that the main job of deconstructive pedagogy is to suspend the oppressive forces of discursive language—to loosen, baffle, or lighten its power. And once more, he devises a strategy to accomplish the job—a strategy that attempts to textualize discourse, to transform speech into writing. In place of "floating," discourse is now "fragmentation," "digression," "excursion." Pedagogical discourse, ideally, should become chronic linguistic sidetracking—randomized movement. The discourse of the professor, partial rather than totalized, should be, at its best, discontinuous.

Near the end of his *leçon,* Barthes observes that the practice of deconstructive digression or excursion describes "the comings and goings of desire" (p. 15). And he notes that the professor of desire—this body—occupies, not the place of the Father, but that of the son. Barthes here links the project for a deconstructive pedagogy with his well-known contemporaneous psychoanalytic project for a libidinal textuality.[11] He seeks, in effect, a pedagogical practice of *jouissance* (libidinal bliss) beyond simple *plaisir* (pleasure). In Barthes's view: "Pleasure is linked with the consistency of the self, of the subject, which affirms itself. . . . As opposed to this, *jouissance* is the system of reading, or of enunciation, by means of which the subject, instead of affirming, abandons itself. . . ."[12] Here we find an extension of the earlier ideas of the "generalization of the subject," of the drug state, of the ascetic posture ("WIT," pp. 214–15). *Jouissance,* in the scene of pedagogy, names a system of enunciation in which the teaching body abandons itself: this excursion of the blissful son's discourse is staged in opposition to the coherent and steadfast speech of the authoritarian, violent Father.[13]

Barthes's whole pedagogical project goes in the direction of deracination and desedimentation, on one hand, and pleasure and play, on the other: uproot the frozen text; break down stereotypes and opinions; suspend or baffle the violence and authority of language; pacify or lighten oppressive paternal powers; disorient the law; let classroom discourse float, fragment, digress; seek ascetic or libidinal abandonment of the teaching body/self. Between its early expression in

Tel Quel and its later formulation in the Collège de France *leçon*, this project, like Barthes's texts, becomes increasingly libidinal and "lyrical" while remaining antiauthoritarian and "anarchist."

Playful and mischievous, Barthes's project for a deconstructive pedagogy, for the depropriation of discourse, contrasts with Derrida's contemporaneous project for a critique of institutional structures that leads to the taking of positions. Derrida's activist and engaged commitment, unlike Barthes's solitary radicalism in its mobility and libidinal floating, aims to take or to stick so as to alter existing hierarchies and pedagogical institutions. To transform only personal classroom practice is to limit the effort; Derrida maintains solidarity with the workers of GREPH—a group that seeks to criticize and transform *the* system. Yet both deconstructors attempt to break down the prevailing cycles of educational (re)production, and both manifest a certain stubborn joy or gaiety in their struggles. Finally, both men, playing at moralist, call all teachers to their consciences—to the obligation to extend critical inquiry beyond a textual hermeneutics and toward a critique of institutional values, arrangements, and practices.

TOWARD A PRACTICE OF DECONSTRUCTIVE TEACHING

In the United States during the early 1980s a growing interest not only in deconstruction but also in its potential pedagogy manifested itself in several ways. *Yale French Studies* devoted an issue to pedagogy—which consisted of fifteen essays, many of which were deconstructive critiques of educational theories and practices. In the same year the Society for Critical Exchange offered a session on "deconstruction and pedagogy" at its annual meeting, which was held in conjunction with the Modern Language Association. In 1983 the International Association for Philosophy and Literature convened a conference on "Deconstruction and Its Alternatives," which featured a panel and discussion on "Deconstruction and the Institutions of Learning in Philosophy and Literature." The journal *Social Text* began a special series in 1982 on "Critical Theory of Education," aiming to clarify "the political stakes of the struggle over education."[14]

What would a pedagogical practice, derived from the "principles" of deconstruction, entail? Can one teach deconstructively? If so, how?

A preliminary step would require something akin to "attitude adjustment" or, more grandly, "epistemological transformation." We can start by affirming an obvious, though sometimes forgotten or overlooked, point: in the realm of knowledge, everything is constituted during a certain time by one or more people. Some "things" are included, some are excluded, some are marginalized. Boundaries are set up. The "made up" quality of knowledge, its fictitious character, evidences itself as inscription. Knowledge is recorded or registered in some way—even if only in an individual's memory cells. In deconstructive terms, everything that we know is written, or, more dramatically, *writing* produces all our knowledge. The adjustment, the transformation, here is twofold: first, traditional epistemological matters are transferred to the ground of philosophy of language or to linguistics; second, *writing* is understood, in the widest possible sense, to include all forms of inscription, ranging from carving a path through a forest to recalling a dream to penning a legal code. The incommensurability of our "written texts" and the "things and ideas" that are written about reveals, once again, the "fictitious" quality of our knowledge: its differential character. The effect of this whole operation—which traces a key paradigm shift of our time from the world as an orderly array of substances and things to the world as a differential text—the effect is to defamiliarize or denaturalize our knowledge. Knowledge is constituted as *historical* writing. Our knowledge, in its present and past formations and branches, could have been, and may yet be, constituted in other ways. Our relation to "facts," disciplines, departments, and hierarchies of knowledge is less "natural" or "normal" than it is concocted and thus alterable.

Out of such deconstructive thinking comes a certain strategic stance and practice for pedagogy. Nothing is ordained, natural, unalterable, monumental. Everything is susceptible to critique and transformation. "Arrangements," whether traditional or contemporary, can be "rearranged." To criticize is to cause crisis. In order to be successful this teaching—suspicious, critical, discriminating, optimistic—must pass to students. What distinguishes such pedagogy is its grounding in *writing*. It is precisely the power of *writing*—to ordain, create, naturalize, and monumentalize—which produces the grounds for critique and transformation.

As classroom discourse, deconstructive teaching ought in turn to submit its own language to depropriation. There might follow tactical assaults on and transformations of pedagogical grammar and syntax through excursive rhetorics and impure styles. Socratic dialogue, dialectical conversation, would probably be disrupted. Intelligibility would be put in constant jeopardy. If not "depropriated," pedagogical discourse risks ordaining and naturalizing its own critiques. In this case, criticism would remain discreet cultural conversation.

Another tactic for classroom discourse is possible. Here, relentless lucid inquiries into the constituting powers of *language* would reveal its "creative" and "monumentalizing" functions, teaching active suspicion of all language formations. All writing, one's own especially, would become subject to depropriation—deconstruction. Lucidity, if pushed far enough, engenders vigilance about language—its productions, slippages, congealings.

The *politics* of such "deconstructive teaching" moves beyond traditional liberal tolerance; it is usable with certain socialist, libertarian, and anarchist ideals. That this pedagogy could serve "rightist" or "leftist" political ideologies is, one would suppose, incriminating. Such heterogeneity or undecidability, however, is the hallmark of deconstructive productions. To purify such duplicity, to turn this new pedagogy toward *a* political doctrine or dogma, would be precisely to turn away from deconstruction—to end its teaching, which, nevertheless, is not apolitical, as Derrida makes clear.

The focus of deconstruction on language, on its potential to "make up" and "maintain," to create and monumentalize, is inherently historicist. Language is historical. Not surprisingly, the archeological examinations performed by deconstructors are frequently corrosive insofar as the formations of history are subject to irreverent critiques of founding categories and operations. (The deconstructive trajectory is from text to textual system as historically constituted.) What we get is often a sort of counterhistoriography. This revisionist impulse, respectful of history in an unconventional way, must lead to a certain pedagogical embrace of cultural history. Thus, deconstructive teaching would be characterized precisely by a "historical," as well as a "linguistic," orientation.

NOTES

1. Jacques Derrida, "Où commence et comment finit un corps enseignant," in *Politiques de la philosophie*, ed. Dominique Grisoni (Paris: Bernard Grasset, 1976), p. 65, my translation. All subsequent French quotations have been translated by me. For a brief overview of the mission of GREPH see James Kearns and Ken Newton, "An Interview with Jacques Derrida," *Literary Review*, no. 14 (18 April–1 May 1980): 22.

2. Jacques Derrida, "L'Age de Hegel," in *Qui a peur de la philosophie?* (Paris: Flammarion, 1977), p. 91. This text lists no editor, containing instead the names of seventeen contributors on its title page and the designation "GREPH." A "Liminaire" (pp. 5–11) offers a short history of GREPH, and a fourth section (pp. 427–71) collects ten GREPH documents, ranging from statutes to interviews to manifestos.

3. GREPH, "Modes de fonctionnement du GREPH (Statuts)," in *Qui a peur*, p. 441.

4. GREPH, "Prise de position contre la Réforme Giscard-Haby," in *Qui a peur*, p. 459.

5. Jacques Derrida, "Philosophie des États Généraux," in *États Généraux de la philosophie (16 et 17 juin 1979)* (Paris: Flammarion, 1979), p. 43, no editor listed. A Committee of Preparation—twenty-one members listed on pp. 16–17—compiled this book from tapes of conference sessions. Among the committee members were Derrida, Gilles Deleuze, Philippe Lacoue-Labarthe, Jean-Luc Nancy, and Paul Ricoeur.

6. Jacques Derrida, "The Conflict of Faculties: A Mochlos," trans. Cynthia Chase, Jonathan Culler, Irving Wohlfarth (Columbia University, New York, 1980), p. 56. I thank the author for the loan of this English-language typescript. This text is forthcoming in a collection edited by Michael Riffaterre entitled *Languages of Knowledge and of Inquiry* (to be published by Columbia University Press).

7. See Jacques Derrida, Letter to Colleagues, 18 May 1982, published in *Sub-Stance*, no. 35 (1982): 80–81. This letter by Derrida, on stationery from the State Minister of Research and Technology, is an international call for suggestions, advice, and participation. On the program of the new college see François Châtelet, Jacques Derrida, Jean-Pierre Faye, and Dominique Lecourt, *Rapport pour le Collège International de Philosophie* (Paris: Ministre de la Recherche et de l'Industrie, 1982).

8. Roland Barthes, *Le Grain de la voix: Entretiens 1962–1980* (Paris: Seuil, 1981), p. 141. This text collects more than three dozen interviews given by Barthes during a two-decade period.

9. Roland Barthes, "Writers, Intellectuals, Teachers," in *Image—Music—Text*, ed. and trans. Stephen Heath (New York: Hill & Wang, 1977), p. 192 (hereafter cited as "WIT"). On this topic see also Jean-François Lyotard and Jean-Loup Thébaud, *Au juste: Conversations* (Paris: Christian Bourgois, 1979), pp. 16–19. See also Lyotard's reflections on contemporary university education in his *La Condition postmoderne* (Paris: Minuit, 1979), pp. 78–88.

10. Roland Barthes, "Lecture" (in Inauguration of the Chair of Literary Semiology, Collège de France, 7 January 1977), trans. Richard Howard in *October* 8 (Spring 1979): 15. Consider also Michel Foucault, "The Discourse on Language" (*Leçon* Presented at the Collège de France, 2 December 1970), trans. Rupert Swyer, in Foucault's *The Archaeology of Knowledge*, trans. A. M. Sheridan Smith (New York: Harper & Row, 1972), p. 227: "Every educational system is a political means of maintaining or of modifying the appropriation of discourse, with the knowledge and the powers it carries with it."

11. See my "From a Poetics to an Erotics of the Text," in *Deconstructive Criticism: An Advanced Introduction* (New York: Columbia University Press, 1983), pp. 102–15.

12. Roland Barthes, "Vocabulary," no trans. listed, *Semiotext(e)* 4, no. 1 (1981): 206. ("Vocabulary" is excerpted from a 1975 interview—see *Le Grain de la voix*, pp. 195–96.)

13. Barthes contrasts older paternal theories of literature as *mathesis* and *mimesis*, with the new theory of literature as *semiosis*, which produces "jouissances du symbolique," in his "Littérature/enseignement" (1975), in *Le Grain de la voix*, p. 225.

14. To sample American reflections on "deconstruction and pedagogy" see, for instance, J. Hillis Miller, "The Function of Rhetorical Study at the Present Time," in a special issue of *ADE Bulletin*, no. 62 (Sept.–Nov. 1979): 10–18;

Jonathan Culler, "Literary Theory in the Graduate Program," in *The Pursuit of Signs: Semiotics, Literature, Deconstruction* (Ithaca, N.Y.: Cornell University Press, 1981), pp. 210–26; "The Pedagogical Imperative: Teaching as a Literary Genre," a special issue of *Yale French Studies*, no. 63 (1982), edited by Barbara Johnson; Michael Ryan, "Reason and Counterrevolution," in *Marxism and Deconstruction: A Critical Articulation* (Baltimore, Md., and London: Johns Hopkins University Press, 1982), pp. 132–58, esp. pp. 152–58; William V. Spanos, "The End of Education: 'The Harvard Core Curriculum Report' and the Pedagogy of Reformation," *Boundary 2* 10 (Winter 1982): 1–33; and Paul de Man, "The Return to Philology," *TLS*, 10 Dec. 1982, pp. 1355–56, which is one of nine contributions to a symposium entitled "Professing Literature."

To sample British thinking about contemporary critical theories and pedagogical practices see *Re-Reading English*, ed. Peter Widdowson (London: Methuen, 1982), which contains sixteen essays by diverse hands. One essay in this collection is particularly concerned with deconstruction—Peter Brooker, "Post-Structuralism, Reading and the Crisis in English," pp. 61–76.

Reading the World:
Literary Studies in the 1980s

Gayatri Chakravorty Spivak

After my public lecture on "Literature and Life" in March 1980 at the Riyadh University Center for Girls [*sic*], a student asked me with some asperity: "It's all very well to try to live like a book; but what if no one else is prepared to read? What if you are dismissed as an irresponsible dreamer?" I found an answer to her question at the tail end of a metaphor: "Everyone reads life and the world like a book. Even the so-called 'illiterate.' But especially the 'leaders' of our society, the most 'responsible' nondreamers: the politicians, the businessmen, the ones who make plans. Without the reading of the world as a book, there is no prediction, no planning, no taxes, no laws, no welfare, no war. Yet these leaders read the world in terms of rationality and averages, as if it were a textbook. The world actually writes itself with the many-leveled, unfixable intricacy and openness of a work of literature. If, through our study of literature, we can learn ourselves and teach others to read the world in the 'proper' risky way, and to act upon that lesson, perhaps we literary people would not forever be such helpless victims." It is difficult to say that very last bit to a woman in Saudi Arabia. So I added, half to myself, and with a sense of failure: "Mere literary studies cannot accomplish this. One must fill the vision of literary form with its connections to what is being read: history, political economy—the world. And it is not merely a question of disciplinary formation. It is a

This paper, which was first delivered as a talk to the Association of Departments of English in June 1980, is reprinted from *College English* 43, no. 7 (Nov. 1981): 671–79.

question also of questioning the separation between the world of action and the world of the disciplines. There is a great deal in the way."

In that exchange I was obliged to stress the distinction between my position and the position that, in a world of massive brutality, exploitation, and sexual oppression, advocates an aesthetization of life. Here I must stress that I am also not interested in answers to questions like "What is the nature of the aesthetic?" or "How indeed are we to understand 'life'?" My concern rather is that: (1) The formulation of such questions is itself a determined and determining gesture. (2) Very generally speaking, literary people are still caught within a position where they must say: Life is brute fact and outside art; the aesthetic is free and transcends life. (3) This declaration is the condition and effect of "ideology." (4) If "literary studies" is to have any meaning in the coming decade, its ideology might have to be questioned.

If the student and critic of literature is made to believe in and to perpetuate the received dogma of my second point, then the work of the "world" can go on without the interference suggested in my fourth point. But the disciplinary situation of the teacher of literature is inscribed in that very text of the "world" that the received dogma refuses to allow us to read. As a result, even as in classroom and article we mouth the freedom of the aesthetic, in bulletin and caucus and newspaper and meeting we deplore our attenuation and betrayal by society. The effort to invite a persistent displacement of the bewildering contradiction between life and art relates to the displacement of the bewildering contradiction between the conditions of life and the professions of our profession.

I have recently described our unwitting complicity with a world that efficiently marginalizes us in the following way:

> We are the disc jockeys of an advanced technocracy. The discs are not "records" of the old-fashioned kind, but productions of the most recent technology. The trends in taste and the economic factors that govern them are also products of the most complex interrelations among a myriad factors such as foreign relations, the world market, the conduct of advertisement supported by and supporting the first two items, and so on. To speak of the mode of production and constitution of the radio station complicates matters further. Within this intricately determined and multiform situation, the disc jockey and his audience think, indeed are made to think, that they are free to play. This illusion of freedom allows us to protect the brutal ironies of technocracy by suggesting either that the system nourishes the humanist's freedom of spirit, or that "technology," that vague evil, is something the humanist must transform by inculcating humanistic

"values," or by drawing generalized philosophical analogies from the latest spatio-temporal discoveries of the magical realms of "pure science." ("Explanation and Culture: Marginalia," *Humanities in Society* 2, no. 3 [1979]: 209; modified.)

In the context of this marginalization our in-house disputes seem not only trivial but harmful. I refer, of course, to the disputes between composition and literature, and between practical criticism/literary history and "theory."

In the case of the dispute between composition and literature, the bewildering contradiction I speak of above is clearly to be seen. Teaching composition is recognized inside and outside the academy to be socially useful. If indeed the pages of the *ADE Bulletin* are to be believed, since 1976 the number of jobs in composition has doubled, and the area has held steady as the largest provider of jobs in the profession. Yet in terms of the politics and economics of the university, the college, the department, and the profession, it is the composition teacher whose position—with some significant exceptions—is less privileged and more precarious. The culprit is not far to seek. It is the received dogma of the freedom of the aesthetic and literature's refusal to soil itself by rendering service to the state—when that very refusal is the greatest service that it can render to a polity that must disguise the extraction of surplus value as cultural dynamism.

Although my general argument and my metaphor of the humanist as disc jockey directly question this illusion of freedom from the "world" and the state, it is in the matter of the dispute between theory and practical criticism/literary history that I find myself most directly touched. I should of course admit that my concern reflects my own increasing specialization in "theory." (By "theory" is meant un-American activities that employ a vocabulary and sometimes methods belonging to the history of ideas rather than strictly to the domain of literary criticism, such as those of phenomenology, structuralism, deconstruction, semiotics. "Psychological" and "Marxist" criticism, long accused of reductivism and determinism, have entered "theory" through Jacques Lacan, Louis Althusser, and the Frankfurt School. The preferred and "American" side of the dispute endorses "pluralism," according to which some points of view are clearly delineated as more equal and more fundamental than others. The terms can be seen outlined in such exchanges as "The Limits of Pluralism," M. H. Abrams, Wayne Booth, J. Hillis Miller, *Critical Inquiry* 3 [1977]: 407–47; such works as Gerald Graff's *Literature against Itself: Literary Ideas in Modern Society* [Chicago: University of Chicago Press, 1979]; and such forums as most of the "theoretical" sessions at annual conventions of national or regional literary organizations.)

Unfortunately enough, what I call the received dogma of the discipline of literary study affects the so-called theoretical field and the so-called practical-historical field equally. The two sides of the dispute in fact leave our general marginalization intact. When "theory" brings up questions of ideological "interest," or the limitations of the merely aesthetic norm, the terminology becomes fearfully abstract. On the other hand, when "theory" seeks to undo this situation by attempting a reading of a hidden ethical or ideological agenda in a literary text, a curious *topos* rises up to resist: the critic is accused, if only by implication, of being a charlatan, of playing Pied Piper to the young, while mature wisdom consists in leaving Business as Usual.

I was troubled by this at our own conference when, after an excellent talk on the resources and techniques for getting grants in our profession, Professor Steven Weiland remarked about Robert Scholes's performance the previous night: "I confess that the paragraph I am about to quote could perhaps be read to mean quite another thing by a semiotician. I suppose I am just not young enough to be able to learn that sort of reading." (I cannot quote his exact words, of course. It was an unrehearsed aside. Scholes had attempted a delicate reading of the theme of the inexhaustible volubility of nonintellectual women as a *topos* of masculinist ideology as it operates in the discourse of Hemingway's "A Very Short Story.")

The same veiled accusation appears at the end of Denis Donoghue's ill-considered review of the most notorious "theory" stalking the halls of American literary criticism today—"deconstruction": "I think Deconstruction appeals to the clerisy of graduate students, who like to feel themselves superior to the laity of common readers" ("Deconstructing Deconstruction," *New York Review of Books* 27, no. 10 [1980]: 41).

The fear of a critical reading that would question the writer's direct access to his or her meaning is related to the received dogma of the illusion of freedom. Strictly speaking, received dogma is another name for ideology. Ideology in the critical sense does not signify an avowed doctrine. It is rather the loosely articulated sets of historically determined and determining notions, presuppositions, and practices, each implying the other by real (but where does one stop to get a grip on reality?) or forced logic, which goes by the name of common sense or self-evident truth or natural behavior in a certain situation. What I have been talking about so far has been the displacing of the ideology of our discipline of literature.

Such an effort need not involve questioning the individual good will of author or critic. The fear of critical reading ill-concealed in the following words is what an ideology-critical pedagogy would constantly question: "The wretched side of this is that Deconstruction encourages [graduate students] to feel superior not only to undergraduates but to the authors they are reading" (Donoghue, p. 41). Wasn't it the "intentional fallacy" that did that? "Wordsworth's Preface to the *Lyrical Ballads* is a remarkable document, but as a piece of Wordsworthian criticism nobody would give it more than about a B plus" (Northrop Frye, *Anatomy of Criticism: Four Essays* [Princeton, N.J.: Princeton University Press, 1957], p. 5).

A pedagogy that would constantly seek to undo the opposition between the verbal and the social text at the same time that it knows its own inability to know its own ideological provenance fully is perhaps better understood in the American context as a dearchaeologized and deteleologized version of the Baconian project to discover the idols of the mind, which would constitute rather than lead to, in a fragmented rather than continuous way, a New Philosophy or *Active* Science.[1] It is an experiment in using an expertise in reading literature to read the text of a world that has an interest in preserving that expertise merely to propagate, to use the Baconian word, an *idolatry* of literature, perhaps even a species of self-idolatry as the privileged reader.

Rather than continue in this abstract vein, let me beguile you with some examples. I taught a seminar for first-year Plan II students at the University of Texas last fall. Plan II is an interdisciplinary, four-year honors program for exceptionally gifted liberal-arts undergraduates; everything else in the college is Plan I.

At the first class meeting, the young men and women sat, as did I, in movable chairs around a hollow square of four oblong tables. I was a little late for the second class meeting. The students had left the same chair empty, and thus given me a chance to introduce to them the theme that is my subject tonight. Here is a gist of my homily: "You are amazingly intelligent young people of unquestionable personal good will. The university has rightly rewarded your outstanding merit by adjudicating some extra freedoms for you. You have, for example, been granted a serious degree of freedom by the arrangement of furniture. You sit with your teacher in a small group in movable chairs around a center; your less gifted peers are in large, well-monitored classes in fixed seats gazing upon authority on a dais. But history and the institutions of power and authority are stronger than the limits of personal good will. If you deny them, they will get in through the back door. Because I warmed that particular chair with my bottom the last time, I seem to have baptized it as the seat of authority and you have left it empty for me. Your historical-institutional imperatives are proving stronger than your personal good will. Since our topic this semester is going to be 'Images of Woman and Man in the Texts of Men and Women,' what I am saying now might be useful for us. We will read some great texts of the past—such as *The Eumenides, The Vita Nuova*, and *Émile*—and see in them the blueprints for rather questionable sexual attitudes. Now you must remember, every day in class, and as you write your papers, that this is not to belittle Aeschylus, Dante, or Rousseau as individuals, but to see in and through them something like their 'age,' to take into account how we are ourselves caught in a time and a place, and then to imagine acting within such an awareness.''

I made some good friends in that class—although I could not always be sure of a chair if I was late—partly because they saw repeatedly that the readings advanced by their teacher, that figure of authority, were not authoritatively backed up by the traditional readings of, say, Aeschylus, or Dante, or yet Rousseau. There was, however, a certain problem the class could not get over.

Since our theme was so clearly sociohistorical, I would often ask these students to write their papers from a point of view that was not only that of private but also of public individuals. After a variety of valiant efforts, nearly every paper faced with that specific charge ended in variations of the following argument: In the final analysis, no public generalization of this question is possible or even desirable, because we are all unique individuals.

I think I had made it clear to my students that although I was often critical of European or American ideology, I was in no way at all offering them, as a native of India, a so-called "Indian spiritual" solution. I was able to talk to them about the problem in their papers, therefore, in a dialogue resembling what follows:

"Do you know what indoctrination is?''

"Yes.''

"Do you know where it is to be found?''

"The Soviet Union and the Islamic world.''

"Suppose an outsider, observing the uniformity of the moves you have all sketched in your papers, were to say that you had been indoctrinated? That you could no longer conceive of public decision making except in the quantified areas of your economics and business classes, where you learn all about rational expectations theories? You *know* that decisions in the public sphere, such as tax decisions, legal decisions, foreign-policy decisions, fiscal decisions, affect your *private* lives deeply. Yet in a speculative field such as the interpretation of texts, you feel that there is something foolish and wrong and regimented about a public voice. Suppose someone were to say that this was a result of your indoctrination to keep moral speculation and decision making apart, to render you incapable of thinking collectively in any but the most inhuman way?''

For my second example I will go back to Saudi Arabia, this time to the male faculty of the Riyadh University Faculty of Arts. I met a group of faculty members twice—I think it was the first time a woman had run what amounted to a faculty-development seminar there. The impression I carried away strengthened my conviction about not only literature, but the humanities in general in the service of the state.

Since 1973, Saudi Arabia has been one of America's strongest allies among the OPEC countries. As a result of the incredible boom following the surprise defeat of Israel that year, Saudi Arabia is ''modernizing'' itself at an extremely rapid pace. Part of the ''modernizing'' package is, quite properly, education; most of it, for reasons much larger than individual enthusiasm for American education, from the United States. As far as I could tell, the methodologies of the humanities that were being imported through visiting or U.S.-trained faculty sustain and are sustained by the ideology or received dogma of disinterestedness and freedom that I have been describing in the case of literature. I compiled this checklist while I was there: analytical and speech act theory in philosophy; quantitative analysis, structural functionalism, and objective structuralism in history and anthropology; mathematization on a precritical psychological model in linguistics; descriptive and biologistic clinical approaches, behaviorism, and delibidinized ego-psychology in psychology; objective structuralism, New Criticism, history- and ideology-transcendent aestheticism in literature—and so on. (I received such lavish hospitality from my hosts that it seems churlish to add that I had probably been invited to add to this package the message of Deconstruction American Style.)

Following my general viewpoint, I would not for a moment suggest that one or more evil geniuses here or in Saudi Arabia are necessarily planning this export-import business in methodologies. My entire pedagogic approach would then come to nothing. The point is, first, that the ideological/material concatenation that produces this can be read and acted upon, although not once and for all, but rather constantly, persistently, like all repeated gestures of life sustenance. Saudi Arabia, with American help, is in fact slowly fabricating for itself a ''humanist'' intellectual elite that will be unable to read the relationship between its own production and the flow of oil, money, and arms. A diversified technocratic elite whose allegiance to humanism, if at all in evidence, will be sentimental, will take care of those dirtier flows. The apparent lack of contact between rational expectations in the business world and freedom and disinterest in the humanist academy will support each other, as here, and to America's advantage. To call it "cultural imperialism" is to pass the buck, in every sense. I am attempting to suggest our pedagogic responsibility in this situation: to ask not merely how literary studies, more correctly the universitarian discipline of English studies, can adjust to changing social demands, but also how we could, by changing some of our assumptions, contribute toward changing those demands in the very long run.

An Arab-American linguist trained on the American West Coast asked me at one of the meetings in Riyadh, "How do you propose to fit, say, Shakespeare, into this pedagogic program?" I did give him an answer, in some detail, referring to my experience as a student in India and a teacher in the American Middle West and Texas. That reply will have to wait till next time. However, I have outlined an answer with reference to Wordsworth's *The Prelude* in an essay—"Sex and History in Wordsworth's *The Prelude* (1805): Books Nine to Thirteen" (*Texas Studies in Language and Literature* 23 [1981]: 324–60).[2]

The point of these far-flung digressions has been, then, that a literary study that can graduate into the 80s might teach itself to attend to the dialectical and continuous crosshatching of ideology and literary language. Further, that such an activity, learned in the classroom, should slide without a sense of rupture into an active and involved reading of the social text within which the student and teacher of literature are caught.

The after-dinner speech as genre allows me to add another story. Toward the beginning of May this year, Sir James Cavenham, the English financier, was looking to buy out "35 percent of Diamond [International]'s stock." He already owned "nearly 6 percent." This was in opposition to Diamond's "proposed acquisition of Brooks-Scanlon Inc., a forest products company" (*New York Times*, 13 May 1980, sec. 4, p. 4), because it would reduce Cavenham's share to a much smaller percentage. Diamond is a paper company.

"As the battle intensified," the *Times* reported the next week, "Wall Street professionals eagerly watched the in-fighting on both sides. The highly respected Merrill Lynch Whiteweld Capital Market Group had assured Diamond a month ago that the merger terms were fair to Diamond's stockholders. The equally prestigious house of Warburg Paribas Becker gave the same assurance to Brooks-Scanlon investors." In the same issue of the *Times*, an advertisement covering an entire page exhorted Diamond's stockholders to vote "no" on the merger, assuring them that it would be to their benefit and advantage.

We have here what the latest literary theory would call—borrowing a word from the Greek—an aporia, an unresolvable doubt. We show our ideological acceptance of error-as-truth when we say, no, one is a paid ad, the other is news, the first therefore is more liable to be false. Is it? If the exchange of money allows for lie-as-truth, what are Diamond, Brooks-Scanlon, Merrill Lynch, and Warburg Paribas Becker working in the interest of? Where is there a decidable truth free of the circuit of exchange to be found? What about the fact that most people would rather read the full-page ad and believe it than read the details of printed news and understand it? Has that fact anything to do with the self-marginalizing dogma of the teaching of literature? Is there an active-philosophical (to remind you of the Baconian term) analysis of that? On May 14, Diamond's annual meeting took place in Bangor, Maine, where Cavenham's French Company Générale Occidentale, S.A., planned to oppose the Brooks-Scanlon-Diamond merger. In nearby Orono, the International Association for Philosophy and Literature met from May 8 to 11. Considerable amounts of paper—Diamond's direct and Brooks-Scanlon's indirect product—were consumed. A considerable amount of intellectual energy and acrimony was spent on the work of a French philosopher who had suggested that "truth" is indeterminate and always "interested"; it was advanced that he and his followers were undermining the seriousness of the American academy. Would the assembled philosophers and literary critics have been capable of drawing a lesson from the accepted indeterminacy, conventionally and by tacit agreement presented as factual truth, that operates and informs the "serious" business that determines the "materiality" of their existence?

The after-dinner speech demands by definition a certain vague euphoria. If you think I have fulfilled that demand only too well, let me hasten to assure you that I am well aware of the complicated organizational assumptions underlying my suggestions. To mention only a few of the heavies: faculty development, fundamental curricular revision, overhauling of disciplinary lines until the term "English literary studies" changes drastically in meaning. I am indeed foolhardy enough to look forward to a struggle for such painstaking and painful transformations. But I do not suggest that the struggle should begin at the expense of our students' immediate futures. I think rather that our efforts should be on at least two fronts at once. We should work to implement the changes even as we prepare our students to fit into the job market as it currently exists. It is merely that we should not mistake the requirements of the job market for the ineffable determinants of the nature of literary studies.

To explain what I mean, I will offer you a final example, a diffident and humble one, the description of a course that I found myself designing on my feet—largely because of the predilections I have elaborated so lengthily above. It is a required course for incoming graduate students: Practical Criticism.

You will have gathered that I am deeply doubtful of the isolationist ideology of practical criticism—to explicate the text as such, with all "outside knowledge" put out of play,[3] even as I think its strategies are extremely useful in interpreting and changing the social text. How can one launch a persistent critique of the ideology without letting go of the strategy? I put together a working answer to the question *while* I taught the course for the first time.

We begin with a situational definition of "practical criticism": a criticism that allows for departmental qualification for the Ph.D. (My department no longer has the qualifying examination, but the standards for qualification remain implicitly the same.) A little over the first half of the course is a criticism workshop, where we read each other's work and learn to write in the approved institutional way, trying to cope with its difficulties and to reveal its subtleties. The rest of the course is given over to readings and discussions of texts that offer fundamental critiques of the ideology that would present this technique as *the* description of the preferred practice of the critic—the list can be wide enough to accommodate Percy Shelley, Walter Benjamin, and Michel Foucault. What I hope to achieve through such a bicameral approach is to prepare the student for the existing situation even as I provide her with a mind-set to change it. A very minor individual effort that looks forward to the major collective efforts that are on my mind.[4]

I have so far tried to follow the notes of the talk I gave at the ADE Seminar in Iowa City. I would like to end by recalling a moment after the talk. Lawrence Mitchell, chairman of the English Department at the University of Minnesota and a friend of long standing from his graduate-student days at the University of Iowa, asked if perhaps my critical attitude did not reflect the fact that I, like him—he was born in England—was an outsider? I have thought about that question. Even after nineteen years in this country, fifteen of them spent in full-time teaching, I believe the answer is yes. But then, where is the inside? To define an inside is a decision, I believe I said that night, and the critical method I am describing would question the ethico-political strategic exclusions that would define a certain set of characteristics as an "inside" at a certain time. "The text itself," "the poem as such," "intrinsic criticism" are such strategic definitions. I have spoken in support of a way of reading that would continue to break down such distinctions, never once and for all, and *actively* interpret "inside" and "outside" as texts for involvement as well as for change.[5]

NOTES

1. I apologize for this awkward sentence. The production of language is our practice. The received dogma asks that our language be pleasant and easy, that it slip effortlessly into things as they are. Our point of view is that it should be careful, and not take the current dogmatic standard of pleasure and ease as natural norms. As for Bacon, I am rueful that, given his spotty record, that is the best one can do for the American literary-critical sensibility. As Stuart Hall has argued, "The concept of 'ideology' has never been fully absorbed into Anglo-Saxon social theory. . . . An interesting essay could be written on what concepts did duty, in American social theory, for the absent concept of 'ideology': for example, the notion of norms in structural functionalism, and of 'values' and the 'central value system' in Parsons" ("The Hinterland of Science: Ideology and the 'Sociology of Knowledge,' " *Working Papers in Cultural Studies* 10 [1977]: 9). As for the "New Philosophy," I hastily disclaim any connection with the young philosophical aesthetes in Paris whose passionate effusions are sometimes known by that name. It is "active" that I want to stress, and "science" in the sense of "state or fact of knowing" (*OED*).

2. Because the essay was too long, those pages outlining the argument were edited out. That decision in itself might provide food for thought on the norms of pertinence for scholarly journals. I hope to include the argument in my forthcoming book on theory and practice in the humanities.

3. I understand and sympathize with that part of the impulse behind New Criticism which wanted to focus attention upon deciphering the text in its context. My point is that, as with my Plan II students, the dominant ideology, slipping in through the back door, has a lot to do with determining a seemingly "free choice" and that a degree of freedom of choice can be achieved if that determination is recognized.

4. The effort is minor also because, since we are gathered here together to discuss the problems for our profession, questions of race, sex, and class—the common threads of the social fabric—have had to be laid aside. I am reminded of a two-and-a-half-hour-long conversation I had with a group of feminist women and some men on the West Coast earlier this year. Many of them were students of English or French literature. They spoke to me emphatically of an issue of faculty development. Our most prestigious professors, they said, will have nothing to do with so "localized" an issue as "feminism," at least not in the matter of reading the canon. Since we must try to pass the examinations, get recommendation letters, and to get jobs in this impossible market, we write our papers with our feminist consciousness and conscience strangulated, with a deliberate and self-contemptuous cynicism. If an advanced degree in literary studies requires and trains in such divisive compromise, its "humanistic" value comes to very little. Even this is a restricted example. The larger questions—Who can make use of a method such as I outline? Where?—must always loom as immediate correctives for the delusion that "to defend the autonomy of culture [provisionally defined as the total body of imaginative hypothesis in a society and its tradition] seems to me the social task of the 'intellectual' in the modern world" (Northrop Frye, *Anatomy of Criticism*, p. 127).

5. If I admit that the simple expression "break down" is doing duty for the hated and feared and derided word "deconstruct," the possibility of reading my speech as being about deconstructive practice in the academy is opened.

Textshop for Post(e)pedagogy

Gregory L. Ulmer

Perhaps we might agree at the outset that a decision to rethink pedagogy in the humanities should not depend upon one's attitude toward Derrida, deconstruction, or any other figure, concept, or method identified with New French Theory. The situation in which the disciplines of language and literature find themselves today is the result, rather, of two major revolutions, the consequences of which are finally beginning to affect the academy. I am thinking of the avant-garde movements in the arts, which broke with the Renaissance tradition of representational realism, and the development of film and television, which brought about a shift in the dominant mode of communication in our culture.

The stylistic and rhetorical peculiarities of New French Theory are manifestations of the inevitable transformation of the discourse of schooling in an age of mechanical reproduction. The principal lessons to be learned from much contemporary theory go beyond any particular critical technique to address, first, the formalist and postformalist problematics of referentiality as they affect the relation of pedagogy to an object of study and, second, the psychological insights into the cognition appropriate to, or necessary for, the comprehension of heterogeneous or multichanneled texts. Briefly stated, what has been learned about how one understands an experimental art text or a film narrative has influenced our approach to lecture and discussion in the classroom. Classroom discourse now is responsible for experimenting with its own realist, representational conventions and for taking into account its own heterogeneous nature (being a scene that is rich in nonverbal and performance supplements to verbal communication). The transformations that may follow from this tendency extend to every aspect of the profession, including curriculum and evaluation as well as pedagogy, and even to the very concept of the university as it is presently constituted. But rather than indulging in speculations or generalizations about these implications, I shall turn instead to a more specific consideration of several examples of what teaching might be like in an experimentalist electronic paradigm.[1]

LEC(RI)TURE

The contemporary theory of textuality is often associated with Derrida's notion of *écriture*, or Writing, understood in the grammatological sense that includes all manner of inscription. It might be useful, in rethinking pedagogy, to consider the possibilities of applying *écriture* to the lecture format. When these two terms are joined in a portmanteau, the *"ri"* stands out, signifying the laughter (in French) that the text proposes to add to teaching. To continue this line of macaronic punning which serves as an invention strategy in applied grammatology, I should add that postmodernized education approaches child rearing as child-*rire*-ing (*rire* = to laugh, laughter). I shall have more to say about this attitude later. For now, let me note that a *lecriture* (a term that will be anglicized by the end of this essay)—lecture as text, rather than as work, hence textshop rather than workshop—operates by means of a *dramatic*, rather than an epistemological, orientation to knowledge.

An example of the effect involved in such a shift may be seen in the strategy that Jacques Derrida uses to deconstruct the academic lecture. A good example of Derrida's technique is "Title (to be specified)," first delivered at St. Louis College, Brussels, in 1979.[2] Derrida began by pronouncing, in the place of the title, the words "the t-i-t-l-e-e-r" (*le titrier*), followed by this sentence: "Were I to venture stopping here, to pronounce this, the t-i-t-l-e-e-r, had I audacity enough to be satisfied with it, or be convinced to leave you with what I have just uttered, no doubt you still could not tell how to take it." He does not stop there, however, thus acknowledging his fundamentally conservative nature. He does not stop with the title, as he explains, because he has entered into an implicit contract—whose law, involving the whole question of *universitas* as institution, he wishes to investigate—to appear on a specific date and to deliver a lecture the title (topic) of which was left unspecified (he was given *carte blanche*, a dangerous risk with a speaker who reads *carte* as an anagram of *trace*, *écart*, and so on).

Having opened with a threat to leave the audience adrift, puzzling over the opening sounds (*le titrier*), struggling to attach them to a meaningful term or phrase (thus performing the action of closure, whose operations textuality is designed to expose), Derrida increases the tension by further threatening to break the promise or contract (speech act), by defying the conventions and the audience's expectations, couched as the scenario of an "imminent catastrophe":

> In the audience there is someone who, sitting in the back, under very polished amenities and despite the display of evident civility, does not always respect the fundamental contracts. And what would happen if he were not to come tonight? And, in coming, if he were to speak? Or, if in speaking, he spoke about anything? Or if in speaking of this or that or one thing or another, he were not to give a title to his speech, if he were to leave the title blank ("to be specified") or if he were to invent a title bearing rapport neither with what he says nor with what we have the right to expect from him in these premises—that is to say, truly nowhere? And were this intolerable situation to last one or two hours without anyone daring to interrupt him? ("Title," p. 7)

Although his next sentence is "So I warn you that this is about to happen," Derrida in fact carries out his threat (to never begin his talk, to remain on its border) only technically, in that he confines his discussion to a theory of titles (which, he argues, have the grammatical status of proper names). In other words, he does fulfill the contract, and he satisfies the audience after all with an intelligible discourse. The discourse is "dramatic" rather than conceptual in that, as Derrida remarks, "having decided to proceed in a more reflective than definitive manner, by way of exemplum, story or samples of tales rather than by concepts," he shows how the titles function in certain works by Baudelaire, Ponge, and Blanchot ("Title," p. 9). (My own approach to this account of a new pedagogy borrows its strategy from Derrida.) With these examples he shows *how* to violate the law of genre and even offers a rationale for doing so, even while his own lecture remains finally obedient to the law.

Derrida's performance suggests, then, that a teacher must finally, and at some level, explain himself. A lecriture that *does* violate the law of genre is exemplified in the "speech" given by the German performance artist Joseph Beuys at the "matriculation ceremony" for the fall term of the Düsseldorf Art Academy in November 1968.[3] In place of the customary address (the responsibility for which rotated among the faculty from term to term), Beuys, holding an axe and dressed in his shamanistic "uniform" (felt hat, flyer's jacket, blue jeans, and boots), made the "sound of the stag" (ö-ö-ö) for ten minutes. By substituting one of his "Actions" for the conventional speech, even though it did have a title—"ö-ö program"—Beuys broke the law of genre and scandalized the academy authorities (not to mention the regional minister of education), even though the performance conformed to his by then well-known art mode.

The immediate rationale for the specific nature of his "talk" was that Beuys, responding parodically to the political tension of the period (1968), had founded the German Student Party and had declared himself King of the Reindeer (since most of the members of the party, he said, were animals, giving him thus a decided majority on an ecology ticket). The German Student Party was an organization designed to "deconstruct" the art/life opposition; and as such, it demonstrates a version of "semiotic art"—the "nonfunctional" exercising of a system (although Beuys later actually stood for election as a candidate for the Greens, the ecology party). Beuys further explains his shamanistic pose in these terms:

> I experienced it in the war and I feel it now every day: this state of decay that comes with a one-sided understanding of the idea of materialism. When people say that shamanistic practice is atavistic and irrational, one might answer that the attitude of contemporary scientists is equally old-fashioned and atavistic, because we should by now be at another stage of development in our relationship to material. So when I appear as a kind of shamanistic figure, or allude to it, I do it to stress my belief in other priorities and the need to come up with a completely different plan for working with substances. For instance, in places like universities, where everyone speaks so rationally, it is necessary for a kind of enchanter to appear. (Tisdall, p. 23)

But Beuys's colleagues were not "enchanted," and as Tisdall reports, the "ö-ö program" was "held against Beuys at the time of his dismissal four years later" (for admitting excessive numbers of students to his class—a dismissal that, after several years of litigation, was overturned).

A valuable example of the unreceivability that is always a risk of the performance mode is the jeering response that Antonin Artaud once received when, delivering a lecture at the Sorbonne on "The Theater and the Plague," he attempted not just to tell *about* the topic, but to give the audience "the experience itself, the plague itself, so they will be terrified and awaken."[4] Artaud, that is, performed his text by enacting a "death agony" at the podium, a presentation that must have resembled the murder scene in *Pierrot Murderer of His Wife*, the mimed play described by Mallarmé in "Mimique."[5] Anais Nin, who attended this lecture, reported in her diary that Artaud was "hurt and baffled" by the audience response (people hissed, laughed, or left).

41

A possible model for the lecriture, existing somewhere between the strategies of Derrida and Beuys, is John Cage's "Lecture on Nothing."[6] Cage, who, I should note, is one of Beuys's tutor figures, was himself once associated with Fluxus, the international avant-garde movement to which Beuys belonged. Cage's link with New French Theory is less direct, although Roland Barthes's analogy (in *S/Z*) relating modernist writing to atonal music (writing that eliminates the hermeneutic and proairetic codes, comparable to the tonality of melody and harmony) suggests the articulation with textuality. Postmodern texts, that is, would correspond to Cage's "step beyond" even serial concepts to the principle of accepting all audible phenomena as the material proper to music (a step made possible by the advent of electronic tapes). Derrida's suggestion (in the closing of "Speculer—sur 'Freud' "—*La Carte postale*) that *rhythm* might replace dialectical development as the principle of textual "arrangement" (*dispositio*), indicates the potential usefulness or relevance of Cage, who uses rhythm as the structuring device for his lectures as well as for his musical compositions (modes that, in any case, begin to lose their distinctness in his work). Cage, that is, "scores" his talks, based on pure "time" or "duration" (one meaning of the "signature" in Derrida). Beuys also works with a musical analogy, describing his "signature" text—a mass of fat applied to the corner of a room—as the "score" of all his other Actions.

A note prefacing "Lecture on Nothing" announces its structure: "There are four measures in each line and twelve lines in each unit of the rhythmic structure. There are forty-eight such units, each having forty-eight measures. The whole is divided into five large parts, in the proportion 7, 6, 14, 14, 7" (*Silence*, p. 109). Beginning with a statement similar to Derrida's opening in "Title"—"I am here [pause] and there is nothing to say"—Cage goes on to explain how the rhythmic or syntactic principle of composition liberates the lecturer from the anxiety of content:

> This is a composed talk, for I am making it just as I make a piece of music. It is like a glass of milk. We need the glass and we need the milk. Or again it is like an empty glass into which at any moment anything may be poured. As we go along, (who knows?) an i-dea may occur in this talk. I have no idea whether one will or not. If one does, let it. Regard it as something seen momentarily, as though from a window while traveling. (*Silence*, p. 110)

Cage's purpose is to *show* the structuring process while it is functioning ("How could I better tell what structure is than simply to tell about this, this talk which is contained within a space of time approximately forty minutes long?'' [*Silence*, p. 112]). *What* he shows (similar to what Barthes calls ''structuration'') is comparable to the framing that Derrida modeled with the picture matting (*passe-partout*) in which any illustration whatever (the examples juxtaposed in the montage of the lecriture) could be mounted. Structure, for Cage, ''is a discipline which, accepted, in return accepts whatever'' (*Silence*, p. 111). The mathematical (musical) character of structuration is associated with dissemination in Derrida's discussion of Sollers's *Numbers*, in which the text—the column of words running down the page—is described as a kind of frame (resembling the window in Cage's account): ''The transformations of meaning no longer hinge on any enrichment of 'history' and 'language' but only on a certain squaring of the text, on the obligatory passage through an open surface, on the detour through an empty square, around the column of fire'' (an allusion, perhaps, to the light beam of a film projector; *Dissemination*, p. 351). As in ''Lecture on Nothing,'' ''the column *is not*; it is nothing but the passage of dissemination.''

Making a similar point from the reader's perspective, Barthes explained (using a shamanistic analogy relevant to Beuys's persona as shaman) his procedure for dividing Balzac's ''Sarrasine'' into lexias as a ''starred text.'' ''The text,'' that is, ''in its mass, is comparable to a sky, at once flat and smooth, deep, without edges and without landmarks; like the soothsayer drawing on it with the tip of his staff an imaginary rectangle wherein to consult, according to certain principles, the flight of birds, the commentator traces through the text certain zones of reading, in order to observe therein the migration of meanings, the outcropping of codes, the passage of citations. . . . The lexia and its units will thereby form a kind of polyhedron.''[7]

As these examples suggest, the lecture as text is a certain kind of placing or spacing, the point being to refocus our attention, as composers or auditors, to the taking place of this place. At issue in these lectures is the extent to which the *performance* aspect of the lectures (the scene of lecturing, rather than the referential scene, the ''diegesis'' of the lecture) is foregrounded, violating the students' expectation of information as message or content. There always is content, of course (the lecriture is not nonobjective in that sense), but the matter of that content is left open. Derrida is the most sympathetic to the traditional demand in that he embeds his performance in a discourse, while Cage embeds, inscribes, his discourse in a performance. Derrida *performs* to the extent that he gives the audience a moment of anxiety (even if only in jest), and in playing with the pun in *le titrier*, which is transformable into the phrase *''le titre y est''* (approximated by the pun in English on "titleer" as "title here"). He shifts this play to the explanatory level, however, closing with a review of the ambiguities involved in one of Blanchot's titles, *"la folie du jour"* (finding seven levels—an allusion to Empson?—to which he adds a "further step," the history of the title itself). To fully perform "Title" as a lecriture might require an exercise of tonal play of the kind that Roman Jakobson has described as an "emotive" (as opposed to a referential or cognitive) function:

> A former actor of Stanislavskij's Moscow Theater told me how at his audition he was asked by the famous director to make forty different messages from the phrase *Segodnja vecerom,* "this evening," by diversifying its expressive tint. He made a list of some forty emotional situations, then emitted the given phrase in accordance with each of these situations, which his audience had to recognize only from the changes in the sound shape of the same two words.[8]

A simplified version of this tonal experiment might be tried in a lecriture by reading a conventional academic paper with a variety of emotional tones ranging from sarcastic to plaintive.

Roland Barthes noted the importance of this musical or tonal dimension of instruction, designated as the "rhetorical system": "My teacher's speech, is, so to speak, never neutral; at the very moment when he seems simply to be telling me that red signals an interdiction [the example involves instruction in the traffic code], he is telling me other things as well: his mood, his character, the 'role' he wishes to assume in my eyes, our relation as student and teacher; these new signifieds are not entrusted to the words of the code being taught, but to other forms of discourse ('values,' turns of phrase, intonation, everything that makes up the instructor's rhetoric and phraseology). In other words, another semantic system almost inevitably builds itself on the instructor's speech, i.e., the system of connotation."[9]

As a final example of the lecriture, I should note one of Beuys's Actions which may be understood as a commentary on literature, structured according to the "chiastic invagination" of Derrida's "double science" and manifested in such essays as "Living On: Borderlines" (in which Derrida wrote "along side" Shelley's "Triumph of Life" with a discussion of Blanchot) or *Glas* (the double-columned book juxtaposing pieces on Hegel and Genet). Here is Tisdall's account of Beuys's performance of *Iphigenie/Titus Andronicus*:

> At the Frankfurt theater festival 'experimenta 3' in May 1969, Beuys was invited to design sets for *Iphigenie* and *Titus Andronicus,* but he offered to perform them simultaneously instead. Just as in the Theory of Sculpture, the poles of chaos and order are linked by sculptural

movement [the process by which fat, packed into the corner of a room, stains the walls, the fat representing creative chaos, the corner representing rational order] so here German "idealism," Goethe's *Iphigenie*, and English "realism," Shakespeare's *Titus Andronicus*, were brought together on the stage. Over the loudspeaker came pre-recorded versions of both, read by actors. Beuys recited *Iphigenie* independently. One side of the stage was empty—that represented Titus—while the other was occupied by a white horse, standing on a sheet of iron so that the stamping of hoofs was amplified very loudly. Beuys himself, wrapped to begin with in a shining white fur, represented Iphigenie, mirrored by the horse. . . . On the *Iphigenie* side of the stage were chalk diagrams and scores for the action, lumps of fat which Beuys periodically spat over into the *Titus* area, and sugar lumps with which he beat out another rhythm. The acoustic emphasis of the whole action is clear from the preparatory drawings illustrating the sculptural potential of the voice. (Tisdall, p. 182)

Another commentator considers the staging of this Action typical of Beuys's productions: "Beuys starts with well-known material whose meaning is fixed and whose presentation always remains the same. He then abandons these restricted forms and replaces them with his explorative methods in which, through the inclusion of unusual materials, he makes usable lost connections of meaning for his consciousness-raising process."[10] Beuys has noted that there is no concept available with which to bring together the materials thus juxtaposed into a unity. But this very impossibility provokes the pedagogical effect that he wants (his texts being didactic), through which the audience activates the natural capabilities of the mind to seek and achieve closure. As Barthes reminds us, "text is produced in the space of the relations between the reader and the written, and that space is the site of a productivity: 'écriture' ('writing')."[11] *Iphigenie/Titus Andronicus* is a good illustration of the fact that the lecriture is a mode in which the teacher *does* something *with* literature, rather than *saying* something *about* it. And the sense of this drama is determined by the students who receive it.

Beuys's use of props in his commentary on Goethe and Shakespeare brings me to the second major aspect of a textualist post(e)pedagogy—the use of models.

MODELS

Confining myself to the level of the minimum difference between post(e)pedagogy and conventional pedagogy, I might mark one other aspect, besides the foregrounding of performance, which distinguishes the new approach—shifting from exclusive reliance on discursive or verbal presentations (no matter how baroque the style) to the use of objects as models: the introduction of "apparatus" into the classroom for purposes of demonstration. On the surface, considered exclusively in terms of "technique," this use of models might be viewed as the extension to the humanities of procedures that are commonplace in science instruction. Gerald Holton has raised this question of pedagogy in its largest sense—how the knowledge, techniques, and attitudes of any topic may be conveyed by one individual to a group (a situation that shares features of the relationship between mother and child, actor and audience, as well as teacher and student).[12]

Part of the value of Holton's discussion (in addition to the virtue of providing a less controversial context for the concept of models) is that he calls attention to the special nature of pedagogical space (its discontinuous relationship with "everything else"). Hence what might seem to be faults in a "mimetological" (realist) theory of pedagogical representation—the distortions, dissociations, and displacements that mark the gap between the whole of physical reality and what is presentable in a classroom (the "abjectness" of a sign that bears no resemblance to what it "stands for")—are accepted and exploited in Holton's demonstrational mode. The purpose of the didactic demonstration according to Holton echoes the goal of Jacques Lacan's seminars—to stimulate the love of learning first of all—which can be achieved, Holton says, by making the student "a participant rather than a consumer" (in short, the textualist goal of a "writerly" classroom). Chief among the stimulating devices that are meant to provoke the student into the writerly attitude is the use of experiments that the students manipulate themselves and models that supplement discourse and aid memory. While Holton acknowledges the difference between the lived and the didactic levels of reality, the "messiness" of the former is to be introduced into the latter in certain fragmented ways, such as the presentation of "relics"—obsolete scientific equipment (similar to Beuys's use of outmoded electronic apparatuses in some of his Actions) that evokes the history of knowledge.

Holton points out that at least seven levels of reality are operative in the pedagogical situation, all of which must be taken into account and which may be exploited for indirect conveyance of what is inaccessible in the natural (or cultural) world: lived experience; the didactic; depiction (film, video); analogon (models); coding (graphics, words, writing); metasymbolic abstractions (technical rather than ordinary language); unconscious (intuitive) apperceptions. Although I agree with Holton's view that the effective class attempts to work on all these levels, I do not share his assumption that the use of physical apparatus (models and equipment) is exclusive to the sciences, which is due, Holton argues, to the "external" focus of science on the natural world, as distinct from the focus of the humanities "on man himself."

In fact, a fundamental dimension of post(e)pedagogy is precisely what might be termed a humanities "laboratory," concerned with providing a visual track to supplement the verbal dialogue of teaching, whose function is at once mnemonic and analytic. The actual manipulation of an item, for example, the toy slate that Freud uses as his model of the psyche (in the case of a class assigned to read Freud, or Derrida on Freud), serves not only to impress the theory on the memory but also allows the class to consider possible alternatives to Freud's application of the model. The principle of this strategy is related to one of the features of paleological thinking (cf. Derrida's paleonymic deconstruction of concepts) defined by Silvano Arieti: namely, "the concretization and perceptualization of the concept," an operation that allows the class to interrogate the material or vehicular level of the analogies and metaphors found in critical writing.[13]

Derrida, in any case, has suggested that the mind may not be so easily distinguished from the machines with which it supplements itself. In "Freud and the Scene of Writing," Derrida departs from Freud on the question of the Mystic Writing Pad as a model of mind at the point at which Freud abandons the model and reverts to the distinction between living and artificial memory. The analogy between the prototype and the organ ceases to apply, Freud says, to the extent that the Mystic Pad is "dead," as opposed to the wax of psychical memory, which is living. Freud, in other words, rejoins here the Platonic tradition and its attempt to separate anamnesis from hypomnesis (against the sophists' exploitation of mechanical aids to memory, such as writing itself). Derrida remarks that Freud failed to think through the problem in terms of the very unity of life and death which he himself conceptualized speculatively in his metapsychology (the merger of the life drive and the death drive formulated in *Beyond the Pleasure Principle*). "Far from the machine being a pure absence of spontaneity," Derrida states, "its *resemblance* to the psychical apparatus, its existence and its necessity bear witness to the finitude of the mnemic spontaneity which is thus supplemented. The machine—and, consequently, representation—is death and finitude *within* the psyche. Nor does Freud examine the possibility of this machine, which, in the world, has at least begun to *resemble* memory, and increasingly resembles it more closely."[14] In other words, by means of deconstructive procedures, it is just as easy to reverse the analogy, to draw the conclusion that the memory *also* resembles the *mechanical functioning* of the prototype (just as much as it resembles the other features of the model such as the double inscription and so forth), rather than to break off arbitrarily the analogy at a point dictated by the traditional notion of the spontaneous nature of living memory (consciousness). Derrida's strategy, typically, is to examine and to revise analogies or metaphors encountered in an object of study in terms of the elements of the vehicle that are *excluded* from the comparison (in this instance Freud wanted to exclude the mechanical nature of the Mystic Pad).

The rationale for Derrida's determination to elaborate on Freud's mechanical model has to do with the advent of electronics after Freud, which requires a systematic interrogation of the interpenetration of the psyche, writing, and technology. "Here the question of *technology* (a new name must perhaps be found in order to remove it from its traditional problematic) may not be derived from an assumed opposition between the psychical and the nonpsychical, life and death. Writing, here, is *technē* as the relation between life and death, between present and representation, between two apparatuses. It opens up the question of technics: of the apparatus in general and of the analogy between the psychical apparatus and the nonpsychical apparatus. In this sense writing is the stage of history and the play of the world" (*Writing*, pp. 228–29). Derrida is alluding, of course, to the ever-greater role that computers are playing in contemporary thinking, and his interest in the tendency of the psyche to imitate the machines that extend the psyche's powers is supported by those who suggest that a civilization tends to think by means of the forms that are available in the dominant apparatus of communication. In this context, logocentrism simply names the era of alphabetic writing that replaced oral civilization and that is given way, in turn, to an electronic era, in which we are beginning to think filmicly.[15] Thus, Derrida extends Freud's original mind/machine analogy (thinking/writing) to more complex devices, such as the printing press. He superimposes the vocabularies of the discourses relevant to each domain, using polysemy and the homophone to guide this articulation. Terms such as "signature" and "tympanum," used in the technical vocabulary of printing as well as having reference "to man himself" (as Holton put it), become organizing terms for a theoretical program for the reconceiving of "mind." This search has yet to be applied to the technical vocabularies of television and computers, but one point of departure might be the homonym articulating "console" as the control unit of an electrical system (being introduced into schools and homes at a phenomenal pace) and "console" as "giving comfort or cheering up" (the effect often reported as the emotional association with learning machines).

Relevant to the value of objects and apparatuses as models in a humanities laboratory, Gyorgy Kepes argued for the need to "regain the health of our visual sensibilities," to educate our inner and social vision such that they might better cope with the new scale of life created by science and technology. With respect to this aim, Kepes suggests that it is now possible (or at least necessary) to fulfill Tommaso Campanella's dream (in the utopian *City of the Sun*, which also served to inspire Beuys) that knowledge might be made *public* through the cooperation of artists and scientists in finding visual analogies for abstract concepts. Of course, the entire theory of representation with which post(e)pedagogy works is different from the one understood by Campanella (and by Kepes, for that matter), but the goal of "popularizing" knowledge is the same.[16]

It may be worth noting, as a further context supportive of a humanities laboratory (or textshop), Gaston Bachelard's assessment of the principal pedagogical problem of our era (made as early as the 1930s). Noting the discontinuity brought about by modern science separating formal space (the space in which we think) from phenomenological space (lived experience), Bachelard called for a new pedagogy that would introduce into the humanities epistemological models derived from science (especially from the new physics). Although post(e)pedagogy, operating in a postmodern era, has a different relation to science than did Bachelard (deconstructive rather than reproductive), there remain several major points of contact between the two (grammatology and surrationalism), not to mention the fact that Derrida (citing *La Formation de l'esprit scientifique*, one of Bachelard's works on the philosophy of science) suggests Bachelard as a possible guide for a study of analogical thinking in science.[17]

The essential task of Bachelard's new pedagogy was to be the generalization of the "uncertainty principle" from physics to general education (cf. Derrida's generalization, metaphorically, of Gödel's undecidability proof); its organizing goal was *invention*, to be approached by a "psychoanalysis of objective knowledge" (with which Derrida sympathizes in "White Mythology") in order to determine the intellectual as well as the emotional blockages in the learning process. One of the more interesting elements in Bachelard's program (which is relevant to the identification of precedents for a humanities laboratory) is the designation of Alfred Korzybski as the vanguard figure of a new pedagogy (circa 1940):

> In America, indeed, the movement of extensional logic has been gaining in importance for some time. A renewal of human thought is

looked for, and a whole group of thinkers (unencumbered, to be sure, by strenuous technical demonstrations) is relying on non-Aristotelian logic to renew the methods of pedagogy, following the inspiration of Korzybski. This amounts to demonstrating the value of non-Aristotelian logic even for walking around, for living itself. . . . We shall therefore follow the work of Korzybski even to its pedagogical applications.[18]

In Korzybski, the founder of General Semantics (a controversial educator who apparently was the "Jacques Lacan" of his day),[19] Bachelard admired his revision of logic (against Aristotle's principle of Identity and of noncontradiction), adding a third value—the *absurd*—to the existing values of "true" and "false" (thus bringing logic into line with the principles of new physics, then proposing that light be comprehended in terms of the "wavicle"). A propos of an education for invention (creative rather than reproductive), and relevant to the matting frame (*passe-partout*) structure of pedagogical space (textual space—"because of its empty square, its open surface, its discounted face, it does not enclose but rather leaves the way open for the intersection of meanings. The square proliferates" [*Dissemination*, p. 349]), Bachelard provides a justification for his selection of Korzybski as an exemplary pedagogue:

> By and large the direction taken by this latter technique [of non-identity] is to exceed the principles of the psychology of form by giving a systematic education in deformation. Animal psychology has proved that by the use of mazes one could constitute new behavior patterns in very rudimentary psychic organisms. The task of non-elementalism would be to train human psychology in some way with the assistance of sequences of concepts (intellectual mazes) in which, essentially, crossroad concepts would yield a prospect of at the very least, two usable concepts. Having once reached the crossroad concept, the mind would not simply have to choose between a true and useful concept on the one hand and a false and harmful one on the other. It would be faced with a duality or a plurality of interpretations. Thus all psychological blockage would be impossible at the level of concepts, but, even better, the concept would be essentially a crossroads at which one would become conscious of one's freedom in metaphorical activity. (Bachelard, p. 110)

The Bachelard-Korzybski notion of an "intellectual maze" corresponds to more recent models describing the mechanical generation of ideas (invention) on the basis of information theory (the computer paradigm), such as Michel Serres's *ars interveniendi* (proposed in his *Hermes* series), or Umberto Eco's remark that "the project of an encyclopedia competence [of which he is an advocate] is governed by an underlying metaphysics or by a metaphor (or an allegory): the idea of labyrinth."[20] Eco's labyrinth, however, is neither "plain" (a straight line) nor a maze; it is a net, best imaged, he says, as a rhizome (a tangle of bulbs and tubers), the main feature of which is "that every point can be connected with every other point."

Some of Korzybski's insights into the consequences of the new science (physics and mathematics) for logic and language anticipate certain deconstructionist notions, such as the general denial of the "is" of identity, accepting "difference" in its place, requiring (Korzybski says) a fourth-dimensional language, a new space-time (Einsteinian) vocabulary (which Derrida in fact provides with "*differance*," defined as a differing and deferring).[21] Korzybski also believed in the possibility of teaching creativity and of popularizing theoretical knowledge by means of simple visual models. What he has to say about his chief model, the apparatus called the Structural Differential ("it is an apparatus made of perforated slabs which can be attached to a series of labels furnished with strings. This apparatus translates to the eye the various conceptual connections which are possible" [Bachelard, p. 110]), both in its description and in the rationale for its use, recalls Derrida's theory of models. Indeed, Korzybski's "machine" was designed to teach something similar to what Derrida models as the chiastic interlace of the shoelaces (alluding to, as a model, the partially laced shoes depicted in Van Gogh's painting) in "Restitutions."[22] Here is Korzybski's description (accompanied by a diagram):

> The Structural Differentials are manufactured in two forms: 1) in a printed map-like scroll for hanging on the walls or black-board; 2) in relief, broken off to indicate its limitless extension. The disk symbolizes the human object; the (other) disk represents the animal object. The label represents the higher abstraction called a name (with its meaning given by a definition). The lines in the relief diagram are hanging strings which are tied to pegs. They indicate the process of abstracting. The free hanging strings indicate the most important characteristics *left out*, neglected, or forgotten in the abstracting. (Korzybski, p. 399)

The purpose of the Structural Differential was to reeducate people to think in a desubstantialized world consisting not of objects but of *events* (i.e., quantum physics). The model visualizes the levels of abstraction involved in the simplest act of perception/conception—for example, the perception of a pencil—beginning with the event ("the mad dance of electrons"), which possesses an infinite number of characteristics, through the object itself, which has a large but finite number of characteristics, to the label or name attached to the object, to which a smaller number of characteristics are assigned "by definition," and so forth (the chain of labels, forming a kind of kite tail, suggests the infinite regression or succession of open semiosis).

Korzybski's goal, however laboriously achieved, is to shift the student's experience of language from the old naming theory to a kind of structuralist view of systematic, relational difference. The difference that the model stresses is that between words and things, reminding the student of the great number of *properties* excluded during concept formation and in description, definition, and all discourse. In the case of an object such as a pencil—that is, to the label "pencil"—"we would ascribe its length, thickness, shape, color, hardness. But we would mostly *disregard* the accidental characteristics, such as a scratch on its surface, or the kind of glue by which the two wooden parts of the objective 'pencil' are held together" (p. 387). Part of Korzybski's concern is that "every individual object has individual peculiarities" that have to be taken into account in research (p. 414). Deconstruction, for its part, is not concerned with the analytical point of the model (intended to devalue ordinary language), but with the exposure of the properties left out of account in the discourses of knowledge.

Roland Barthes perhaps best summarized the value of models for a textshop when he remarked that "the text can be approached by definitions, but also (and perhaps above all) by metaphors" ("Text," pp. 35–36). The metaphor, as part of a dramatic pedagogy, is an alternative to the reliance, in an epistemological pedagogy, on definitions, whose inadequacy for dealing with difference/differance is demonstrated by the Structural Differential. And like Bachelard and Korzybski before him, Barthes finds in science a storehouse for metaphorical invention (he is particularly attracted to the correlation between the proverb about lifting oneself by one's own bootstraps and the recent theory of the bootstrap in physics, having to do with the way in which particles are self-engendered out of relationships at a given moment).[23] The idea, according to Barthes, is to develop concepts that function as metaphors (*Grain*, p. 260).

In short, we might conclude that Barthes's admonition with respect to criticism—"*Let the commentary be itself a text*" ("Text," p. 44)—is, in post(e)pedagogy, extended to the teacher's discourse in the classroom. Pedagogy must itself be a text.

AS-SIGN-MENTS

The post(e)pedagogue communicates the ideas of a discipline by means of a lecriture in which are mounted certain models. But it may not be possible, or even desirable, to shift completely to a postmodernized pedagogy. The textshop, rather, may serve as a supplement to current practice. Indeed, part of its effectiveness depends on its juxtaposition with conventional approaches, its structure being, as Barthes stressed, that of parody. Parody can be "revolutionary," Barthes argues, because it simultaneously presents the object and contests it: "a simple, beautiful formula—the 'along side' " (alluding to the etymology of *parody* as "beside" + "song"; see *Grain*, pp. 49, 56, 126).

My own application of the lecriture has been sparing, strategically tentative, and eclectic. To give one example, I have assayed the technique in the genre of the "introduction" for a visiting lecturer. The organizing principle of such presentations is "dramatic"—not only to tell the audience about the speaker's essential method or orientation, but to *show* it, to demonstrate it by using parodic exaggeration as a means to enlarge it (the close-up or *blow-up* of filmic montage, hence at once denotation and detonation). The first time that I tried this approach was when Harold Bloom visited our campus. My introduction to his address consisted of an attempt to perform the anxiety of influence. After explaining briefly the rhetorical strategies by which a poet or critic establishes his own priority, I cited a passage from "The Breaking of Form" in order to prepare for what was to follow:

> Literary prophets teach us that the Greeks and the Renaissance were fiercely competitive in all things intellectual and spiritual, and that if we would emulate them, we hardly can hope to be free of competitive strivings. But I think these sages teach a harsher lesson, which they sometimes tell us they have learned from the poets. What is weak is forgettable and will be forgotten. Only strength is memorable; only the capacity to wound gives a healing capacity the chance to endure, and so to be heard. Freedom of meaning is wrested by combat, of meaning against meaning. . . . Reading well is therefore *not necessarily a polite process*, and may not meet the academy's social standards of civility.[24]

The next step was to demonstrate the strong poet-critic's final strategy—apophrades,

> a style that captures and oddly retains priority over their precursors, so that the tyranny of time almost is overturned, and one can believe, for startled moments, that they are being *imitated by their ancestors.* . . . The triumph of having so stationed the precursor, in one's own work, that particular passages in *his* work seem to be not presages of one's own advent, but rather to be indebted to one's own achievement, and even (necessarily) to be lessened by one's greater splendor.[25]

I then claimed that my monograph *The Legend of Herostratus* (University Presses of Florida, 1977), a study of envy in Rousseau and Unamuno, which was published after Bloom's *Anxiety* and which was a work that Bloom (like most other people) was entirely ignorant of, had in fact rendered Bloom's publications superfluous, or at best made them mere auxiliaries. With great economy (my one text to his many), *Herostratus* went directly to the essence of the phenomenon that Bloom described by identifying its "anxieteme" in the legend of my title. In order to usurp the occasion of his lecture for my demonstration, I expressed my gratitude to Bloom for having popularized my theory and declared him an honorary Herostratus, in recognition of which I awarded him an autographed copy of my monograph. Bloom's talk, then, constituted an acceptance speech. Bloom did come forward to accept his award (feeling the pressure, no doubt, of the contract that Derrida referred to; in any case that seemed preferable to the possibility that I might carry out my earlier threat to refuse him the stage altogether).

The purpose of this experiment was as much to expose the conventions of the "introduction" as it was to dramatize Bloom's theory. The audience, after some hesitation, honored the performance with laughter (you had to be there), which brings me back to the "ri" of the lecriture. For what remains to be dealt with is the question of the assignments appropriate for a textshop. Barthes again shows the way, suggesting that pedagogy need not be magisterial, that it could be "amorous," meaning that the *pleasure* of the text might become the pleasure of the assignment. To use pleasure as the guide for rethinking the function of the assignment is to seek a solution for the problem identified by Michel Serres: "At its birth, knowledge is happy, delivered natively from all culpability. It is, perhaps, happy by nature. However, in the institutions which direct it, exploit and transmit it, for the individuals it overwhelms, it fosters, in fact, the death instinct. Throughout my youth, I believed I discerned, on the walls of amphitheaters or on the brows of the learned, the hideous word, Renan's absurdity: sadness alone is fruitful. How the change came about, I don't know. By whatever means its own nature might be restored, it is urgent, on pain of death, to respond to this question."[26]

The echo of the opening of Rousseau's *Social Contract* indicates the seriousness with which Serres views the academy's lack of frivolity. The unreceivability of Serres's appeal may be measured by the extent to which contemporary educators agree with Plato's suspicion of play and his condemnation, therefore, of writing. Behind the apparent *logophilia*—the esteem of discourse—that seems to characterize our culture, Michel Foucault observes this Platonic emotion: "It is as though these taboos, these barriers, thresholds and limits were deliberately disposed in order, at least partly, to master and control the great proliferation of discourse, in such a way as to relieve its richness of its most dangerous elements; to organize its disorder so as to skate round its most uncontrollable aspects. It is as though people had wanted to efface all trace of its irruption into the activity of our thought and language. There is undoubtedly in our society a profound logophobia, a sort of dumb fear of these events."[27]

Educators in this Platonic tradition attempt to contain the frivolousness of writing (its potential for "play") by assigning "play" to the "innocent and inoffensive" category of "entertainment" or "fun." "Amusement: however far off it may be," Derrida remarks, "the common translation of *paidia* by *pastime* [*divertissement*] no doubt only helps consolidate the Platonic repression of play" (*Dissemination*, p. 156). Derrida submits *paideia*, then, to the same desedimentation that is undertaken with other philosophemes (founding metaphors), such as *eidos* and *theoria* (based on metaphors of sight): "It is simply a question of being alert to the implications, to the historical sedimentation of the language which we use."[28] Desedimentation in this case serves to expose the sublation of *paidia* (play) into *paideia* (culture). "In Greek," Werner Jaeger notes, "the two words have the same root, because they both originally refer to the activity of the child (*pais*); but Plato is the first to deal with the problem of the relation between the two concepts. . . . It was taken up by Aristotle, and serves to illustrate his ideal of culture— scientific leisure as opposed to pure play. Plato is anxious to include the play-element in his paideia: the guards' children are to learn their lessons through play, which means that paidia helps paideia [supplement]. Dialectic, however, is a higher stage. It is not play, but earnest. Since many modern languages have taken over this classical contrast of the two concepts, it is difficult for us to realize what an effort of abstract philosophical thinking created it."[29]

Derrida explicitly associates writing with *paidia* (play) to show that both have undergone a similar repression in logocentrism. At the beginning of "Plato's Pharmacy," for example, Derrida observes: "Since we have already said everything, the reader must bear with us if we continue on awhile. If we extend ourselves by force of play. If we then *write* a bit: on Plato, who already said in the *Phaedrus* that writing can only repeat (itself), that it 'always signifies (*semainei*) the same' and that it is a 'game' (*paidia*)" (*Dissemination*, p. 65). Plato is committed to the "science of measure," to the *episteme*, as the "antidote" to writing as *pharmakon* (poison/elixir), which puts its user into the double bind of the "supplement" (there can be no intelligibility without "writing"—

representation, sign, symbol, mediation—the intelligible being that which repeats, is recognizable as the same); and yet, by its very nature as simulacrum, writing continually threatens to carry off "being" into "mask" and "festival" (*Dissemination*, p. 140). The "magic" of imitations (writing, painting) is like the cosmetics, colors, and perfumes that are used to make presentable the corpse at funerals. "Death, masks, makeup, all are part of the festival that subverts the order of the city, its smooth regulation by the dialectician and the science of being. Plato, as we shall see, is not long in identifying writing with festivity. And play. A certain festival, a certain game" (*Dissemination*, p. 142). The advent of mechanical reproduction exacerbates the issue, of course, increasing the possibility that voice and *paideia* will lose control of their supplements, writing and *paidia*.

Throughout his interviews and essays, Barthes reiterates that Bertolt Brecht is his primary tutor figure, remarking that Brecht saw no need to leave the realm of entertainment to accomplish his intellectual aims. That is, for its part, education should move in the same direction that Brecht set for theater. "But this makes it simpler for the theater to edge as close as possible to the apparatus of education and mass communication," Brecht argued. "For although we cannot bother it with the raw material of knowledge in all its variety, which would stop it from being enjoyable, it is still free to find enjoyment in teaching and inquiring. It constructs its workable representations of society, which are then in a position to influence society, wholly and entirely as a game."[30]

Barthes translates Brecht's attitude into the pleasure of the text by calling for a "civilization of amateurs" (*Grain*, p. 193), meaning that we need to reestablish the relation between the reader and the world of production of texts, to introduce the reader to the pleasure of writing, of fabricating a text (*Grain*, p. 227). What Barthes's amateurization implies for post(e)pedagogy is that we approach our undergraduates, not as specialists, but as amateurs (in the best sense of the term). As such they might be introduced to the real issue of our material: not what literary works mean, but why one writes in the first place; not the work of analysis, but, first of all, the pleasure of the creative process. Imagine if athletic programs taught only the analysis of sports, and not the playing of them. And yet we relate to the imagination and creativity analytically, never as faculties in need of exercise. By reproducing our specialist's pedagogy for our undergraduate majors, and even for general education, we form only consumers, spectators, very few of whom desire the pleasure, which they must accept on our authority.

The avant-garde revolution in the arts offers a way out of this dilemma. The general principle for the pedagogy of amateurs is Beuys's slogan "Every person an artist," which may be understood as a summary of the lesson of the arts in this century, beginning with Marcel Duchamp's ready-mades, passing through the aleatory techniques developed in surrealism, and coming up to contemporary textuality. The lesson of this history should be remarked from the perspectives of both the arts and criticism. Avant-garde and experimentalist art (as distinct from modernism)[31] has demystified the artist and dematerialized the art object as part of working through the separation of "art" from "craft" or "skill." The point of this development is that anyone *can* "do" art in this experimentalist sense, in which the only requirement is to actively make something. "This is where the sentence: 'Everybody is an artist' becomes interesting," Beuys says, discussing his "multiples" (simple, mass-produced items, on the order of ready-mades). "And that is precisely what, to my mind, people can experience with the help of such objects. They can realize that everyone is an artist, because many people will ask themselves: 'Why don't I make something like that, something similar.' The sentence 'Everybody is an artist' simply means that the human being is a creative being, that he is a creator, and what's more, that he can be productive in a great many different ways."[32]

From the side of criticism, this creative option, due to the absence of any metalanguage, is couched as a necessity. Literature or art, as understood within postmodern criticism, has no need of interpretation and cannot be demystified in any case, since it is already "self-conscious." Literature, Paul de Man notes, "is the only form of language free from the fallacy of unmediated expression. . . . But the fiction is not myth, for it knows and names itself as fiction. It is not a demystification, it is demystified from the start. When modern critics think they are demystifying literature, they are in fact being demystified by it."[33] In this crisis of criticism, de Man says, the "well-established rules and conventions that governed the discipline of criticism and made it a cornerstone of the intellectual establishment have been so badly tampered with that the entire edifice threatens to collapse." The alternative to criticism in this situation, providing the model for assignments just as it did for lectures, is textuality. "With the writer of bliss (and his reader) begins the untenable text, the impossible text," Roland Barthes remarks. "This text is outside pleasure, outside criticism, *unless it is reached through another text of bliss*: you cannot speak 'on' such a text, you can only speak 'in' it, enter into a desperate plagiarism."[34] The only response to a "text of bliss" (experimental arts, whether generated by automatic techniques—collage, frottage, aleatory devices, free associa-

tion—or linguistic theory) is another text, alongside an originary plagiarism or parody. In the textshop this approach may be extended to any
work.

The advantage of beginning with the textualist assignment in the
context of models drawn from the avant-garde is that the principle of
"everyone an artist" is explicitly part of the experimentalist aesthetic.
Texts produced by students using "mechanical" or automatic means
have the same status as the tutor text. A student's ready-made is "as
good" as one by Duchamp. But the issue in the textshop is not the
quality of the product, but the quality of the process, the goal being to
simulate, if you like, the experience, the pleasure, of creativity. Oulipo,
the Workshop for Potential Literature, offers a practical strategy for
realizing the poststructuralist lesson that each text is its own model and
hence, potentially, a generalizable form for the production of other texts.
By way of example of how these principles might function as assignments, let me cite a work (text) sheet that I distributed as the instructions
for a project:

> Principle: creativity as transformation (generative and transforma-
> tional poetics); the use of individual poems as if they were generic
> forms. The point of the Humanities Laboratory is to take one step back
> from the information and skills relevant to the discipline in order to
> attend to the fundamental experience of creativity that motivates the
> production of literature in the first place. By using an extant poem (of
> your choice) as a generative form, the student has a short-cut to the
> production of a complete, finished creation. Even though the stu-
> dent's participation is "mechanical," the resultant text is an authentic
> invention. The exercise may be compared to using belts and ropes to
> learn difficult moves on the trampoline (the exercise as springboard).
> The chief lesson of such an exercise should involve the "fun"
> (FUNdamental) or pleasure of linguistic invention, but there are also
> several practical benefits, including the lessons to be learned about
> rhetorical effect from the commutation of a given poem into alternative
> versions (testing the romantic and formalist claims that a finished
> poem is "perfect"). The function and effect of diction, style, syntax,
> semantics, parts of speech, etc. in literature may be observed in the
> reworking of the poem. Sample Text: The first stanza from "The
> Tyger," William Blake.

> > Tyger! Tyger! burning bright
> > In the forests of the night,
> > What immortal hand or eye
> > Could frame thy fearful symmetry?

1. Transformation by antonymy (use a Thesaurus).

> Rabbit! Rabbit! freezing dull
> In the plains of the day,
> What mortal foot or ear
> Could copy thy timid disproportion?

2. Transformation by displacement (generated by looking up Blake's word in the dictionary, then replacing it with the first word above it of the same type [noun, verb, etc.]. The substitution formula may involve any number, above or below the original term).

> Tiffin!* Tiffin! burlesquing brigandishly
> In the foreskin of the niggling,
> What immoral hanaper** or eyas***
> Could fragmentise thy feal**** symmetalism*****

(*lunch. **receptacle for documents or case for drinking vessel. ***a young falcon. ****faithful. *****the use of two or more metals, such as gold and silver, combined in assigned proportions as a monetary standard).[35]

Many other generative and combinatory formulas are possible, of course. What gave me pleasure in preparing the textsheet was that the second sample made sense. The laugh that such exercises elicit (the result is similar for visual productions, using Duchamp's modified ready-mades as the model) is best described in Brecht's *Galileo*:

ANDREA: Then all things that are lighter than water float, and all things that are heavier sink. Q.E.D.
GALILEO: Not at all. Hand me that iron needle. Heavier than water? (*They all nod*) A piece of paper. (*He places the needle on a piece of paper and floats it on the surface of the water. Pause.*) Do not be hasty with your conclusion. (*Pause.*) What happens?
FEDERZONI: The paper has sunk, the needle is floating. (*They laugh.*)
VIRGINIA: What's the matter?
MRS. SARTI: Every time I hear them laugh it sends shivers down my spine.[36]

The distance that separates the textshop from current practice may be measured by the fact that two of the worst faults, according to the latter, become guidelines for the former—misreading and plagiarism. These practices may seem contradictory in that misreading (of which Harold Bloom gives the best description) is motivated by the desire never to reproduce the given but always to innovate, to produce something *other*, while plagiarism is necessitated by the postmodern understanding of creativity that rejects Romantic theories of ''genius'' and "originality" while reviving something like the medieval sense of *inventio*—invention as (hypomnemic, mechanical) *discovery* rather than as "creation" (something out of nothing). Derrida's notion of differance, which eliminates at every level any claim to priority of originality, is just one version of the general postmodernist rejection of Romantic creativity. Collage is the appropriate procedure in this situation, taking over what one finds, misreading it in citation. Misreading is an operation that is applied to plagiarized material, a dynamic that is governed by the principle of iteration (the repetition constitutive of the identity/difference pair). "As soon as a sign emerges, it begins by repeating itself. Without this, it would not be a sign, would not be what it is, that is to say, the non-self-identity which regularly refers to the same" (*Writing*, p. 297). Such is the "sign" in as-sign-ment.

"Logokleptism" is the term that has been used to describe this new attitude (fulfilling the general aesthetic of the age of mechanical reproduction); it is exemplified in its purest form by the work of Sherrie Levine, who literally "takes" pictures, borrowing the work of other artists for her productions. "At a recent exhibition, Levine showed six photographs of a nude youth. They were simply rephotographed from the famous series by Edward Weston of his young son Neil, which was available to Levine as a poster published by the Witkin Gallery. According to the copyright law, the images belong to Weston."[37] Similarly, the "autobiographical" statement that Levine attached to "her" work was an unacknowledged citation (the strategy that Barthes recommends, to cite without quotation marks) of a novel by Alberto Moravia (a passage containing an erotic confession). The articulation of Weston's photographs and the Moravia fragment constitute the writing of Levine's piece. Derrida has provided the theory for a logokleptic aesthetic, especially in his critique of "copyright" in "Limited Inc" and in his various discussions of the "Cretan Liar" paradox that undermines the decidability of first-person utterances. Whatever the ultimate practicality of logokleptism might be, the procedure is well suited to the pedagogical situation (it may even be the product of the contemporary tendency of artists to become teachers), in which teachers and students alike are always in the position of working with the intellectual and artistic "property" of others.

Post(e)pedagogy is a response to the electronic paradigm, whose chief characteristic, with respect to education, is information overload, or knowledge explosion. "The knowledge explosion, both in quantity of data and speed of transmittal, has suddenly brought the world to our doorstep. With an overwhelming deluge of information, it has been suggested there is about 100 times as much to know now as there was in

1900. By the year 2000 there will be more than 1,000 times more knowledge of all kinds than there is now."[38] By the late 1960s "there were approximately 50,000 journals containing about one million separate scientific papers per year," supplemented by secondary journals abstracting the primary level, a task that is now being transferred to computers (Howard, p. 13). As Jean-François Lyotard has remarked, the individual professor in the postmodern situation will have to find a new function or become obsolete, given that "he is no longer as competent as the memory machines for transmitting established knowledge, and he is not as competent as interdisciplinary teams for imagining new moves or new games."[39]

The function that Walter Ong once attributed to the avant-garde arts—"a vacation from oppressive rationalism"[40]—may be extended by post(e)pedagogy to the humanities in general in order to meet the needs of students working in the postmodern condition of information overload. The *inventio* of the textshop, then, allows the student to *write* with the mass of data that already exists (bricolage). It is a mode intended for a world dominated by a science and a technology that have made us realize, as one critic said, that it is not the *sleep* of reason that breeds monsters any longer, but the attentiveness of scholarship, an insomniac knowledge, and the gray patience of genealogy.[41] Post(e)pedagogy, finally, is a nomad—it has no discipline base but is the exploration by means of art and autography of the relation between the student and knowledge.

The textshop, then, functions best as general education, being to the sciences what the carnival once was to the Church. The ultimate goal is to deconstruct the work/play, serious/frivolous opposition and to redesign the current college catalogues that reserve for language and literature its own ghetto of specialization. Meanwhile, let us promote the pleasure of the text, in order to shake loose the powerful strategies of hypomnesis (all the more powerful because artificial memory is now electronic) from the control of *Prudence,* which held them captive during the Christian era (mnemonics used to inventory the virtues and vices), enlisting them instead in the subversive games of festival. In terms of curriculum, carnival disrespect means the inversion of the "order" of disciplines (the "pharmacy" is a classic mnemonic image—an apothecary arranging his boxes stood for *dispositio,* arrangement, concerning the constraints of succession, the problem of beginnings and endings). As it is now, only a select few, after passing through years of replicating the known and of being socialized into discipline loyalty, are allowed to learn the actual nature of a discursive field, allowed to see its *frame*: the inner "mystery" of any discipline is not its order or coherence but is its

disorder, incoherence, and arbitrariness.⁴² The textshop permits the
student to by-pass initiation as a specialist (the "specialist" is to
modernism what the "genius" was to Romanticism), to confront
simultaneously the provisional, permeable character of all knowledge,
the creative "ground" (*apeiron*) of the formation of a discipline. This
confrontation is achieved by removing the disparity between the history
of knowledge and its transmission through the pedagogy of a given
moment, between the private experiences of discovery and the public or
collective institutionalization of a canon.

The problem with this pedagogy, however, may be identified by
one of Nietzsche's queries: Who will teach the teachers?

NOTES

1. The "Post(e)pedagogy" in my title is an allusion to my book *Applied Grammatology: Post(e)Pedagogy from Jacques Derrida to Joseph Beuys* (Baltimore, Md.: Johns Hopkins University Press, 1985). The French "e" is included to indicate that this approach is not only "beyond" the old pedagogy but that it is also a pedagogy designed for the age of video and computers (*poste* as "set").

2. Jacques Derrida, "Title (to be specified)," trans. Tom Conley, *Sub-Stance* 31 (1981).

3. Caroline Tisdall, *Joseph Beuys* (New York: Solomon R. Guggenheim Museum, 1979), p. 266. This is the catalogue for Beuys's one-man show at the Guggenheim Museum.

4. Rodolphe Gasché, "Self-Engendering as a Verbal Body," *Modern Language Notes* 93 (1978): 689–90.

5. Derrida discusses Mallarmé's piece and the mime in "The Double Session," in *Dissemination*, trans. Barbara Johnson (Chicago: University of Chicago Press, 1981).

6. John Cage, *Silence* (Cambridge, Mass.: MIT Press, 1970).

7. Roland Barthes, *S/Z*, trans. Richard Miller (New York: Hill & Wang, 1974), p. 14.

8. Roman Jakobson, "Linguistics and Poetics," in *The Structuralists from Marx to Lévi-Strauss*, ed. R. and F. De George (Garden City, N.Y.: Doubleday, 1972), p. 91.

9. Roland Barthes, *The Fashion System*, trans. M. Ward and R. Howard (New York: Hill & Wang, 1983), p. 31.

10. G. Adriani et al., *Joseph Beuys* (New York: Barron's, 1979).

11. Roland Barthes, "Theory of the Text," in *Untying the Text: A Post-Structuralist Reader*, ed. Robert Young (London: Routledge & Kegan Paul, 1981), p. 31.

12. Gerald Holton, "Conveying Science by Visual Presentation," in *The Education of Vision*, ed. Gyorgy Kepes (New York: Braziller, 1965).

13. Silvano Arieti, *Creativity: The Magic Synthesis* (New York: Basic Books, 1976), p. 82.

14. Jacques Derrida, *Writing and Difference*, trans. A. Bass (Chicago: University of Chicago Press, 1978), p. 228.

15. See Gavriel Salomon, *The Interaction of Media, Cognition, and Learning* (San Francisco: Jossey-Bass, 1979).

16. See Kepes's introduction to *The Education of Vision*.

17. Jacques Derrida, *Marges de la Philosophie* (Paris: Editions de Minuit, 1972), pp. 309–10.

18. Gaston Bachelard, *The Philosophy of No: A Philosophy of the New Scientific Mind*, trans. G. C. Waterson (New York: Orion Press, 1968), p. 90. Michel Serres has argued for the importance of Bachelard's philosophy of science, whose influence should be distinguished from his phenomenological poetics.

19. For a review of the General Semantics movement see Theodore Longabaugh, *General Semantics: An Introduction* (New York: Vantage Press, 1957); and Adam Schaff, *Introduction to Semantics* (New York: Pergamon Press, 1962).

20. Umberto Eco, *Semiotics and the Philosophy of Language* (Bloomington: Indiana University Press, 1984), p. 80.

21. Korzybski, *Science and Sanity* (Lancaster, Pa.: International Non-Aristotelian Library, 1958), pp. 57, 93, 513. He stresses throughout the relational as "betweenness." For Derrida's definition see "Differance," in *Speech and Phenomena*, trans. D. Allison (Evanston, Ill.: Northwestern University Press, 1973).

22. Derrida, *La Vérité en peinture* (Paris: Flammarion, 1978).

23. Roland Barthes, *Le Grain de la voix: Entretiens, 1962–1980* (Paris: Seuil, 1981).

24. Harold Bloom, "The Breaking of Form," in *Deconstruction and Criticism* (New York: Seabury Press, 1979), pp. 5–6.

25. Harold Bloom, *The Anxiety of Influence* (New York: Oxford University Press, 1973).

26. Michel Serres, *Hermes III: La Traduction* (Paris: Editions de Minuit, 1974), p. 75.

27. Michel Foucault, "The Discourse on Language," in *The Archaeology of Knowledge*, trans. A. M. S. Smith (New York: Pantheon, 1972), pp. 228–29.

28. Derrida, "Structure, Sign, and Play in the Discourse of the Human Sciences," in *The Structuralist Controversy*, ed. R. Macksey and E. Donato (Baltimore, Md.: Johns Hopkins University Press, 1975), p. 271.

29. Werner Jaeger, *Paideia: The Ideals of Greek Culture*, trans. G. Highet, vol. 2 (New York: Oxford Univesity Press, 1943), p. 317.

30. *Brecht on Theatre: The Development of an Aesthetic*, ed. and trans. J. Willet (New York: Hill & Wang, 1964), p. 186.

31. On this distinction see Matei Calinescu, *Faces of Modernity: Avant-Garde, Decadence, Kitsch* (Bloomington: Indiana University Press, 1977).

32. Joseph Beuys, *Multiples* (New York: New York University Press, 1980), pp. 8–9.

33. Paul de Man, *Blindness and Insight* (New York: Oxford University Press, 1971), pp. 17, 18.

34. Roland Barthes, *The Pleasure of the Text*, trans. R. Miller (New York: Hill & Wang, 1975), p. 22.

35. On Oulipo see Paul Fournel, *Clefs pour la littérature potentielle* (Paris: Denoël, 1972).

36. Bertolt Brecht, *Galileo*, trans. C. Laughton (New York: Grove Press, 1966), p. 90.

37. Douglas Crimp, "The Photographic Activity of Postmodernism," *October* 15 (1980): 99. Cf. the theme of the "purloined letter," passed from Poe to Lacan to Derrida to Barbara Johnson, and so on. "But the theft of speech is not a theft among others; it is confused with the very possibility of theft, defining the fundamental structure of theft. And if Artaud makes us think this, it is no longer as the example of a structure, because in question is the very thing—theft—which constitutes the structure of the example of such" (*Writing*, p. 175). The *inventio* of the example derives from Hermes the thief. See Norman O. Brown, *Hermes the Thief* (Madison: University of Wisconsin Press, 1947).

38. Robert Howard, *Performance in a World of Change: Perspective on Learning Environments* (Washington, D.C.: University Press of America, 1979), p. 7.

39. Jean-François Lyotard, *La Condition postmoderne* (Paris: Editions de Minuit, 1979), p. 88.

40. Walter Ong, *Rhetoric, Romance, and Technology* (Ithaca, N.Y.: Cornell University Press, 1971), p. 325.

41. Donald F. Bouchard, in the introduction to Foucault, *Language, Counter-Memory, Practice* (Ithaca, N.Y.: Cornell University Press, 1977).

42. Michael Young, "Curricula as Socially Organized Knowledge," in *Knowledge and Control: New Directions for the Sociology of Education*, ed. Michael Young (London: Collier, Macmillan, 1971), pp. 57–61. Cf. Morse Peckham, *Explanation and Power: The Control of Human Behavior* (New York: Seabury Press, 1979).

2

DECONSTRUCTION AND THE TEACHING OF COMPOSITION

To Write Is to Read
Is to Write, Right?

David Kaufer and Gary Waller

PROLEGOMENA

Like influenza in winter, deconstruction is in the air. Some of us will catch it, others will panic and take shots against it, a few of us will ignore it and assimilate its attendant discomforts along with our other minor and major irritants. A few of us will go stoically on and wonder what the fuss is all about—it's always been here, even if we've called it by other names. The question that a few of us are starting to ask is, "Can we use it?" It's easy enough for department heads or full professors, bought out of their teaching by prestigious grants, to speculate on self-indulgent play, dehierarchizing hierarchies, finding the tracks along which meaning may (or may not) be possible; but what of those of us who must teach the 8:30 A.M. freshman composition or literature class? What relevance do discussions of differance, decentered selves, and grammatology have to what the educational acts we (or our teaching assistants) perpetrate in Strategies for Writing or Reading Literature? Or are such questions misplaced? Are the deconstructive mysteries, perhaps, necessarily the province of an elite whose arcane mystifications need never descend into the material practices of history?

Too often, perhaps, the advocates of many varieties of the New New Criticism have indeed presented themselves as being insular and self-indulgent, their work the last refuge that the liberal mind has in which to play, as Terry Eagleton has taunted.[1] So to ask about the "relevance" or "application" of deconstruction to the teaching of literature and composition may be a useful deconstruction of deconstruction's own claims. In any case, to ask is to acknowledge for our time the inescapability of the deconstructive questions—that they are making us reflect on the very foundations of our discipline and its pedagogy.

We will start with the seemingly "natural" activities of reading and writing. It seems commonsensical to see both as unmediated, straightforward activities, whereas, in fact, both are culturally acquired, "unnatural" activities. Deconstructive critics have not always acknowledged this. J. Hillis Miller speaks of deconstruction simply as another term for close reading—in this case a particularly close form of reading in which we observe how "the text performs on itself the act of deconstruction without any help from the critic" except (presumably) from his observing the process.[2] Eric Gould suggests that deconstructive reading in such a guise is a little like watching a text masturbate.[3] But other deconstructive critics speak less naïvely about a very active mode of reading wherein the reader focuses intently on the dislocations between a text's intentions and its language, on the problem of "meaning," on the way in which texts undermine their premises. Such a reader moves around within a text, juxtaposing passages with one another, showing how figure and argument are contradictory, and acknowledging that only by ignoring or mystifying textual contradictions can we sustain the illusion of "meaning." In such a view, deconstruction is, in Barbara Johnson's words, "the careful teasing out of [the] warring forces of signification within the text."[4]

Reading thus obviously connects with writing, both in the sense of *écriture*, the dissemination and *glissage* of textuality, and the seemingly more mundane kind which we inculcate in such courses as Introductory Composition, or what we at Carnegie-Mellon call Strategies for Writing. Writing in this latter sense has so far generally shied away from the Derridean extravagance of the former. Yet parallel to the rise of poststructuralist theory in our universities, although surprisingly rarely overlapping with it, there has grown up the equally sophisticated New Rhetoric, which places strong emphasis on writing-as-process, on the play between discourse and contexts, on how goals undermine or define "meaning" in discourse. Paul de Man has written about how literary criticism inevitably dissolves into the study of rhetoric; Jonathan Culler argues that deconstruction describes "a general process through which texts undo the philosophical system to which they adhere by revealing its rhetorical nature." So the connection between high literary and rhetorical theory, between "reading" and "writing" in their arcane senses, may be seen as relevant to and intersecting in the seemingly mundane activities of the teaching of reading and writing. If, as deconstruction suggests, we probe the rhetorical figures of a text, then the systematic of metaphor and logic and the interplay of linguistic practice in reading and writing are deeply interconnected with what deconstruction has been (to return to this essay's opening metaphor) infecting us with.

Deconstruction, at least in its common American guise, has been widely criticized (by one of the present writers, for instance) because it sometimes becomes merely a trendy New Criticism—a formalist sheep in a snappy new wolf-suit. Derrida Himself (as we are wont occasionally to say) speaks of the "commonsensical" reading of a text as an "indispensable guardrail" protecting a reading, and argues that "doubling" commentary "should no doubt have its place in a critical reading" but that we should be urged to read, as he puts it, differently, with *differance*.[5] But the notion of a "commonsensical" or "straightforward" reading is itself suspect: one of the many services that the deconstructive posture can provide is to direct us and our students towards the always already interpreted nature of interpretation. As Terry Eagleton (hardly a deconstructive critic but one who, like many of us, sees the inevitability of working through the deconstructive challenge) puts it, "straightforward" readings are made up of many unacknowledged, ideological strands.[6] Our reading and our writing alike are made up, constructed, by the intersection of models, paradigms, sign systems, and conventions mediated by our culture. To adapt Derrida's celebrated formulation, writers write and readers read *"in* a language and *in* a logic whose proper system, laws, and life" their "discourse by definition cannot dominate absolutely."[7] So we might teach our students to ruthlessly subvert their own (and our) discourse, to use the "play" (in both the mechanistic and the ludic senses) in language in order to insert themselves creatively and effectively into the discourses that envelop them. Thus might deconstruction become part—or acknowledged as always already part—of the teaching of literature and composition. Deconstruction, in short, can be a powerful ally to teachers of literature and composition, apart or together, to direct students to the omnipresent, untrustworthy, yet unavailable, power and powerlessness of language. It can also help to dislocate the ideologies with which our students so often commence their university studies. As Fredric Jameson notes, our students bring sets of previously acquired and culturally sanctioned interpretive schemes of which they are unaware and through which they read the texts prescribed to them. What we can do is to encourage them to become more self-aware of the power of such schemes, to become, in short, theoreticians (even deconstructionists, though we would not necessarily use the term).[8] What follows in the rest of this paper are suggestions to such an end.

DECONSTRUCTING ASYMMETRIES BETWEEN READING AND WRITING

First, then, to reading and/as writing: to read is to write is to read is to—. A fundamental tenet underlying work in deconstruction is that every interpretation must make systematic omission of incompatible, though no less possible, interpretations. This assumption has long been associated with an attitude of critical play, the sense of amused exhilaration that one feels when firm midriffs show their soft underbellies; when sheep turn into wolves and wolves into sheep; when figures first expose and then are swallowed by their grounds; when confident assertions are routed by the very assumptions that they were meant to protect. Hegel saw in this tenet—and in the playful attitude that it inspires—the most philosophical of all comic insights: the unmasking of putative universals for the particulars they really are. And he characterized the attitude of dwelling in this playful pose as "the factor of negativity in general."[9] Deconstruction sees this turn into negativity, this undecidability of truth, as necessarily producing a celebration, the possibility of "free play."

Among their various contributions, deconstructionists have shown how playful poses can enrich criticism, how infinite negativities can add fresh air and space to theories that had become stale and confined. But the notoriety of these contributions has made it easy for people to underestimate, if not to disregard, the instructional value of deconstruction (or at least some key assumptions of deconstruction) to researching and teaching the basic processes of reading and writing. We prize our instruction as "serious business," and we can't easily fathom how "playful" techniques can serve important functional ends. We represent pedagogy as a "positive" and "constructive" effort, and we can't easily imagine how fostering an attitude of infinite negativity can lead to anything positive or constructive.

In fact, the principles of deconstruction can be harnessed to practical ends. Indeed, in teaching processes as complex as reading and writing, we may have no alternative but to resort to fundamentally subversive methods in order to teach students to read and write. Purely positive techniques would serve as well if our students were merely lacking information that could be appropriated into a superior skill—if our students were like beginning billiards players who could improve their game simply by being told to "think ahead" when they tried a shot.

69

Yet there is reason to believe that many college students are victimized as much by their comfortable (though nonproductive) beliefs about reading and writing as by a lack of skill; in particular, students are wont to view reading as "processing linguistic units to uncover *the* theme" and to view writing as "manipulating linguistic units to describe *the* summary."

Even when we succeed in squeezing the life out of these student beliefs, we find that they die a slow death. Recognizing that their reading or writing is not approaching the standards that we set for them, students are still likely to do whatever they can to improve *within* their limiting conception of these skills. They are likely to look for "better" themes and for "better" summaries. Our direct appeals to abandon this limited vision only fall on puzzled, if not disbelieving, ears. Would a decent person tell you to stop breathing? Why then has the reading teacher told me to stop reading? The writing teacher, to stop writing? We are trying to change an ideology—but students think we are trying only to undo whatever small successes their secondary teachers were able to claim.

In this context, we might better understand the value of teaching students playful poses and infinite negativities. We might better understand why it is of the utmost educational importance for us to structure assignments so that students are made to confront the limitations of their own assumptions about reading and writing and are made to bracket those assumptions so that they can inspect them with playful— albeit embarrassed—amusement.

What makes these educational epiphanies so important is that students don't dare risk giving up their old beliefs until they feel intellectually and emotionally primed to embrace viewpoints that they have previously failed—or couldn't afford—to notice. Students who are drowning have no inclination to feel embarrassed—or at play. Embarrassment is as much a sign of relief as it is of shame. And in this context, feeling "at play" is the relief of knowing that one has abandoned a sinking ship on what seems to be—for the moment at least—a sturdy lifeboat.

We have been suggesting that our students' limiting beliefs about literacy can't be cast off or stripped away in the manner of tired, isolated, and discredited falsehoods or stereotypes. We forget, at our peril, that these beliefs appear to be coherent and well integrated and that they have proven to be extremely functional. That is, as Louis Althusser and others have shown, how ideology works—as a kind of sociocultural epoxy resin, designed to bond us together. Ideologies are clusters of beliefs and practices that predispose, direct, and naturalize action in enormously powerful ways. Our students' assumptions about literacy determine how they represent and act upon writing and reading assignments; these assumptions determine what skills students try to practice when engaged in acts of writing and reading and what skills they think these acts *make available* for practice; these assumptions also determine the identities that our students try to adopt as writers and readers as well as the identities that our students believe readers and writers *can* adopt.

Dominant ideologies thus not only prescribe actual behaviors but also define or "naturalize" possible ones. The act of deconstructing an ideology is thus an act of examining possibilities that have been systematically repressed or undefined—and thus not explored. We would be remiss, however, only to charge college students of reading and writing with unexplored opportunities. As college teachers of reading and writing, we are caught in the same ideological bind. We have often been guilty of seeing our task as "offering instruction" within the limited ideology that students bring with them from elementary and secondary schools. Like our students who learned that writing and reading are distinct intellectual activities, we have often been guilty of trying to teach writing or reading as if they were divorced from one another: as if writing were the exclusive business of composition; reading, the territory of literature.

Even those of us who respect such boundaries readily grant that there is reading in writing (or what would we write about?) and writing in reading (or who would know what—or more to the point, that—we have read?). The Derridean insistence that Reading *is* Writing and vice versa is maybe not too far away. But insofar as we or our students have allowed that these skills can include each other, we have usually made this allowance under the assumption that reading and writing serve one another *asymmetrically*. Reading is the way in which we evaluate (not develop or complete) writing skill; writing is the way in which we evaluate or express (not develop or extend) reading skill. Small wonder that college freshmen understand little of the possibility that one learns to write to read to write—that, in short, language flows endlessly, that its business is not complete when the final term paper is marked or the grades are posted. Freshmen are far more sensitive to a personal history in which they have read not to write to read but to recite. Nor can they understand what it means to write to read to write nearly as clearly as they "understand" that the purpose of writing is to express one's "reading" and to provide "samples" for evaluation. For many of our students, giving a writing sample is like giving blood—the donor finds little point to it, but knows that others will.

71

Under these asymmetrical assumptions, reading and writing become their own intellectual ends, each divorced from the interaction of reading to write to read, which we know to be essential for reasoned and sustained inquiry. Student readers, working within these asymmetries, do not see texts as occasions for being provoked, extracting information, sifting, interpreting, or regenerating it. They rather see them as occasions (even pretexts) for displaying knowledge. Each text is a locked box. As taught conventionally, the *theme* is the key that opens this box in an act called *understanding*. Teachers are privileged sorts who hold thousands of keys in their pockets (and many up their sleeves). The trick of reading is anticipating (if you have the skill; guessing, if you don't) what the teacher's key will look like. If you anticipate (or guess) incorrectly, no *understanding* is achieved, and no knowledge can be displayed. Writing has a place, but merely as a vehicle for displaying knowledge. Writing serves no autonomous function as a vehicle for discovery, because everything that needs to be discovered already exists (somewhere in the teacher's pocket).

Not surprisingly, student writers, working under these same asymmetries, represent writing as a comparably sterile process, but now with a change of emphasis from the *knowledge* displayed (in reading) to the *display* of knowledge (in writing). Under these asymmetries, writers typically see texts as offering a different kind of pretext—an occasion for showing off the patterns of syntax and diction that reflect their knowledge of standard edited English. For these students, each "perfect writing specimen" is an image locked away in the mind's eye of the teacher. The rules of grammar and usage are the windows that reveal these images—however faintly. Should one memorize these rules, the target images, presumably, will come into sharper focus—can even, perhaps, be duplicated on the page (as duplication of "favored forms" seems characteristically to be the goal). Reading has a place, but merely as the "content" needed to fill up the syntactic and lexical slots that match this image.

We have sketched these extreme positions only to suggest that teaching students to read or to write without also teaching them to read to write (to read—) is not to teach them how to read or to write or all. It is only to teach them the thin parodies of reading and writing represented by these extremes. Nonetheless, a dominant ideology that has endured in the schools and in the colleges (certainly at the freshman level) contends that writing and reading are complementary but nonetheless asymmetric skills, meaning that "essentials" of writing can be taught sans the "essentials" of reading, and vice versa.

Having sketched something of the problem as we see it, the purpose of the rest of this paper is to outline techniques in introductory literature and composition courses which we use to subvert this ideology of asymmetry for our students—an ideology that has brought them to the college curriculum but now leaves them helpless before it.

PRAXIS

The Ideology of Asymmetry Made More Concrete: Writing

How about, then, the introductory writing course? Before turning to practical cases, we need to get more concrete about the commitments of an ideology that makes reading and writing only asymmetrically related. So far, we have associated assumptions of asymmetry with the belief that skills of reading and writing are essentially independent. The assumption of independence allows that reading and writing are isolated (receptive or generative) "appendages" to thought and reason. In computer jargon, reading and writing are looked upon as isolated "peripherals," channels for funneling knowledge but not for representing or modifying it. People read, in other words, to funnel knowledge *from* the external world; they write to channel knowledge *to* it. These computer metaphors give rise to a host of other more concrete and consequential metaphors and beliefs that haunt our students.

1. *Knowledge is incorrigible.* This belief stems from the fact that, as peripherals for channeling knowledge, neither reading nor writing can affect knowledge in any significant way. Indeed, our students are more likely than not to associate "poor" writing and reading with activities that try to "tamper" with knowledge—either by failing to understand the author correctly or by failing to portray his or her thoughts accurately on paper.

2. *Knowledge is manipulated via the outer shells of words and sentences.* This may seem at variance with belief number 1, but beliefs 1 and 2 are in fact surprisingly consistent. As we hinted above, our students are prone to think of knowledge as incorrigible only because they think of it as inaccessible and untestable. Yet while belief 1 acknowledges that knowledge can't be examined and tested (much less changed), belief 2 allows that the "outer shell" of knowledge (i.e., the surface marks used to express words and sentences) is easy to manipulate.

Students think of themselves as being able to "manipulate" this outer shell much in the way that one can be said to "manipulate" electricity when one moves an appliance from socket to socket. As writers and readers, they can "carry" knowledge, push it from place to place (i.e., from, say, the library to the teacher's desk), but they have few, if any, tools with which to study the "innards" of knowledge, with which to examine, destroy, or reconstruct it. Lacking the tools of expert writers and readers, students are often innocent of the logical and epistemic devices that would make it possible for them to see beyond (and more deeply within) these outer shells.

A growing empirical literature attests to this innocence. One of us has found that student readers have great difficulty seeing beyond (or more deeply into) words when tracking arguments in a text.[10] The words seem to be what a deconstructive critic would call unregeneratedly logocentric words. When, typically, we ask students to "evaluate" a textual argument, we receive, instead, surface criticisms (e.g., "I think the writer should have used a comma here") or formulaic ridicule ("the author's position is crazy"). The significant number of studies (including those by Sommers and by Faigley and Witte) that show the proclivity of student writers to make only surface-level revisions also attest to their association of the "text" with the outer shell of words and sentences.[11] "Knowledge" remains inviolate, finished, something requiring only minor adjustments to express when adjustments are needed at all.

3. *The manipulation of these outer shells is governed by rigid and external rules.* This belief helps to explain the surprising cooccurrence of beliefs 1 and 2. It helps to explain, that is, how student readers and writers can harbor grave doubts about their ability to seriously access, alter, or test knowledge. They retain much more confidence, however, about their ability to manipulate the surface text. It explains how so many student profiles reveal persons who have never seriously cared about or acted upon reading/writing tasks under their own authority or curiosity, who, in spite of indifference or timidity, nonetheless regard themselves as "superior" because they "know what's in the grammar books."

The roots of this belief can be traced to our students' earliest experiences with writing/reading—and their tendency to overgeneralize from these experiences. In early training, reading is a matter of recognizing; writing, a matter of generating words and sentences under tight constraints imposed by the teacher. It is tempting for students, even in later years, to succumb to the belief that these images describe writing/reading at its mature stages; tempting to think that the regularities of skilled writing or reading practice remain "rules" in the manner of agreement between subject and verb or the conjugation of verbal tense and aspect; tempting to think that "good" writing or reading is a matter of following rules, and "poor" writing or reading is a matter of violating them; tempting to think, therefore, that "good" reading or writing need not be driven by internal goals but by the external advice of textbooks and teachers. Such attitudes, of course, betray a fear of language, a fear of play, of *glissage*. Such attitudes may be fine for the sandbox, but not for the serious business of life.

These temptations are nearly impossible for students to avoid. By succumbing to them, after all, students turn a highly anxious, risk-filled situation into a comforting one. They are able to define reading and writing as activities at which they can't fail—for who can fail at following the textbook prescriptions or teachers' advice? (If the advice is vague [e.g., "be clear, be coherent"], then students can't be refuted when they claim to have followed it; as it becomes more concrete ["don't split infinitives"], the advice becomes trivial to follow.) Think how comforting life becomes when we assume that meeting a goal is just a matter of following advice to achieve it. It makes us feel just a "split infinitive away" from Shakespeare, a "dangling participle" away from Milton.

Revision is another area in which the repressiveness of logo-centricity can be observed. As Cheryl Geisler and David Kaufer have observed,[12] student writers and readers tend to confuse external advice with the goals that they must set for themselves. This confusion explains why students feel so frustrated when they dutifully (but unimaginatively) follow our advice for a first or second draft and then find us no more happy with the results. As teachers, *we* thought our remarks were intended (and were recognized as intended) to help students meet their *own* needs. But our students tend to misidentify our advisory statements with goal-setting statements in their own right. And so they can't easily understand how we can continue to balk when they think they have met (what they have mistaken as) our goals for them. "But I did *exactly* what you told me to do!" is a comment we often hear, and when we hear it, we sigh (under our breath), "Yes, that's *exactly* the problem."

We have seen, then, that the ideology of asymmetry breaks down more concretely into beliefs about the incorrigibility of knowledge, beliefs about the easy manipulability of knowledge via the outer shells of words and sentences, and beliefs about the inflexible and external rules that govern the "appropriate" manipulation of these shells. These are the beliefs that our students carry with them both to freshman composition and to freshman literature.

As we mentioned earlier, however, subversion won't meet with lasting success unless there is a constructive plan with which to follow it up. Unlike the logical positivists, who took up the "incorrigibility of knowledge" thesis to express a (now discredited) point of view about the domain of "truth," our students believe in it because they have no alternative: if you have no confidence that you can manipulate or test knowledge resourcefully, what commitments toward knowledge, other than incorrigibility, can you seriously entertain? Furthermore, if you don't write or read to access, explore, and test knowledge, how do you

75

justify to yourself or to others what you *do* do when you read and write—unless, of course, you interpret (as our students are inclined to do) reading and writing simply as "recognizing and producing marks on a page"?

Much ideological blindness arises from the lack of food, money, or power. The ideological limits that we have been discussing arise from a lack of skill—not necessarily the lack of reasoning skill (which the manipulation of knowledge is all about and which many of our functional illiterates handle admirably in their nonwriting courses) nor the lack of writing or reading skill in the narrow senses that we have been considering, but certainly from an incapacity to *integrate* one's reasoning with one's reading and writing, to let reading and writing become integrated with each other and with the textuality of the world. Our students are led to impoverished understandings of reading and writing because they are still mostly innocent of the reasoning that goes into the tasks of reading and writing.

Consequently, we have found it advantageous, both in freshman writing and in freshman literature, to design practical reading/writing tasks in which students are first left to their own devices and then, having found these devices lacking, are given "new" stratagems to bring the task to a more fruitful resolution. More specifically, in each of the practical cases that we discuss below, the following general procedure applies:

1. Each case allows, even encourages, the student to embark upon a reading/writing task using his or her limiting assumptions of reading and writing.
2. Then the subtle deconstruction starts, for each case exposes the limitations of the student's assumptions by showing that, with them as guides, the student won't, can't, meet the goals of the task—or will be able only to fulfill alternate goals (i.e., vapid summaries or paraphrases) that are considerably lower than the challenge presented by the task.
3. Each case offers the students strategies for analyzing, for deconstructing their previous "knowledge" and transcending it so as to be better equipped to meet the task challenge.

This procedure, of course, implies that there are ripe ambiguities, rich translation problems, in what it means to "do the task." A child who sees a mannequin leaning forward on a chair, hand resting on chin, may say that the dummy is "thinking." To dismiss this assertion without also trying to refute it is to deny the child an important bit of feedback about what it means to be "thinking." A refutation in this instance is kinder than a dismissal because only *it* takes the assertion seriously and on its own terms. How much more enlightened the child might feel were an adult, taking the assertion seriously, to place a problem in addition before the "thinking" dummy and ask it to add! Such actions make visible the amusing, though uncomfortable, lifeboats that remain afloat when a discredited position sinks into the ocean.

Resisting the natural inclination to dismiss our students' beliefs, we assign tasks that can show them to their lifeboats. We exploit the fact that the demands placed on writers and readers are richly ambiguous and subjectively defined, that one person's understanding of the behaviorial implications of "having read" or "having written" something can be very different from another's, and that intellectual enrichment takes place when we take the time and the trouble to discuss these alternative understandings and to evaluate their respective strengths and weaknesses, when we make it clear to students that no one need drown should a position go under, because there will always be others within swimmable reach.

Each of the cases that we present below is defined by a task. Each task, in turn, becomes the locus of discussion for alternative understandings and systematically omitted possibilities.

"FIND A PROBLEM IN THE TEXT TO WRITE ABOUT."

In freshman composition, we typically ask students to "find a problem in a text to write about." This may seem to be an unambiguous directive, but, in fact, we have found that freshman students seldom if ever interpret it as we might expect. In the high schools, writing assignments are never driven by problems. Writing thus becomes reified in its self-contained, replete presence. Writing assignments *are* the problems. Professional writers see completing a writing task as a means to a goal (to inform, persuade, entertain), but student writers seldom have writing goals beyond "finishing the assignment." Closure is primary. If we assume that problems are discrepancies between one's present state and one's goals, then the problem of the student writer is the writing assignment. Once it is completed, then what is desired is, presumably, somehow "there." Thus the logocentric tradition and the need for closure remain triumphant.

Students are typically discouraged from using writing assignments as genuine occasions to complain about writing assignments. More often than not, they have learned that writing problems are best defined as occasions for displaying knowledge, or what Marlene Scardemalia and Carl Bereiter call "knowledge-telling strategies."[13] The student conjectures: "The teacher knows something and expects me to know it too. Therefore the teacher has given me an opportunity to write to confirm this expectation.'' In this guise, the student sees ''writing problems'' as lengthier short-answer questions, true/false tests, or fill-in-the-blanks exercises. Ambiguity, open-ended inquiry, puzzles, anomalies are, too often for students, not prompts for writing but diversions from ''getting the assignment done.''

Let us now consider very concretely what happens when our directive ''find a problem in the text to write about'' collides with these students' expectations for ''finding a problem to write about.'' In *Strategies for Writing*, we assign a short piece by Paul Hout, an educational psychologist, who argues that I.Q. tests are hopelessly invalid measures of intelligence. When we ask students to find a problem in Hout's text to write about, almost 95 percent of our students across all sections assume that we are asking them to ''summarize Hout's position'' or to ''tell us what Hout saw his writing problem to be.'' As a result, they offer up writing problems such as ''Our country relies heavily on I.Q. tests, but people have to be informed that they are invalid.''

Taking their answers seriously, we try to get students to see that they have appropriated Hout's problem and, in so doing, are restricting themselves to writing a paper that may be only a paraphrase away from Hout's attempts to limit, rather than to open up, thinking. Of course, initially, paraphrase is exactly the strategy that our students had in mind, since that is an essential ingredient of the knowledge-telling strategy. But it proves to be quite a revelation to them when they find that they have been blindly identifying ''the finding of a writing problem in a text'' with strategies that will consign them only to ''paraphrasing its author.'' It is at this point that students understand why instruction in problem analysis and formulation (as offered in texts such as those by Young, Becker, and Pike and by Flower) proves to be so powerful.[14]

''CONSIDER YOUR OPPONENT IN YOUR ARGUMENT.''

Our freshman composition program focuses on reading and writing argumentative discourse, and so this directive is frequently voiced. But the directive seems to puzzle students. It doesn't neatly fit into their residual stratagems of knowledge telling. Knowledge telling seeks harmony. It seeks to live out the parody of the motto of the *New York Times* with a vengeance: ''all the news (or knowledge) that fits.'' Yet to tell a student to ''consider the opponent'' seems to punch holes in this strategy. Opponents, after all, are people who *don't* fit. Opponents directly question the knowledge that ''needs to be told.'' Opponents make a frontal assault on the incorrigibility of knowledge, for opponents don't know precisely what advocates do.

A common practice is to have students read a strongly argued, highly persuasive text representing one side of an issue, such as abortion, the I.Q. controversy, reverse discrimination, teenage driving, and so on. The information in the text is relatively one-sided, so that students see only a faint image of the opponent(s). This exercise is enough to put each student's universe in order. All is well for knowledge telling, since the student now has constructed (and needs to write out) a narrative of what the author had known and written. Students are then given a text in which the image of the opponent is far stronger and now rivals in attractiveness the image of the original advocate. The "same" narrative is now shown up as being "different."

The reactions of students, in our experience at least, have been remarkably consistent—as if out of a Bill Perry script. When students discover disharmonies in their knowledge, they retreat into the view that, as writers and readers, they are dealing, not in knowledge at all, but in the "outer shells" that only reflect "opinion." As if to protect the incorrigibility assumption at all costs, they now deny that any participant (including themselves) can do more than "express an opinion" and that all opinions are equally valid or invalid. It is a bizarre parody, indeed, of one issue of deconstruction—but it is an impasse that the student has been indoctrinated to repress. Some tend to qualify every assertion with "in his [her or my] opinion" just to assure the teacher that nothing so weighty as knowledge is being brokered.

One way in which we undermine this subjectivism is to tell students that they must analyze the views of both authors and show the ultimate superiority of one over the other. This constraint intensifies student anxiety, because it forces them to proceed without the cover of "incorrigibility." It forces them to acknowledge that knowledge is at issue, that there are things that writers and readers can come to know, things that they can continue to know, and, no less importantly, things that they can stop knowing. Yet we find that students make this acknowledgment only with great reluctance.

How do students fare when left to their own devices to overcome the incorrigibility assumption? Often they interpret the directive "consider your opponent" to mean "ridicule your opponent." If knowledge can't be all of a piece, they seem to reason, let's expose part of it as counterfeit and then slander it to death. Students are led to see that this strategy won't work if we restrict "consider your opponent" to contexts in which the opponent is considered competent and credible and in which the opponent himself or herself must be viewed as a potential target of persuasion. "Truth" is never one; reading and writing are always complex.

But once this restriction has been made, students are left with obstacles that can seldom be overcome without additional training. For what this restriction asks them to do is to abandon entirely any semblance of "incorrigibility." It asks them to countenance aspects of knowledge standing toe to toe, incompatible but still worthy, functional but still revisable. This is a hard fight for students to witness—especially when knowledge-telling practices have discouraged them from trying to represent, much less to weigh and consider, conflicting knowledge. At this point, we offer students training in discrimination, or training in how to classify conflicting knowledge. Is the conflict a matter of semantics (which forces them to dig into the insides of words and expressions), of factual evidence (which forces them to consider the observable facts that bear on resolving the conflict), or of value (which forces them to consider the larger goals of the parties to the dispute)? How we represent conflict has a great deal to do with how we try to overcome it—and how we try to accommodate our opponent in the process.[15]

"APPLY GOOD PRINCIPLES OF STYLE."

One of the great deceptions foisted upon our students is perpetrated through the sheer bulk and quantity of textbooks on grammar and style. The inference is that such texts need to be heavy (and expensive) in order to be complete. The deception is that students think they know what "complete" means in this context. "Complete" to them commonly means "the total decision maker," the executive who not only shapes expressions at the point of utterance but who plans them as well. This generous construal derives in large measure from the observation, empirically documented,[16] that writers in grades kindergarten through twelve seldom distinguish composition planning from the actual point of utterance at which pen meets paper.

It is easy—in a one-hour discussion of planning—to persuade college writers that rules of grammar and style have little to say about the planning that does not take place at the point of utterance. It is more difficult, however, to convince them that these rules are worth very little *even at* that critical point. Students tend to misidentify these rules as detailed road maps for producing or perceiving sentences, rather than what they more likely seem to be—perceptual (i.e., visual, auditory) landmarks that tell you what is "seemingly okay" and what is not.

Unfortunately—and this seemingly elementary observation bears out, ironically, what many Derrideans have been saying over and over—rules of grammar and style turn out to be much less reliable landmarks than, say, "the church on the corner of Maple and Elm Streets." At least, with the church on the corner, you can reliably infer "I am three miles from home" or "I am a block from the drugstore." Landmarks of this kind seem relatively stable and unambiguous. Rules of grammar and style, when used as perceptual cues to trigger the judgments "this seems okay" but "this does not," are neither right nor wrong. Such terse judgments simultaneously monitor many layers of writing goals: syntactic, semantic, interpersonal, intrapersonal, phonetic, metrical, cultural goals (just to name a few).

One can conjecture that rules of grammar and style become codified only when their systematic violation leads to writers' failing to fulfill changing combinations of these goals. When language starts to slip, then panic and repression enter. Manuals on grammar and style offer pat solutions that have brought writers in particular writing contexts closer to the manuals' goals. But since the manuals can't begin to delineate the infinity of contexts in which these rules would help, we must make up for this lacuna by introducing an "all things being equal" clause. That is, we must read a rule of grammar or style (call it *x*) not simply as stating "Do *x*!" but as stating, "All things being equal, do *x*!" And in this case, the "all things being equal" clause is shorthand for "If it is consistent with your syntactic, semantic, phonetic, interpersonal, intrapersonal, and cultural goals to do *x*, then Do *x*!"

All this is to suggest that it is highly misleading to identify the "learning" of a grammatical or stylistic rule with the learning of the right-hand side (Do *x*!) if the writer has yet to learn the contextual antecedents (the "if" clause) that must be identified prior to applying the rule. Writers must learn, paradoxically, how to apply a rule of grammar or style only by learning how *not* to apply it. They can't appreciate rules of grammar and style as reliable perceptual landmarks for "good writing" without also understanding how they may be unreliable landmarks.[17]

For this reason, we teach students rules of style and grammar by teaching them how to deconstruct them. A standard assignment has students work through Joseph Williams's *Style: Ten Lessons in Clarity and Grace*.[18] Each of the first six chapters in Williams's text introduces various rules of style and then contains exercise sentences that "need to be revised according to the rule." We direct students to examine the exercise sentences very closely and to investigate for each sentence (and for an implicit context in which the sentence might be produced) how Williams has made the application of the rule seem attractive. We then ask students to come up with counter examples, by producing either new sentences or new contexts, in which applying the rule would not move a writer closer to his or her expressive goals.

An example will make this more concrete. On page 91 of his text, Williams writes, "Normal English word order is subject-verb-object. All things being equal, we should avoid breaking the connections between those sentence parts." On pages 92 and 93, he offers nine example sentences in which there are "unfortunate interruptions" between the subject and the verb, and he asks the students to revise them accordingly. Should the students follow the exercises by rote, however, they may be led to the incorrect generalization that all such interruptions are unfortunate ones. We therefore ask students to consider carefully how Williams has "stacked" the exercises so that the interruptions appear to be unfortunate.

Students soon realize that the exercise sentences have many more specific problems than "interruptions between the subject and the verb." Some of Williams's exercises contain interruptions that are logically out of sequence: for example, effects are placed *after* causes, as in "The construction of the interstate highway, owing to . . . Congress did not. . . ." Other exercises contain interruptions that lead to dangling, illogical, or ambiguous modifiers, as in "Such conduct or behavior, for whatever reasons offered, is rarely . . ." (where the interrupting clause seems to modify the noun-phrase subject when it can only reasonably modify the whole proposition).

After isolating specific causes of "unfortunate interruptions," students are asked to generate contexts in which interruptions are welcome. They discover that interruptions used as subject modifiers are common. Indeed, relative clauses are inevitable interrupters: "The man, who lived in the forest, died." And nonrestrictive elements, like appositives, used as subject modifiers, are highly functional when they build up premises that explain the predicate: "John Smith, the inventor of the mini-skirt, deserves our thanks." Some students even recognize functional value in delaying the predicate for reasons of building up to very important information: "Joe Blo, curator of the Carnegie Museum for the last twenty years and father of twelve, received the Nobel prize today." After this exercise, students understand that the injunction to "apply good principles of style" is just as easily an injunction, in many circumstances, not to. Language and writing are rendered more problematic—and, it is hoped, more interesting.

Reading: A Different Case?

The relevance of deconstruction to courses in reading literature seems, at first, to be more obvious and more intimidating. As we have outlined the praxis above, the teaching of writing classes can be reinforced or redirected by the teacher's scheming and theorizing, and thus persuading or manipulating the students into becoming more critical and subversive about their residual assumptions about writing. But deconstruction is surely better known as a way of reading (or misreading) literary texts. In fact, it is primarily a set of theories, not always consistent, about the ways in which language functions, in and beyond textuality. But if we announce that deconstruction can be harnessed in the teaching of writing, as we did above, it may seem merely cute and certainly less threatening than if we say we wish to institute a freshman literature course in deconstruction. Oh horrors! that Chaucer, Shakespeare, Milton, Wordsworth, and others should be forced to suffer such indignities! Worse, that students should be encouraged to let *Macbeth* or "In Memoriam" mean "anything."

So we are asking how deconstruction can aid in the practice of a freshman literature course. Let us begin by supposing a world in which "deconstruction" no longer provokes a knee-jerk reaction, no longer calls forth a symbol of anarchy loosed upon us—but, instead, evokes a world that an increasing number of writers are now arguing for, one in which self-consciously aggressive theorizing can live alongside praxis.

Two ways in which deconstruction can be usefully appropriated strike us immediately. The first is that the teacher of literature who in his secret moments has dabbled in deconstruction (if only to see what distinguished colleague X is doing, or despising) should find a strikingly potent way by which to show how reading and writing have inextricable ties to each other. Deconstruction gives substance to that widely felt experience that to "read" a text is always to be thrown into language, into its flow and surprises, and to recognize that we are part of that flow, that "writing." Reading and writing, within deconstruction's premises, move as a linguistic and cultural yin and yang: we read each other, the signs of the world, the nuances or blatant assaults of political, commercial, cultural signs; and to "read" is to find ourselves within "writing."

The message is potent. Now how do we make it stick? Because of their conditioning, students generally find it difficult to see multiple, let alone endlessly disseminated, meanings in what their schooling has indoctrinated them into accepting as "literary texts," "the canon," the "masterpieces of our culture," and so forth. But it is reasonably easy to get them to acknowledge that Pat Benatar's "Love Is a Battlefield" and *Star Wars* and the machinations in the State Department and double talk on campus about liquor policy are all signs, making demands, requiring "reading" (and therefore capable of misreading), multiple interpretation, and infinite argument. They (and we) are parts of a discursive reality, a "writing" that must be read necessarily from within and can be done so only by falling into the deceptions and traps of writing—and by searching for ways out. In short, we can speak of the interactive nature of textuality, of the ways in which languages rewrite one another.

But in the classroom it is surely important (many will say) not to disrupt a freshman course by interjecting chunks of alien theory. Discussions that are laden with strange talk should best be left to the theoretical closet. Perhaps. But a reluctance to discuss, even relatively simply, what we do when we read complex texts, either "literary" or "cultural," tends to beckon the kind of self-defeating asymmetries that we have already dismissed. It cuts off the study of "literary" interpretation from the study of real interpretative acts. It denies to literary interpretation the very reflexiveness that makes such interpretation meaningful, even possible. It leaves us on theoretical grounds that are no more substantial than are the profit motives that spur the makers of mass-produced Notes to the Great Works of the Canon. It reinforces the notion of English as a "service" department of "curators," rather than "theorists of interpretative acts" who are no less vital to the behavioral and natural sciences than they are to "liberal learning."

Deconstruction can help the teacher of a literature course by encouraging him or her to come out of the closet, to talk and mediate methodological issues—the philosophy of the discipline—with students. What is it that we *do* when we read? What difference is there, indeed, between reading each other and reading *Emma* or *Macbeth*? Why are so many writers seemingly so frustrated with the language of which (at least we teachers have for so long asserted) they are supposedly, as writers, in control? Does that frustration have anything to do with our frustration at our own writing? Why do so many of the greatest writers—Shakespeare, Hopkins, Eliot—so often see language as frustration and failure?

One especially good example, drawn from actual teaching practice, is related to the deconstructive insistence that writing never achieves presence, that language can only point to, but never bring into final presence, its user's frustrations. In a freshman literature class, a great example to work with is a love poem. Most students in that class will have written one, even sung one in the shower, and can recognize both the deceptiveness and the frustration of language. What do Donne's "Now I Have Loved Thee One Whole Day" and Jay Geils's "Love Stinks" (or Nazareth's "Love Hurts") have in common? All are expressions of language's desire to achieve presence. All express desire. As generations of Petrarchan scholars have pointed out in their scholarly way, the Petrarchan sonnet is written only because the beloved is absent—"o present absence" cries Sidney's *Astrophil* (104). And when a love poem ends, does the beloved suddenly materialize? Alas rarely, and if so, what happens is that the words of the poem cease, and other words or other practices take over. The poetry usually continues until the speaker is exhausted (not, note, the discourse, which always already exists, which flows ceaselessly before and after any particular attempt to buttonhole it).

Making a fool of oneself in a classroom over a love poem is therefore not merely a fun way to wake up an overcast February day; it is a way of introducing, without intimidating labels, the frustration of language—its real emptiness and its ceaseless desire to persuade us of its plentitude. And of course, our ceaseless willingness to be so fooled. If solemnity is to be replaced by jocularity, it doesn't explicitly have to be of the "Well, folks, that's what we call the tragic emptiness of language" kind of crassness. It can be a way into both the fun and the fascination of language—and an opportunity to show how deconstructive strategies are "natural." The power of New Criticism was always its assumption that its strategies were "natural," "commonsensical." A deconstructive rhetoric can adopt, provisionally, the same strategy.

What the deconstructive teacher of literature is bringing to such a strategy is a desire to give his or her students not only a powerful new vocabulary but also the excitement that comes with the iconoclasm of initiation into the ways in which language *really* functions. Once again, a "way in" may be to side-step, at least at first, what we have reified as literature. Advertising is as good a starting point as rock music. "Close reading" of any text has traditionally tried to make that text cohere so that, all too often, the marveling student will be encouraged to replicate the sophisticated reading of the teacher, whose skill and patience have just "proved" that *Among School Children* is a great poem, a worthy embodiment of the canon, and so forth. But language is (as we know) always contradicting itself; texts are replete only because we will them to be. What our students invariably bring into the classroom is, as we noted in discussing composition, an ideology. In literary study, it is manifest in an inculcated belief that texts "mean" something, that the best texts are coherent and organic, and that they hold together. In that they are, supposedly, better than something vulgar, easy, and disgusting—as Dr. Johnson remarked of *Lycidas*—something like advertising, the texts of which are certainly all round us.

But with the language of advertising, students are attuned to something else: there is no reverence assumed, as with the canonical masterpieces. So what can we do with them? First, enjoy them: after all, some of the greatest literary, theatrical, and musical talent of our age has mastered the distinctive demands of the 30-second TV commercial as thoroughly as Webster or Jonson mastered the five-act play (Shakespeare we'll tactfully leave aside). But after enjoyment, what else? We suggest a little deconstruction by means of cultural semiotics. Today we're all attuned to having ads ask, "What are they *really* after?" Usually the student's answers to that question will be on the level of the obvious—"they" want to sell more soap, cars, shampoo, beer, Meow Mix, or Pampers. And that's precisely the starting point for the deconstructively attuned teacher. If deconstruction, especially in its American manifestations, is primarily a fiendishly rigorous formalism, then its strengths should be employed to show not only how the ideas or the "intentions" of a text are inconsistent or facile but also how the *language* self-deconstructs. Pit logic against figure, probe the metaphors, ask questions about boundaries. (Why is it that during John Madden's football commentaries, there are clear signs of the narrative build-up to one of his Lite Beer commercials. How do "reality" and "fantasy" overflow and undermine each other there?) On this level, Hillis Miller's disarmingly arrogant claim that deconstruction is really just a name for good close reading operates wonderfully. Our quarrel with New Criticism on this level is that its close-reading habits were just not close enough.

Once the principles (and the praxis) are established in the worldly text, then the literary text can be treated similarly. One of the oddly conservative aspects of much deconstruction is its reverence for the canon—that is, interestingly, a distinctively American phenomenon, one by which deconstructive critics in Britain and in Europe are often rather puzzled. And one consequence of that conservatism is that there is, it is often asserted, a debilitating distinction between the "literary" text and the utilitarian texts by which we function in the world. Hence our suggestion that the deconstructive teacher start with defamiliarizing the familiar may seem unsettling. But to maintain the untouchability of the "canon" for deconstruction and to let the business of the world proceed in its "natural," commonsensical way is to fall prey to the same ideology that vitiated New Criticism. Our object of scrutiny is language and how it both reads and writes us—how it flows through novel, poem, or play into audiences, readers, writers, and beyond, into the world— just as the tapestry in the painting in *The Crying of Lot 49* flows on, for- ever, into the world. All human discourse is one text waiting to be unraveled.

So far we have looked at ways in which students' residual assump- tions about "reading" and "text" can be dislocated and extended by deconstruction; but what of another of those great shibboleths of traditional literary criticism, the "author"? Here deconstruction is up against the residual American belief in the "individual" as an unassailable originator of history and language, and it is intriguing how uneasy the deconstructive formalists have remained towards the poststructuralist emphasis on the "individual" as always already being a subject of discourse. Once again, we are dealing with an enormously powerful residual ideology, one in which our students are, seemingly inextricably, enmeshed. After all, each of them has struggled, perhaps at great cost, to enter college; most are determined to succeed; success is measured by individual achievement and by proven reputation. If, like Nietzsche's madman rushing down the mountain to announce the death of God, we simply assault the reified individual in the guise of our students' ambitions, the result is easy to predict. Karlis Racevskis calls the current deconstruction of the individual "profoundly liberating in its effects," a successful dismantling of "the system of constraints with which Western civilization has established the norms and limits of humanity."[19] Yes, one says, as one prepares for class, how true. And yet, once in the classroom, *how* true? Do we simply walk into the classroom, eyes ablaze with a strange light, and announce to the football team's star linebacker or to the girl by whom "cute" is accepted as a compliment that he and she are no longer transcendent subjects but are parts of a collage of dislocated languages, their sense of "self," that he and she are, like the literature text that they have just bought in the bookstore, the product/ the products of an ideological struggle that must be ruthlessly and endlessly deconstructed? Like Dr. Johnson refuting Bishop Berkeley by kicking a rock, you may, for your pains, receive a particularly persuasive blow (literal or metaphorical) to your decentered center.

This is where the teacher of literature who has seen the power of the deconstructive questions joins with the teacher of composition. This is also where the epistemologies that are battling in this paper are working to stimulate each other. Reading and writing go together on the level of classroom practice because they are inseparable in the problems that they pose for the planner of curriculum, the experimenter with pedagogy, textbooks, student assignments. In short, they go together on that essential level of theorizing which, like its fellow poststructuralist modes of operation, deconstruction forces upon even the seemingly most pragmatic of educational practices—the teaching of literature and composition. Deconstruction forces us to acknowledge that we are theorists; as in the revelation of Molière's M. Jourdain, we have been doing theory all our lives. By not acknowledging that, we have been sucked into the ideology that we must now help our students to extricate themselves from. To deconstruct is to leave the seemingly innocent world of naïve pragmatism; it is to acknowledge that we are always (already) in theory. Or as Lacan might put it, we do not theorize; we are theorized, we are theorizings.

For teachers of reading and writing, then, deconstruction might well be seen as combining a rigorous, even ruthless, attention to the particularities of the ways in which language works in and through us with an insistence on becoming self-conscious about that process. Whether or not we call it "deconstruction" (and that decision is a pragmatic, even political, one perhaps), we can agree with Hillis Miller that it can be seen as a particularly close kind of attention that we should give to both reading and writing.

But as one of us at least would argue, and has argued elsewhere, a caution should be entered. Perhaps the greatest limitation of the older formalism, whether applied to reading or to writing, was its tendency toward an ahistorical aestheticism, a temptation to take reading and writing alike out of the wider networks of our culture and so to create the kind of aesthetic escapism that has been so widely criticized recently as one of the major disasters of American culture and education in the past half-century. Deconstruction can help the teacher of literature, as it can help the teacher of composition, to dislodge ideological presuppositions, to learn to play in language, to ruthlessly examine all claims to truth (especially those of the reified texts of both the literary and the writing traditions). But just as New Criticism tended to escape into a self-concentrated aestheticism, so American deconstruction has tended to be hermetic, to take the text out of culture and history.

It is fascinating to see how Derrida's own stress on history, specifically the historicity of reading, is almost inevitably filtered out by his American disciples—a most revealing misreading of his work. Michael Sprinker has raised the question of whether Foucault's reading of Derrida may not have encouraged this narrowing by attacking what Foucault sees as a Derridean pedagogy which insists that there is nothing beyond the text. Yet Derrida can write of "the internal historicity of the work itself" and of "its relationship to a subjective origin that is not simply psychological or mental."[20] And more surprisingly (if we have learned to read him through Miller or even de Man), Derrida can write about what he terms the determinate force of the author, of intention, and of the productive matrix and historical conditions in the production of meaning. What Derrida often thrusts before us is something that the residual temptation to formalism of American Deconstruction has largely ignored—the double determination of language. In our enthusiasm for the rigor of deconstructing the texts before us, we may be tempted to forget that language is also traversed by the formations and systems of representation that define a particular society's culture and ideological formations.

Fifty years ago, when the classroom praxis of New Criticism was being established, the enemy was seen as a decrepit historicism. That enemy is still around, however, cowering in (admittedly well-protected, warm, and comfortable) caves. It would be ironical if deconstruction's desire to establish its praxis were to produce a similar confrontation with a New Historicism. It would be unfortunate because, of course, historical scholarship is not what *it* was in the 1930s: circumventing the Old Historicism, there has grown up a new, indeed a deconstructive, historicism, one that can be used by deconstructive-minded teachers of literature (and language generally) as an ally, not one to be treated as an archaic enemy.

What seems important to realize is that our students are situated not only in language but also in history, and in *their* history. They are formed, they struggle, and they study where language, culture, and history intersect. A deconstructive pedagogy will remain incomplete—asymmetrical, as we termed it in our previous section—unless it is positioned in the midst of these three forces, and that positioning ought to have both curricular and pedagogical implications.[21]

How, then, does a deconstructive historicism insert itself into this conjunction? Literary texts primarily should be seen as writer's and as cultural practices, which are not simply self-deconstructing but are open to their reader's cultural practices. We can circumvent the reductionism of the older, antiquarian historicism by the deconstructive insistence on textuality, but the Derridean question loses its power unless it is situated, unless we see texts as being produced and always in process within, not outside, our students' history. From deconstruction's insistence that a text never arrives unaccompanied and that a text is always engaged in a perpetual struggle to perform the impossible (an irony that our literature and composition students *may* appreciate that they and we are together caught in), it hardly follows that we are doomed to an endless, irresponsible play of language. Because of physical necessity, sociocultural pressures, and the sheer need to finish this paper, texts are closed, and we label the various instances of their closure as "meanings." Anathema to deconstruction is less the concession of "meaning" than the common failure to understand that "meanings" are arbitrary, culture-specific concessions to a process that is neither arbitrary nor culture-bound, to understand that "meanings" are more aptly conceded than asserted. And so, even as we acknowledge that the "real world" escapes discourse and can never be made to coincide with language, nonetheless in their *aporias*, in the fissures and gaps, we can readily concede, systematically, the ways in which texts are *made* to mean.

This argument leads to an interesting conclusion—that deconstruction can be an ally not only in classroom practices, not only in teaching reading and writing, but also in formulating curriculum and, in particular, in revitalizing literary history. That is a large project and one in which many teachers and scholars are involved—including the present writers' own department, where a large-scale curricular development is under way, designed to produce what in more grandiose moments is being termed the first poststructuralist literary curriculum. Its foundations incorporate many of the arguments that we have broached here. No doubt, like all discourses, these arguments will be revised in their turn; they will be shown how their ideological presuppositions are repressed, their apparent logic undermined by their choice of figure; and their tropes will be troped.

IN WHICH THERE ARE NO CONCLUSIONS, BUT AN OPPORTUNITY FOR DIALOGUE (OR POLYLOGUE)

This paper has been written ostensibly as a dialogue by two members of a department that was recently praised in *College English* as being on the forefront of bringing English studies out of the nineteenth and into the twenty-first century, who are pondering the responsibility accompanying that praise.[22] We have approached the question of the relevance of deconstruction to the teaching of writing and reading, to student writing and literature, and we have found that despite bringing (or at least one of us would argue, because we bring) into our discussion other languages than those that we think we "own," there are inescapable connections among the problems with which we grapple. Deconstructive theory and praxis have reminded us forcefully that what holds us together is language. We are, in Derrida's famous phrase, born into language, and we find that language is given to us by forces and within structures that, in Althusser's famous phrase, interpellate, even, in a very real sense, create us. We find that deconstruction reinforces our realization of something that ought not to need reinforcing—namely, that reading and writing are inseparable, that we are both read and written, just as we struggle to read and write.

But more: deconstruction has forced both of us to theorize, to constantly examine the basis of our studies and our pedagogy. If language is as suspicious and yet as inescapable as we now realize, then deconstruction is helping us to face and to work through both the suspicion and the inescapability. It has forced us to look carefully at the ideological blindspots of our theory and practice. Above all, it has helped push us into forwarding the polylogue. Perhaps, indeed, there lies the basis of the fear of deconstruction, which is so prevalent in the profession—why it is (to return to our opening metaphor) seen as a disease, a pustule on the otherwise clear skin of the discipline—because it forces us back into our unexamined presuppositions, our metaphysical privileging of comforting assumptions, half-examined concepts, and habitual praxis. Even when we have added so many qualifications to what Terry Eagleton calls deconstruction's "hair-raising radicalism—the nerve and daring with which it knocks the stuffing out of every smug concept,"[23] we realize that it has moved to the center of where the profession of language and literary studies must go—not to a particular goal, but to a continuing process. The only stability is instability. To read is to write is to read is to write is to read. Right?

NOTES

1. Terry Eagleton, *Walter Benjamin: Or Towards a Revolutionary Criticism* (London: Verso, 1981), p. 134.

2. J. Hillis Miller, "Deconstructing the Deconstructers," *Diacritics* 5 (Summer 1975): 31.

3. Eric Gould, "Deconstruction and Its Discontents," *Denver Quarterly* 15 (Fall 1980): 101.

4. Barbara Johnson, "The Critical Difference," *Diacritics* 8 (Summer 1978): 3.

5. Jacques Derrida, *Positions*, trans. Alan Bass (Chicago: University of Chicago Press, 1981), pp. 47, 64.

6. Terry Eagleton, *Literary Theory: An Introduction* (Minneapolis: University of Minnesota Press, 1983), pp. 198–99.

7. Jacques Derrida, *Of Grammatology*, trans. Gayatri Chakravorty Spivak (Baltimore, Md.: Johns Hopkins University Press, 1976), p. 158.

8. Fredric Jameson, "Interview," *Diacritics* 12 (Fall 1982): 73.

9. G. W. F. Hegel, *The Phenomenology of Mind*, ed. J. Baillie (New York: Harper Torchbooks, 1952), pp. 96ff.

10. David S. Kaufer and Christine Neuwirth, "The Irony Game: Measuring a Writer's Adaptation to an Opponent," *Journal of Advanced Composition* 2 (1981): 89–102.

11. Nancy Sommers, "Revision Strategies of Student Writers and Experienced Writers," *College Composition and Communication* 31 (Dec. 1980): 378–88; and Lester Faigley and Stephen Witte, "Analyzing Revision," *College Composition and Communication* 32 (Dec. 1981): 400–414.

12. Cheryl Geisler and David S. Kaufer, "Beliefs, Goals, Advice in Writing: How We Confuse Them," *Writing Center Report* (Carnegie-Mellon University, 1984).

13. Marlene Scardamalia and Carl Bereiter, "Assimilative Processes in Composition Planning," *Educational Psychologist* 17 (1982): 81–101.

14. Richard Young, Alton Becker, and Kenneth Pike, *Rhetoric: Discovery and Change* (New York: Harcourt Brace Jovanovich, 1970); and Linda Flower, *Problem-Solving Strategies for Writing* (New York: Harcourt Brace Jovanovich, 1981).

15. See David S. Kaufer, "A Pedagogy for Developing Original Policy Arguments: A Supplement to Instruction in Stock-Issues," *College Composition and Communication*, in press, for more discussion.

16. Scardamalia and Bereiter, "Assimilative Processes."

17. This paradox, so easy to accept in its present form, actually reinforces a more arcane tenet of deconstruction that few teachers of composition have come to appreciate fully: writers can't possibly take control over all the systems of goals that readers *must* ascribe to them as controlling if they are to "make initial sense" of the writing. The attribution of a "writer's perfect control" is, arguably, a highly functional premise for "first readings." While the premise surely needs defeating on closer inspection, it at least gives the reader an initial target to defeat. This same premise, however, seems to have no functional value for the writer. Still, many teachers of composition, harboring naïve notions of reading (confusing a theory of reading with a theory of "first readings"), accept "perfect control" as a coherent goal of skilled writing.

18. Joseph Williams, *Style: Ten Lessons in Clarity and Grace* (New York: Scott Foresman, 1981).

19. Karlis Racevskis, *Michel Foucault and the Subversion of Intellect* (Ithaca, N.Y.: Cornell University Press, 1983), pp. 15–16.

20. Derrida, *Positions*, pp. 47, 64.

21. The next two paragraphs draw upon and adapt some remarks in "Deconstruction and Renaissance Literature," *Assays* 2 (1983): 69–94. See also Gary F. Waller, "Writing the Languages Writing Us," *Denver Quarterly* 16 (forthcoming); and "Post-Structuralist Practice: The Carnegie-Mellon Curriculum," *ADE Bulletin*, Sept. 1985 (forthcoming)

22. See Clinton S. Burhans, Jr., "Writing and the Knowledge Gap," *College English* 45 (1983): 654–55.

23. Eagleton, *Walter Benjamin*, p. 134.

writing and Writing

Sharon Crowley

Here is a way to think about texts.

Texts are discursive bits whose edges, boundaries, beginnings, and ends are marked only by the conventions of reading and bookbinding. Texts are occasioned by other texts. They are produced in order to be read, to be rewritten, and hence to generate other texts. The overt reference or subject of a text is irrelevant; covertly the text is an emblem of the desire to write and a display of one's capacity to insert one's pen into the textual flow. Texts are produced simply because it is necessary that they be, although if one wished to be more specific, one might allow that texts appear because of the human desire to compete with the father, the will to overthrow his text in a fruitless but noble quest to end once and for all the proliferation of meaning by writing the last word.

Here is another way to think about texts.

Each text reflects an Ideal Text. One instance of a text is pretty much like another because they all imitate the formal constraints imposed by the Ideal Text. The boundaries of texts are static and are clearly defined by the Ideal Text and are thus known (or ought to be) by all parties to the textual transaction. Texts are not "real"; they are "practice" for some imagined future production of "real" texts. Texts are produced by people who are trying to get better at it by writing a series of trial texts, each of which attempts to approximate the Ideal Text with increasing degrees of success. The covert subject of each text is the very quest for success; overt subjects are, once again, irrelevant.

No doubt there are countless other ways in which to think about texts. But my crude juxtaposition of poststructural and current-traditional models of textuality does raise a number of interesting questions. Is a poststructural model to be preferred over the current-traditional one as a better or more useful description of texts? True enough, the exhilarating sense of ubiquitous textuality that is espoused by poststructural theory renders it attractive as a possible substitute in instruction about writing. But can such a substitution be managed? Doesn't the obvious pedagogical slant of the current-traditional model render it more suitable to teaching writing than does the poststructural model, which presumes not only a desire to write but the wherewithal to do so?

My juxtaposition of the two models in question was instigated by my observation that they can be held in tandem by the same person (if that person is an English professor) and may be espoused with equal fervor in successive class hours, depending on whether the professor is teaching literature or composition. That poststructural and current-traditional views of the nature of texts can and do coexist comfortably in discussions of reading and writing by professors of English is a remarkable circumstance, to say the least. This circumstance opens the possibility that some sanction permits the harmonious maintenance of at least these two models of textuality, despite their seeming unrelatedness, within the profession. That sanction is, I think, the notion of author-ity, the relative appropriation of privilege by a text through the agency of its author's name. In literary pedagogy, the texts at hand usually carry names on whose author-ity there is substantial agreement, and whose demand on our time is thus deemed worthy. In composition classes, however, the author-ity of texts or, to be more precise, the lack of it, is such that people must be paid to read the texts produced therein. Apparently sound cultural reasons underlie this diversity in the profession's approach to the question of the author-ity of texts, and these need to be laid bare before I can broach the possibility that a workable poststructural model of the writing process might be devised for use in writing instruction.

Current-traditional rhetoric generated its textual model in and for a strictly pedagogical context, despite its proponents' occasional protest that the Ideal Text (the five-hundred-word theme) has value outside the classroom. The notions of "practice" and "trial" are thus crucial in the production of current-traditional texts. Each such effort is expendable, marking, as it does, only a stage in a learner's/writer's progress toward "real" writing. This situation makes for a very strange relation between an author and her text. In each trial, the author is commended to do her best writing, and yet her text is expected to carry no sign of her author-ity. (Indeed, in the more extreme current-traditional class she is taught to erase the grammatical marks of her presence—such as first-person pronouns. And in the discursive gangbangs that are holistic readings, even her name is expunged from her texts.)

It seems possible, then, that some texts may be satisfactorily read in an author's absence, that author-ity is not necessarily granted to a text by virtue of its having been authored. If so, the notion of ethos, as this was advanced by classical rhetoricians after Aristotle, needs to be rethought. Aristotle assumed that the most efficacious mode of proof was the ethical and that it derived its power from two kinds of author-ity: that which emanated from the speaker's use of language to create a persona appropriate to the occasion and that which devolved on a speaker by virtue of his role and reputation in the community. Aristotle thought that both modes were under the speaker's control to some extent; the former could be mastered by the patient study of human character, while the latter had to do with the way in which one lived one's life. But perhaps the ethical situation is different in regard to texts, which, as Plato complained, seem to have no father (mother) and thus may be made to say whatever one wishes them to say. And yet something like Aristotle's antecedent ethos still clings to textuality; furthermore, it has the important cultural function of determining which texts will be written and read.

In our culture, author-ity is freely granted to the Great Works of discourse; it is sometimes achieved by aspiring writers; and it is neither accorded nor aspired to by the texts produced by most members of society, including those designated as "students." That there are sound cultural reasons for withholding author-ity from all but a few texts has been demonstrated by Michel Foucault, who writes that an Author is

> a certain functional principle by which, in our culture, one limits, excludes, and chooses; in short, by which one impedes the free circulation, the free manipulation, the free composition, decomposition, and recomposition of fiction. . . . The author is therefore the ideological figure by which one marks the manner in which we fear the proliferation of meaning.[1]

Unlike Aristotle, Foucault argues that the name of the Author in its cultural role is ultimately irrelevant to the historical person who originally bore it. Rather, the function of this name permits a hierarchical set of value distinctions to operate as braking mechanisms on the otherwise uncontrolled outpouring and consumption of discourse. One does better to read Dickinson or Emerson than Stowe or Rosemary Rodgers and, best of all, to read Milton or Shakespeare, although the relative power of such names to open universes of discourse alters over time. And as these names indicate, there are Authors, and there are authors.

Foucault is concerned with the former class, those writers who, like Flaubert, Proust, and Kafka, are quite literally obliterated by their texts: the

> relationship between writing and death is also manifested in the effacement of the writing subject's individual characteristics. Using all the contrivances that he sets up between himself and what he writes, the writing subject cancels out the signs of his particular individuality. (Pp. 142–43)

Authors have to be invisible; more literally, they have to be dead. The status of Author-ity cannot be freely granted, lest the power that accrues to the name of the Author be centered in a living person. Hence Author-ity is not easy to achieve, involving, as it does, the disappearance of one's person. Also, part of the power that accrues to Authors' names seems to me to derive from the secret nature of the process by which one becomes an Author. The ranks of Author-ity carry about them an aura of mysticism or cabal; they always have.[2] Writers have about them the character of members of a secret society, the rules for admission to which are a carefully guarded secret.

American culture, however, seems willing enough to grant the status of authorship (small *a*) to certain persons who announce their aspiration toward Author-ity by inserting their work into the textual flow in a conspicuous way, a process for which impressive publishing and academic theaters have been erected. Authors (small *a*) regularly get their names into the right journals and reviewing organs. A sort of guru status accrues to such persons, and they are permitted to live in neat places like New York City or Iowa City or Montana or Hollywood and to do pretty much as they please as long as they keep writing and/or displaying their work from time to time for their students and admirers. This authorial hierarchy is extremely fluid; witness the sheer number of Norman Mailer's presences in it and absences from it since 1948. In the American academy, yet another hierarchy of authors' names functions so efficiently that one can betray one's theoretical allegiance simply by dropping some. In a few critical circles one can still raise eyebrows by naming Derrida; in rhetorical circles, one can demonstrate one's with-it-ness by mentioning Elbow or Flower and one's advancing age by uttering the names of Hirsch or Crews.

It should be clear by now that the association of writing with power is not facile. However, the quality of the power that is associated with writing varies with the degree of author-ity granted by a culture to its texts. As Foucault demonstrates, texts that are linked to an Author's name control the very possibility of writing or reading other texts. This is apparently true of authors as well; that one reads (and rewrites) Foucault's text determines one's relation ever after to any text that bears the name "M. H. Abrams." And so on.

We are now in a better position to understand the cultural usefulness of the current-traditional model of textuality. The democratic impetus to make writing available to everybody has been with current-traditional pedagogy since its inception in America. English departments have erected (and in part have been erected by) a vast industry on the promise that the rules of writing can be made explicit. The seminal figure of current-traditional pedagogy, Alexander Bain, opens his influential *English Composition and Rhetoric* (1866) by noting that the "principal vocation" of the composition teacher is to condense the principles of writing so that he "can impart in a short compass, what, without him, would be acquired slowly, if at all."[3] Current-traditional rhetoric began with the aim of "methodizing composition," of putting writing's bones and sinews on public display for everyone's potential appropriation. Such public textuality can come about, however, only through the aegis of the wonderful fiction that texts are somehow walled off from the flow of "real" textuality, having only a reflective and hence dead-end relation to the author-itative texts that model the Ideal Text. Moreover, current-traditional rhetoric enters an important qualification to its claim to make writing public. Instruction in invention—the wherewithal of having something to write—is always already held in reserve. As Bain puts it, to achieve a "command of language" is a lifetime preoccupation, and in its absence, teachers of writing are helpless to instruct their pupils in writing (p. v). Invention is the secret part of writing, the part that cannot be taught but must nonetheless be learned.[4] This hedge, of course, marks current-traditional rhetoric's adaptation to the cultural necessity of putting limits on the sprawl of author-ity.

What has happened, of course, is that in American culture, people correctly conceive of writing as having two manifestations: there's writing, which is the simple ordering and recording of thoughts or information and which can be done as easily by a secretary or a committee or a machine or a technical writer, since its author-ity is not relevant to its status as text; and there's Writing, what Authors (and authors) do.

The cultural implications of moving writing instruction toward a model of writing on which the author-ity of every text is assumed are now obvious. Were all—or even some—of the thousands of students who pass through freshman composition each year in this country to exert author-ity over even one text, the culture could begin to move toward something like Foucault's "absolutely free state, in which fiction would be put at the disposal of everyone and would develop without passing through something like a necessary or constraining figure'' (p. 159; Foucault is aware that this is a purely romantic notion on his part).

However, there is a kind of power associated with writing other than the power of the name. This is the sense of satisfaction that accrues from the experience of doing writing, of exerting, however briefly, control over one's environment. This effect of writing is as powerful an incentive to keep on writing as is the desire for author-ity, I think, and together these elusive promises of power are what keep writers at it. Contemporary composition theorists have devised a pedagogy that attempts to impart this sense of power to student writers. The point of ''process pedagogy'' is to provide students with writing experiences that will permit them to share—more than once and in a controlled environment—the exhilaration that results from mastering the flow of textuality.[5] This pedagogy, however sound and well-meaning, has remained on the fringes of composition instruction in America to date. I suspect that this is partly due to the subversive nature of its aim, which is, ultimately, to teach novice writers what it feels like to produce a text that has author-ity.

The difficulties surrounding the institution of a poststructural model in writing instruction are similar to those facing process pedagogy. Poststructural thought—for all of its avowed occulting of the author—assumes that writing is a manifestation of desire, is a reach for author-ity.[6] Invention begins in the encounter with one's own text or with those of others. Harold Bloom goes so far as to postulate that invention consists in a writer's attempt to defend against culturally strong texts by appropriating and improving them.[7] In poststructural thought, beginnings are acts as well as edges; as Edward Said puts it, the aim ''is to consider the text as a structure in the process of being composed from a certain beginning intention, in the process of realizing a structure.''[8] The notion that authors exert control over at least their own textuality appears implicitly in poststructural writing in its tendency to mess with the conventions of writing, as Derrida's texts repeatedly exemplify. In Derridean textuality the act of inserting his discourse into the flow of textuality is often made apparent not only within the text itself but by its very placement on the page alongside or above or below a companion text. Digressions abound, as do signatures and figures, most of which are (perhaps) intended to remind readers of the mutual referentiality of all discourse. In a neat nose-thumbing at the Saussurean hierarchy, the Derridean voice is displayed graphically, and hence publicly, on the page.

Some readers may be musing at this point that such textual acrobatics are beyond all but the most advanced writers. But that is just another way of saying that students are not ready to grasp textual author-ity. Such a statement is true enough, not in its usual sense that students are intellectually incapable of entering their discourses into textuality (no user of language is so incapable), but in the sense that culture, as it is currently constituted, forbids their doing so. Following Foucault, I do not see this as necessarily a permanent state of affairs. For Foucault, given the constant of societal change, the constraining role of the author function will disappear, to be replaced (perhaps) by another mode of limiting the polysemy of texts. If so, new questions about discourse would have to be formed and answered. Among the questions would be these:

> What are the modes of existence of this discourse? Where has it been used, how can it circulate, and who can appropriate it for himself? What are the places in it where there is room for possible subjects? Who can assume these various subject-functions? (P. 160)

Perhaps, to ask such questions about the texts produced in a writing class is a place from which to begin not only the smaller project of bringing writing pedagogy into line with what writers do, but to initiate as well the larger, the cultural, project.

NOTES

1. Michel Foucault, "What Is an Author?" in *Textual Strategies: Perspectives in Post-Structuralist Criticism*, ed. Josué V. Harari (London: Methuen, 1979), p. 159.

2. See Gerald L. Bruns, *Inventions: Writing, Textuality, and Understanding in Literary History* (New Haven, Conn.: Yale University Press, 1982), especially chapter 1 on the relation between secrecy, writing, and authority.

3. Alexander Bain, *English Composition and Rhetoric* (London: Longmans, Green, 1866), p. v.

4. For a fuller explication of current-traditional rhetoricians' position on the impossibility of teaching invention see my "Invention in Nineteenth-Century School Rhetoric," *College Composition and Communication* 36 (Feb. 1985): 51–60.

5. Process pedagogy was probably inaugurated by Janet Emig's 1971 study *The Composing Processes of Twelfth-Graders* (Urbana, Ill.: NCTE). Since then it has been elaborated into a full-blown approach to teaching composition. See particularly Peter Elbow's two textbooks *Writing without Teachers* (New York: Oxford University Press, 1973) and *Writing with Power* (New York: Oxford University Press, 1980).

6. See, for example, John Sturrock, *Structuralism and Since* (New York: Oxford University Press, 1979), pp. 12–15. Sturrock has done his best to amalgamate the strands of poststructuralist thought with which he is concerned;

but like all commentary on its principal writers (including mine, of course) to generalize about poststructuralism is to sacrifice.

7. See Bloom's *The Anxiety of Influence: A Theory of Poetry* (New York: Oxford University Press, 1973); *A Map of Misreading* (New York: Oxford University Press, 1975); and his essay in *Deconstruction and Criticism* (which he edited), especially pp. 10–14 (New York: Seabury Press, 1979), especially pp. 10–14.

8. Edward W. Said, *Beginnings: Intention and Method* (New York: Basic Books, 1975), p. 194.

The Two Rhetorics: George Eliot's Bestiary

J. Hillis Miller

In an essay published in 1983, "Composition and Decomposition: Deconstruction and the Teaching of Writing,"[1] I argued that all good readers as well as all good writers have always been "deconstructionists." Deconstruction was defined as presupposing a methodical awareness of the disruptive power that figures of speech exert over the plain construable "grammatical" sense of language, on the one hand, and over the apparent rigor of logical argumentation on the other. I concluded from this that rhetoric in the sense of knowledge of the intricacies of tropes should be taught in courses in composition, along with grammar and rhetoric in the sense of persuasion. Knowledge of figures of speech should also be taught in courses in reading. In the process of arguing that more attention should be given in courses both in reading and in writing to knowledge of figures of speech and their disruptive power, I discussed briefly (as examples of the way the great writers are all "deconstructionists" before the fact) a passage from Plato and one from George Eliot. I propose here to analyze those passages in more detail in an attempt to identify their deconstructive rigor. It should be remembered that "deconstruction" is not something that the reader does to a text; it is something that the text does to itself. The text then does something to the reader as she or he is led to recognize the possibility of two or more rigorously defensible, equally justifiable, but logically incompatible readings of the text in question.

The passage from Plato comes from the *Phaedrus*. Plato's rejection in the *Gorgias* and in the *Phaedrus* of empty skill in writing well still has

101

force. It is not enough to learn to write correctly and forcefully about any subject at all, taking any side of an argument, as a gifted lawyer can get the man on trial freed or condemned depending on which side has hired him. Writing well is not writing well unless it is guided by all of those ethical, political, and even metaphysical considerations that cannot be excluded from the teaching of writing. Such considerations involve true knowledge both of the human soul and of language. Here rhetoric as reading or as the knowledge of tropes comes in even for Plato. Plato's discussion of rhetoric in the *Phaedrus* contains a program for both kinds of rhetoric—rhetoric as writing and rhetoric as reading. The latter, too, must be guided by a knowledge of truth and conducted in the name of truth. Here is the crucial passage in the *Phaedrus*:

> *Socrates*: So contending with words is a practice found not only in lawsuits and public harangues but, it seems, wherever men speak we find this single art, if indeed it is an art, which enables people to make out everything to be like everything else, within the limits of possible comparison, and to expose the corresponding attempts of others who disguise what they are doing.
>
> *Phaedrus*: How so, pray?
>
> *Socrates*: I think that will become clear if we put the following question. Are we misled when the difference between two things is wide, or narrow?
>
> *Phaedrus*: When it is narrow.
>
> *Socrates*: Well then, if you shift your ground little by little, you are more likely to pass undetected from so-and-so to its opposite than if you do so at one bound.
>
> *Phaedrus*: Of course.
>
> *Socrates*: It follows that anyone who intends to mislead another, without being misled himself, must discern precisely the degree of resemblance and dissimilarity between this and that.
>
> *Phaedrus*: Yes, that is essential.
>
> *Socrates*: Then if he does not know the truth about a given thing, how is he going to discern the degree of resemblance between that unknown thing and other things?
>
> *Phaedrus*: It will be impossible.
>
> *Socrates*: Well now, when people hold beliefs contrary to fact, and are misled, it is plain that the error has crept into their minds through the suggestion of some similarity or other.
>
> *Phaedrus*: That certainly does happen.
>
> *Socrates*: But can anyone possibly master the art of using similarities for the purpose of bringing people round, and leading them away from the truth about this or that to the opposite of the truth, or again can anyone possibly avoid this happening to himself, unless he has knowledge of what the thing in question really is?
>
> *Phaedrus*: No, never.[2]

Rhetoric as reading, as the knowledge of tropes, is here defined as the only means of protection against the powers of rhetoric as writing, as illicit persuasion, as well as the essential means of composition for those who write successfully. A mastery of the truth about things and a mastery of the various forms of similitude turn out to be the two things that are needed by the rhetorician, both in his guise as writer and in his guise as reader. For Plato, too, reading and writing are intrinsically connected.

But what of Plato himself? What happens if we apply to Plato's discourse the method of reading that he himself advises? It is readily observable that Plato's own argument (or that of Socrates) proceeds by just that persuasion by means of similitude against which he warns—for example, when Socrates expresses his condemnation of rhetoric in the *Gorgias* in what he calls "the language of geometricians": "Sophistic is to legislation what beautification is to gymnastics, and rhetoric to justice what cookery is to medicine." A moment before, Socrates has condemned cookery and beautification as being mere semblances of medicine and gymnastics respectively: "Cookery then, as I say, is a form of flattery that corresponds to medicine, and in the same way gymnastics is personated by beautification, a mischievous, deceitful, mean, and ignoble activity, which cheats us by shapes and colors, by smoothing and draping, thereby causing people to take on an alien charm to the neglect of the natural beauty produced by exercise" (*Gorgias*, 465b, p. 247). By the remorseless logic of the language of geometricians, then, if we condemn cookery and beautification, we must also condemn rhetoric and its brother in false similitude, sophistry. The language of geometricians, however, it is easy to see, is nothing but a somewhat misleading name for that reasoning by similitude which Socrates condemns in the *Phaedrus*.

A is to B as C is to D: this is just the paradigmatic form of a proportional metaphor as Aristotle gives it in the section on metaphor in the *Poetics*. The ship is to the sea as the plow is to the waves, and therefore we say that the ship plows the waves. The basic resources of rhetorical argumentative persuasion are, in Aristotle's *Rhetoric*, said to be the example and the enthymeme. An example is a synecdoche—part used for the whole and then applied to another part—with all the problems appropriate to that trope; and the enthymeme is defined as an incomplete syllogism—that is, once more, argument by similitude or trope, since a syllogism is a formally stated proportional metaphor.[3]

It is all very well for Plato to have Socrates claim that he is dividing things according to their essential nature, as a good butcher cleaves a carcass at the joints—for example, in the distinction between body and soul on which the comparison of cookery to rhetoric depends—but Socrates' argument proceeds as much by similitude as by division. Plato's ''dear gorgeous nonsense,'' as Coleridge called it, is primarily a brilliant gift for arguing by means of similitudes or tropes—for example, in the famous condemnation of writing in comparison with speaking at the end of the *Phaedrus*. Writing is like the stupid farmer who sows his seeds in a barren garden of Adonis, while speaking is like the farmer who sows his seeds in suitable soil, that is, in the souls of living men (276b–77a, pp. 521–22). The wise reader will remember this by-no-means-innocent metaphor of farming when I come in a moment to discuss the passage from George Eliot's *The Mill on the Floss*. In the *Gorgias*, Callicles responds to a metaphor from shoemaking proposed by Socrates, followed by another use of the figure of the farmer who sows seed, by saying in exasperation, ''By heaven, you literally never stop talking about cobblers and fullers and cooks and doctors, as if we were discussing them'' (490e, p. 273). That is to say, Plato never stops talking nonliterally, not least in personifying himself as Socrates, and the result is that readers of Plato need most of all a skill in interpreting arguments based on tropes.

Plato's writings, too, both in what he says about rhetoric and in how he says it, provide an example of the inextricable interinvolvement of the two kinds of rhetoric and of the impossibility of having one without the other. He also provides another example of the way in which the act of reading can uncover directions for reading the text at hand in such a way as to undermine or deconstruct the apparent affirmations of that text, if the reader is cannily attentive to the play of tropes in the text. This is just what Plato tells us to be, along with learning to use tropes cannily in our own compositions. The text warns against the argument by tropes on which the text itself depends. To put this in another way, all discourse about rhetoric, for example Plato's *Gorgias* or a modern textbook of freshman composition, is itself an example of rhetoric and demands to be read as such, if we are not to be bamboozled by its enthymemes. This is another argument for the necessity of teaching reading along with writing.

As an exemplification of what might be meant by a ''deconstructive'' or rhetorical reading or of a reading as such, along with a demonstration of the truth of my claim that all good readers have always been deconstructionists, I shall discuss a wonderfully penetrating and witty passage from George Eliot's *The Mill on the Floss*. The passage reads itself, or gives the reader directions for how to read it. It is not only a text to be read but also a lesson in how to read. Any careful reader of *The Mill on the Floss* is likely to notice this passage. It has not failed to elicit comment.[4] The passage gives oblique hints to the reader about how to read the novel itself, as well as hints about some dangers lurking in the pedagogy of grammar and composition. The passage has to do with poor Tom Tulliver's sufferings at school in the hands of Mr. Stelling. It might have as title "The Beaver, the Camel, and the Shrewmouse":

> Mr. Broderip's amiable beaver, as that charming naturalist tells us, busied himself as earnestly in constructing a dam, in a room up three pair of stairs in London, as if he had been laying his foundation in a stream or lake in Upper Canada. . . . With the same unerring instinct Mr. Stelling set to work at his natural method of instilling the Eton Grammar and Euclid into the mind of Tom Tulliver. . . .
>
> [Mr. Stelling] very soon set down poor Tom as a thoroughly stupid lad; for though by hard labour he could get particular declensions into his brain, anything so abstract as the relation between cases and terminations could by no means get such a lodgment there as to enable him to recognise a chance genitive or dative. . . . Mr. Stelling concluded that Tom's brain being peculiarly impervious to etymology and demonstrations, was peculiarly in need of being ploughed and harrowed by these patent implements: it was his favourite metaphor, that the classics and geometry constituted that culture of the mind which prepared it for the reception of any subsequent crop. I say nothing against Mr. Stelling's theory: if we are to have one regimen for all minds, his seems to me as good as any other. I only know it turned out as uncomfortably for Tom Tulliver as if he had been plied with cheese in order to remedy a gastric weakness which prevented him from digesting it. It is astonishing what a different result one gets by changing the metaphor! Once call the brain an intellectual stomach, and one's ingenious conception of the classics and geometry as ploughs and harrows seems to settle nothing. But then it is open to some one else to follow great authorities, and call the mind a sheet of white paper or a mirror, in which case one's knowledge of the digestive process becomes quite irrelevant. It was doubtless an ingenious idea to call the camel the ship of the desert, but it would hardly lead one far in training that useful beast. O Aristotle! if you had had the advantage of being "the freshest modern" instead of the greatest ancient, would you not have mingled your praise of metaphorical speech, as a sign of high intelligence, with a lamentation that intelligence so rarely shows itself in speech without metaphor—that we can so seldom declare what a thing is, except by saying it is something else? . . .
>
> At present, in relation to this demand that he should learn Latin declensions and conjugations, Tom was in a state of as blank unimaginativeness concerning the cause and tendency of his sufferings, as

if he had been an innocent shrewmouse imprisoned in the split trunk
of an ash-tree in order to cure lameness in cattle.[5]

This admirable passage rises from height to height by a continual
process of capping itself or going itself one better, which is to say it
constantly deconstructs itself. The passage speaks of the activity of
reading, manifests a model of that activity, and invites us to read it
according to the method it employs. In all these ways it is a fine example
of the form of reading that I am calling "deconstructive" or of reading as
such. Though good reading does not occur as often as one might expect
or hope, it is by no means confined to any one historical period and may
appear at any time, perhaps most often in those, like George Eliot, who
are also good writers, masters of composition. The deconstructive
movement of this passage is constituted by the proffering and with-
drawing of one metaphorical formulation after another. Each metaphor
is dismantled as soon as it is proposed, though the sad necessity of
using metaphors is at the same time affirmed. No doubt, most teachers
of English grammar and composition, like teachers of Latin, have
experienced Mr. Stelling's exasperation at the obduracy and denseness
of their students' inability to remember the rules of grammar and idiom
when they try to write or to grasp syntactical concepts, while at the same
time they speak with fluency and force, just as Tom Tulliver "was in a
state bordering on idiocy with regard to the demonstration that two
given triangles must be equal—though he could discern with great
promptitude and certainty the fact that they *were* equal" (p. 215).
Though Tom cannot learn Latin grammar, he uses English with devastating cruelty towards his sister.

It might seem that George Eliot is placing in opposition the use of
literal language and the abuse of metaphorical language and that she is
counseling the former in a way that recalls the late-seventeenth- and
eighteenth-century tradition alluded to in her Lockean figure of the
mind as a sheet of white paper. In fact, the passage demonstrates that
"rarely" or "seldom" seems to be "never." The only weapon against a
metaphor is another metaphor, along with an awareness of our linguistic predicament in not being able—or in being so seldom able that
"rarely" is "almost never"—to declare what a thing is, except by saying
it is something else. Mr. Stelling's problem is not that he uses the
metaphor of ploughing and harrowing for his teaching of Euclid and the
Eton Grammar, but that he takes his metaphor literally, has no awareness of its limitation, and uses it as the excuse for a brutally inappropriate mode of instruction in Tom's case. Mr. Stelling teaches "with that
uniformity of method and independence of circumstances, which distin-

guishes the actions of animals understood to be under the immediate teaching of nature,'' such as that beaver who builds a dam ''up three pair of stairs in London'' in sublime indifference to the absence of water (p. 213). The beaver, like Mr. Stelling, is a literalist of the imagination. To take a metaphor literally is the aboriginal, universal, linguistic error, for as George Eliot says in an often-quoted passage in *Middlemarch*, ''We all of us, grave or light, get our thoughts entangled in Metaphors, and act fatally on the strength of them.''[6]

The escape from this entanglement in the net of a metaphor (another metaphor!) is not a substitution of literal language for misleading figure, but is the replacement of one metaphor by another. The second metaphor may neutralize the first or cancel out its distortions. This is a cure of metaphor by metaphor, a version of homeopathy. So George Eliot replaces the metaphor of ploughing and harrowing with a metaphor of eating. Forcing geometry and Latin grammar on Tom is like curing an inability to digest cheese with doses of cheese, or, the reader might reflect, like curing the disaster bought on by carrying the metaphorical basis in a pedagogical theory into practice by the application of another theoretical metaphor, replacing one kind of cheese with another kind of cheese. It is at this point that the narrator draws herself (himself?) up and makes the exclamation about how astonishing it is what a different result one gets by changing the metaphor.

To the other figures here must be added irony and prosopopoeia, irony as the pervasive tone of the narration and personification as the trope whereby the ironic discrepancy between narrator and character is given a name and a personality in the putative storyteller, ''George Eliot.'' That narrator pretends to have made Mr. Stelling's mistake, or the beaver's mistake—namely, to have used a metaphor without reflection—and then to have been surprised by the results into having a metalinguistic insight into the role of metaphor in pedagogical theory. But of course the narrator, who has been aware of this all along, is manipulating the metaphors in full deliberate awareness. He only pretends to be astonished. The sentence is ironic in the strict sense that it says the opposite of what it means, or rather that it says both things at once. It is astonishing and not astonishing, and the reader is challenged to ally himself with one side or the other, though at the same time he is put in a double bind. If he is not astonished, he may be putting himself unwittingly in the same camp as the beaver and Mr. Stelling, since another way to define a literalist is to say that he is incapable of being astonished by the workings of language. If the reader is astonished, then he is admitting that until a moment ago at least, he was a linguistic innocent, lagging behind the all-knowing narrator, who only ironically pretends to be astonished by something that he or she has known all along.

The digestive metaphor is then followed by two more traditional metaphors for the mind—the Lockean one of the white sheet of paper, and the figure of the mirror, which has had such a long history in expressions of "realism" in the novel: for example, in Georg Lukács or in George Eliot herself in the celebrated chapter 17 of *Adam Bede*, the *locus classicus* for the theory of realism in Victorian fiction.

The next metaphor, that of the camel as the ship of the desert, seems to be irrelevant or nonfunctional, not part of the chain, no more than a textbook example of metaphor.[7] It allows the bringing in of Aristotle and the opposition of the ancients who naïvely praised metaphor, on the one hand, and the moderns, such as Locke, who lament its presence in language and try (unsuccessfully) to expunge it, on the other. Aristotle, by the way, did not, strictly speaking, "praise . . . metaphorical speech as a sign of high intelligence," as George Eliot says. Aristotle said a "command of metaphor" was the "mark of genius," "the greatest thing by far," in a poet, the one thing that "cannot be imparted by another."[8] A command of metaphor is for Aristotle not so much a sign of intelligence as an intuitive gift, "an eye for resemblances" (1495a, p. 87). The poet does not rationally think out metaphors. They just come to him in a flash, or they fall under his eye. In any case, the figure of a camel as a ship accomplishes three moves simultaneously in the intricate sequence of George Eliot's thought in the passage as a whole.

First move: The image of the camel more or less completes the repertoire of examples of metaphor that makes the passage not only a miniature treatise on metaphor but also, unostentatiously, an anthology, bouquet, herbarium, or bestiary of the basic metaphors in our tradition—that is, coming down from the Bible and from the Greeks. No choice of examples is innocent, and it is no accident that metaphors of farming and sowing (for example, in Plato's *Phaedrus* or in Christ's parable of the sower, with the sun lurking somewhere as the source of germination); metaphors of specular reflection, the play of light, of images, of reflection, and of seeing; metaphors of eating, of writing on that blank sheet of paper, and of journeying from here to there (that is, of transport, whether by camel back or on ship board)—all tend to reappear whenever someone, from Aristotle on down to the freshest modern teacher of composition, pulls an example of metaphor out of his pedagogical hat. These remain the basic metaphors still today, and though he will not necessarily have the poet's instinctive command of them, a good reader can learn to thread his way from one to another in their interchangeability and begin to master them as a deliberate reader if not as a writer. If the ship plowing the waves mixes the agricultural with the nautical region of figure, the sowing of seed, for both Plato and Jesus, is at the same time a form of writing, a dissemination of the word. And does not the assimilation of learning to eating appear in that extraordinary image of Ezekiel eating the scroll, as well as in Hegel's interpretation of the Last Supper in *The Spirit of Christianity*, not to speak of the Communion service itself, in which the communicants eat the *Logos*, and of a strange passage in George Eliot's own *Middlemarch*?[9]

Second move: the camel as ship of the desert is not just an example of metaphor. It is a metaphor of metaphor; that is, of transfer or transport from one place to another. This is not only what the word *metaphor* means etymologically but also what metaphor does. It effects a transfer. If George Puttenham's far-fetched Renaissance name for metalepsis is the "Far-fetcher," he elsewhere calls metaphor the "Figure of Transport."[10] Metaphor gets the writer or reader from here to there in his argument, whether by that "smooth gradation or gentle transition, to some other kindred quality," of which Wordsworth speaks in the "Essays upon Epitaphs,"[11] following the Socrates of the *Phaedrus* on "shifting your ground little by little," or by the sudden leap over a vacant place in the argument, of which George Meredith writes: "It is the excelling merit of similes and metaphors to spring us to vault over gaps and thickets and dreary places."[12] Pedagogy is metaphor. It takes the mind of the student and transforms it, transfers it, translates it, ferries it from here to there. A method of teaching, such as Mr. Stelling's, is as much a means of transportation as is a camel or a ship. My own "passages" from Plato and Eliot are synecdoches, parts taken from large wholes and used as figurative means of passage from one place to another in my argument.

Third move: The sentence about the camel brings into the open the asymmetrical juxtaposition between the opposition of literal and figurative language, on the one hand, and the opposition of theory and practice, on the other. The reader may be inclined to think that these are parallel, but this probably depends on a confusion of mind. One thinks of literal language as the clear nonfigurative expression of ideas or concepts: for example, the "abstract" concepts of grammar, such as the relation between cases and determinations in the genitive and the dative, which Tom Tulliver has as much trouble learning as a modern student of English composition has in learning the rules of English grammar. At the same time, one thinks of literal language as the act of nonfigurative nomination, calling a spade a spade and a camel a camel, not a ship. We tend to think of figure as applied at either end of the scale—from abstract to concrete—as an additional ornament making the literal expression "clearer," more "vivid," or more "forceful." As George Eliot's sentence makes clear, however, the trouble with theory is not that it is abstract or conceptual but that it is always based on metaphor—that is, it commits what Alfred North Whitehead calls "the fallacy of misplaced concreteness."

If it is true that original thinking is most often started by a metaphor, as both Whitehead himself and such literary theorists as William Empson and Kenneth Burke aver in different ways, it is also the case that each metaphorically based theory, such as the alternative pedagogical theories that George Eliot sketches out, has its own built-in fallacious bias and leads to its own special form of catastrophe in the classroom. If a camel is not a ship, the brain is neither a field to plough nor a stomach nor a sheet of paper nor a mirror, though each of these metaphors could, and has, generated ponderous, solemn, and intellectually cogent theories of teaching. Neither theory nor literal meaning, if there is such a thing (which there is not), will help you with that camel. As soon as you try to tell someone how to manage a camel, you fall into theory—that is, into some metaphorical scheme or other. The opposition between theory and practice is not that between metaphorical and literal language, but is that between language, which is always figurative through and through, and no language—silent doing. If the praxis in question is the act of writing, the habit of writing well, it can be seen that there are going to be problems in teaching it, more problems even than in teaching someone how to drive a camel or to make a chair. That the terms for the parts of a chair are examples of those basic personifying catachreses, whereby we humanize the world and project arms and legs where there are none, may cause little trouble as the apprentice learns from watching the master cabinetmaker at work, but it might cause much trouble to someone who is writing about chairs.

After what has been said so far, the function of the final animal in George Eliot's bestiary, the shrewmouse—the vehicle for the last metaphor in the segment that I have excised from her narrative—is clear enough. Having seemingly aligned herself with those fresh moderns who would opt for an antiseptic "speech without metaphor," George Eliot, far from speaking without metaphors herself, goes on to present the most ostentatious and elaborate of all the metaphors in this sequence—ostentatious in the sense that the literal elaboration of the vehicle of the metaphor, a bit of Warwickshire agricultural folklore, seems far to exceed its parabolic application to Tom's suffering: "Tom was in a state of as blank unimaginativeness concerning the cause and tendency of his sufferings, as if he had been an innocent shrewmouse imprisoned in the split trunk of an ash-tree in order to cure lameness in cattle." This not only demonstrates once more that "we can . . . seldom declare what a thing is, except by saying it is something else." It also shows that the only cure for metaphor is not literal language but another metaphor that so calls attention to itself that no one could miss that it is a metaphor or take it as innocently "dead." If literal language is possible, it is likely, paradoxically, to occur in the elaboration of the vehicle of the figure, as in this case or as in the parables of Jesus in the Gospels. It is possible to speak literally about shrewmice in Warwickshire or about the details of farming, fishing, and household care in first-century Palestine, but this literal speech almost always turns out, by a kind of fatality intrinsic to language, to be the means of speaking parabolically or allegorically about something else. The most figurative language, it would follow, is the language that appears to be the most literal. The good reader is one who, like George Eliot, brings this sad fact into the open, as a secret writing in sympathetic ink beneath the writing on the surface is brought out by the application of heat or the right chemicals. Bringing it into the open, alas, is not an escape from it or a "cure" for it.

From where does my metaphor of "cure" come? Is it my own licit or illicit addition, the reader's license? No, it is of course already there as one of the places of passage in the quotation from George Eliot. I have said that the shrewmouse is the last animal in George Eliot's bestiary and that the literal details of the shrewmouse's suffering exceed its figurative application. Obviously, neither of these is the case. The last animals are those lame cattle, and they function to make the figure of the shrewmouse, at a second remove, a figure for the failure of teaching to cure lameness in the sense of linguistic incapacity—for example, an inability to write clear and concise English prose. Mr. Stelling's pedagogy, based as it is on the magic literalization of a metaphor, is as much a piece of superstition as is the countryman's beliefs about shrewmice and cattle. Which of us twentieth-century teachers can be sure that our method is not another such blind belief in an unread metaphor?

In any case, the reader at the end of my sequence from *The Mill on the Floss* remains as trapped as ever within the linguistic situation of not being able to say what a thing is, except by saying it is something else. Tom is imprisoned within the obstinate rigors of Mr. Stelling's pedagogy, rigors that result from the literal application of a metaphor. His situation makes him like a poor innocent imprisoned shrewmouse. The melancholy wisdom of this passage affirms that the reader or writer of any sort—you or I—is imprisoned as much as Tom, Mr. Stelling, or the shrewmouse within the linguistic predicament that the passage both analyzes and exemplifies. The most that one can hope for is some clarification of the predicament, not escape from it into the free light of day.

In "Composition and Decomposition" I concluded my brief discussion of the passages from Plato and George Eliot with the claim that both teachers and students of rhetoric as persuasion or as composition must aim to become as good readers as Plato, George Eliot, or Jacques Derrida, as wise in the ways of tropes, or else they will not learn to be good teachers or practitioners of writing either. "Good courses in rhetoric as reading," I concluded, "must always accompany programs in composition, not only in preparation for reading Shakespeare, Milton, Wordsworth, and Wallace Stevens, but as an essential accompaniment to courses in writing." I draw now another, perhaps more radical or disturbing, conclusion. If the medieval trivium of grammar, logic, and rhetoric is indeed a place in which the pathways of those three disciplines come together or cross, as the etymology of *trivium* suggests (*tri-viae*, "three roads"), it may be that rhetoric is not so much the climax of a progressive mastery of language both for reading and for writing as it is the place in which the impossibility of mastery is definitively encountered. The road called "rhetoric" is always marked "impassable" or "under construction; pass at your own risk" or, as it is succinctly put on signs in England, "road up!"

Paul de Man certainly thought this was the case with rhetoric as the wrestling with tropes. In an interview with Robert Moynihan, in answer to a question about irony, de Man asserted that "the claim of control, yes, when it is made, can always be shown to be unwarranted—one can show that the claim of control is a mistake, that there are elements in the text that are not controlled, that it is always possible to read the text against the overt claim of control."[13] And in another essay, "Semiology and Rhetoric," discussing Archie Bunker's question "What's the difference?" de Man asserts: "The grammatical model of the question becomes rhetorical not when we have, on the one hand, a literal meaning and on the other hand a figural meaning, but when it is impossible to decide by grammatical or other linguistic devices which of the two meanings (that can be entirely incompatible) prevails. Rhetoric radically suspends logic and opens up vertiginous possibilities of referential aberration. . . . I would not hesitate to equate the rhetorical, figural potential of language with literature itself."[14]

Certain notorious quarrels among literary critics or between philosophers and literary critics or among philosophers occupy the polemical field of humanistic study today. I am thinking, for example, of interchanges between Jacques Derrida and John Searle or between Paul de Man and Raymond Geuss or between me and Meyer Abrams, or of attacks on "deconstruction" in the name of history and straightforward referential language by Gerald Graff, Frank Lentricchia, and others.[15] The issues at stake in these various quarrels are complex, but it may be possible to understand them better by seeing them as disagreements about the proper relation among the three branches of the ancient trivium. A critic such as Meyer Abrams wants to make grammar, what he calls "construing" of the plain sense of a poem or a novel, the basis for literary study, to which the study of the "perfidious" language of tropes by deconstructionists might be added as an extra frill for a few specialists in advanced courses. Analytical philosophers or logicians (with a few honorable exceptions such as Wittgenstein and Austin) tend to minimize the effect that figures of speech might have on their enterprise, or to believe that logic might, so to speak, reduce, encompass, or master rhetoric. Such logicians or analysts tend to be violently and unreasonably hostile to a philosopher of rhetoric such as Jacques Derrida and even to deny him the name of philosopher (for is not philosophy purely a matter of logical reasoning?).

The claim of "deconstruction," by now patiently (and reasonably) demonstrated with a wide variety of philosophical and literary texts and patiently (and reasonably) argued in "theoretical" statements, is that language is figurative through and through, all the way down to the bottom, so to speak, and that rhetoric in the sense of tropes inhibits or prevents both the mastery of the plain sense of texts, which is promised by grammar, and the mastery of reasoning, which is promised by logic. "Rhetoric radically suspends logic and opens up vertiginous possibilities of referential aberration." If this is the case (and it is), rhetoric is not so much the imperial queen of the trivium and of basic studies in humanities generally, as it is the odd man out, the jack of spades or the wild card, who suspends the game or at any rate causes much trouble in playing it. This is not an argument against the kind of study of rhetoric that I have tried to define and exemplify in this essay. Far from it. Though the truth about language may be a dark and troubling one, it is better to know that truth than to fool oneself or others, since language is an edge tool, and much harm may be done by even the most amiable and well-meaning of mistaken assumptions about it, as the sad story of Mr. Stelling demonstrates.

NOTES

1. In *Composition & Literature: Bridging the Gap*, ed. Winifred Bryan Horner (Chicago: University of Chicago Press, 1983), pp. 38–56.

2. *Phaedrus*, 261d–62b, trans. R. Hackforth, in *Plato: The Collected Dialogues*, ed. Edith Hamilton and Huntington Cairns, Bollingen series 71 (Princeton, N.J.: Princeton University Press, 1963), pp. 507–8. The citations from *Gorgias* are from the translation by W. D. Woodhead in the same volume, pp. 229–307.

3. See Aristotle, *The Rhetoric*, trans. Lane Cooper (New York: D. Appleton-Century, 1932), p. 10.

4. For example, by Joseph Litvak in a recent Ph.D. dissertation in Comparative Literature at Yale University.

5. George Eliot, *The Mill on the Floss*, Cabinet Edition, vol. 1 (Edinburgh and London: William Blackwood & Sons, n.d.), bk. 2, chap. 1, pp. 213–17.

6. George Eliot, *Middlemarch*, Cabinet Edition, vol. 1 (Edinburgh and London: William Blackwood & Sons, n.d.), chap. 10, p. 127.

7. The *OED* gives several examples under "Desert" and "Ship," the earliest dated 1615.

8. Aristotle, *Poetics*, trans. S. H. Butcher (New York: Dover Publications, 1951), 1459a, p. 87.

9. *Middlemarch*, vol. 1, chap. 6, p. 86.

10. Cited by Richard A. Lanham, *A Handlist of Rhetorical Terms* (Berkeley: University of California Press, 1969), p. 100.

11. William Wordsworth, "Essays upon Epitaphs," in *The Prose Works*, ed. W. J. B. Owen and Jane Worthington Smyser, vol. 2 (Oxford: Clarendon Press, 1974), p. 81.

12. George Meredith, *One of Our Conquerors*, in *Works*, Memorial Edition, vol. 17 (London: Constable, 1909–11), p. 189.

13. Robert Moynihan, "Interview with Paul de Man," *Yale Review* 73, no. 4 (July 1984): 580.

14. Paul de Man, *Allegories of Reading* (New Haven, Conn.: Yale University Press, 1979), p. 10.

15. For the first see Jacques Derrida, "Signature Event Context"; John R. Searle, "Reiterating the Differences: A Reply to Derrida," *Glyph 1* (Baltimore, Md.: Johns Hopkins University Press, 1977), pp. 172–208; and Jacques Derrida, "Limited Inc," *Glyph 2* (Baltimore, Md.: Johns Hopkins University Press, 1977), pp. 162–254. For the second see Paul de Man, "Sign and Symbol in Hegel's *Aesthetics*," *Critical Inquiry* 8, no. 4 (Summer 1982): 761–75; Raymond Geuss, "A Response to Paul de Man"; and Paul de Man, "Reply to Raymond Geuss," *Critical Inquiry* 10, no. 2 (Dec. 1983): 375–90. For the third see M. H. Abrams, "The Deconstructive Angel"; and J. Hillis Miller, "The Critic as Host," *Critical Inquiry* 3, no. 3 (Spring 1977): 425–47. For the fourth see Gerald Graff, *Literature against Itself: Literary Ideas in Modern Society* (Chicago: University of Chicago Press, 1979); and Frank Lentricchia, *After the New Criticism* (Chicago: University of Chicago Press, 1980). The literature about, for, and against deconstruction has since 1980 grown to impressive proportions.

Heuristics and Beyond: Deconstruction/Inspiration and the Teaching of Writing Invention

Paul Northam

As Maxine Hairston notes, the teaching of composition in the United States is almost certainly undergoing what she (following Thomas Kuhn) calls a "paradigm shift."[1] The "common body of beliefs and assumptions" shared until recently by the majority of composition teachers—the "current-traditional paradigm"—emphasizes the product of writing over the process that generates it. As a result, those who work under it value style, grammatical/mechanical correctness, and appropriateness of form over other considerations. The process of writing is assumed not to be teachable "because writing is a mysterious creative activity that cannot be categorized or analyzed." One consequence of this assumption is the tendency of the current-traditional practitioner to neglect invention "almost entirely." But this paradigm is becoming less and less trusted. Teachers are recognizing that it is simply no longer working, that large numbers of students "come to them writing badly and . . . leave writing badly" (pp. 76–81). Consequently, a new paradigm is gradually evolving, one that (to generalize) emphasizes the process of writing rather than the product and that carries with it several important implications for the teacher of composition (pp. 82–88).[2] In this paper I will focus on two of these implications, developments from the process-centered paradigm: the newly recognized importance of invention and the call for wider acceptance of the composition teacher as the performer of a significant educational function.

"Invention," according to W. Ross Winterowd, may be defined as "the process whereby a writer discovers ideas to write about,"[3] but all too often, invention theorists neglect an essential step in that process. I shall call that step "inspiration," and I shall define it as the act through which writers discover that they have something worth saying about a topic which they want to write down. Most conventional approaches to invention neglect the essential part of inspiration, as I define it, in the process. One potentially fruitful way to encourage inspiration in writing, however, a means I will suggest in this paper, is to train students in reading texts of all sorts (verbal, social, aesthetic, and so on) with an attitude encouraged by deconstructive literary theory.

I agree with Richard Young's contention that inspiration as such—"the imaginative act or the unanticipated outcome"—cannot be directly taught because "the processes involved . . . are too unpredictable to be controlled by rule-governed procedures."[4] Reading deconstructively, however, provides fresh insights into texts and, more importantly, proceeds with the intention of exploring the oscillations in meaning of the language that embodies them. Deconstruction, then, involves a playful reading, a playful discovery of the text's compromises in meaning. To follow successfully the deconstruction of a text, however, requires also that students read more closely, more analytically, than they are usually asked to do. Practice in reading with a deconstructive attitude will, as a result, lead to an increase in students' reading ability as they learn to play (intellectually) with the many possible significations inhabiting a given signifier or chain of signifiers. By learning to approach a text from a less-rigid point of view and by enhancing their reading ability, students will gain confidence and competence in their writing, and these qualities—parts of an attitude towards language—combined with the fresh insights that deconstructive reading yields, will give students likely stimuli to inspiration. Writers who are confident and convinced that they have original perspectives on a topic will probably be more eager to communicate their thoughts and will probably care more about this act of communication than writers who are mechanically following traditional heuristics.

Three points qualify the following pages. First, I am not advocating deconstruction as an all-purpose heuristic; indeed, it cannot be a heuristic in any literal sense at all (as we shall see). Second, I am not arguing that reading well, deconstructively or otherwise, leads inexorably to writing well. Rather, my contention is that training students in this mode of reading gives them analytical skills and a positive attitude towards language that are more likely than established methods of invention to lead to inspiration. Inspiration will, again, stimulate students to care about their writing, and their caring, I am convinced, will lead to better writing.[5] Deconstructive reading, in other words, provides for a set of intellectual conditions that are likely to lead to inspiration. Third, I wish to emphasize my belief that a pluralistic approach to writing invention is still necessary: we know too little about the composing process to be justified in rejecting out of hand any single method of generating subject matter. It is necessary to keep in mind a cardinal (to my way of thinking) rule of writing pedagogy: use whatever works in the classroom, whatever leads students to greater insights, awareness, or knowledge, no matter what the source or the methodology.

Like all good pedagogical approaches, the one I shall suggest (which I call deconstruction/invention) can benefit both student and teacher. Students, of course, improve their chances to write well. The composition teacher, though, stands to gain not only the satisfaction of doing a job well but also wider acceptance of the significance of his or her role in higher education. Learning the deconstructive mind-set encourages students to examine closely and critically not only their diction and syntax but also their conventions of naturalizing personal beliefs and social and academic experiences. Thus, introducing it into the classroom will stimulate the putting into question of all such conventions. In this way, writing classes will encourage the evaluation of typically accepted metaphysical, ontological, epistemological, psychological, and cultural conventions, thus converting the writing class into an arena in which learning is done in the most esteemed of liberal-arts fashions—for its own sake, for the intellectual growth of the individual. We, as teachers of writing, will then have the means to combat the view "which denies that writing requires intellectual activity and ignores the importance of writing as a basic method of learning," as Hairston puts it, an opinion that relegates writing classes to the status of second-class citizenship in the academic nation as "service courses and skills courses" (p. 79). But before I can exemplify a deconstructive way of reading and thereby suggest its significance to the composition class, it will be necessary to define briefly what I mean by "deconstruction" as an attitude from which reading and writing may be done.

J. Hillis Miller provides perhaps the clearest succinct account of the deconstructive project: it is "an attempt to interpret as exactly as possible the oscillations in meaning produced by the irreducibly figurative nature of language."[6] His statement points the way towards the implications of deconstruction for the teaching of writing. As we shall see, Miller's picture of language as "irreducibly figurative," combined with a Heideggerian view of it as the defining quality of human being, is what makes possible the deconstructive analysis of not only such language-constituted signifiers as essays but also such ostensibly non-language-constituted "social" or "cultural" events as films or a home-coming parade. This interpretation of language is derived from the writings of Jacques Derrida, especially his *Of Grammatology*. Consequently, it is with Derrida that my overview of deconstruction should begin.

Derrida criticizes the privileging of speech over writing in Western civilization from Plato to Saussure;[7] this hierarchization is no doubt a source of the current-traditional paradigm's view of composition as a skills course. "Writing," as Sharon Crowley notes, "is thought of as a recording or representation of speech, and often not a good one at that."[8] The conventional view of language would have it that the signifier is similar to a window through which we can glimpse an extralinguistic concept or referential object known as the signified. According to this perspective, "cat," for example, points as a signifier to an animal whose reality is unrelated to our naming of it. Speech thus becomes simply a convenient means for designating objects in an independently existing phenomenal world. And writing becomes a recorded substitute for speech; it thus, notes Crowley, "is taught in schools not as a means of tapping the power and charm of the word but as a less-than-satisfactory representation of speech" (p. 284). Given writing's third-rate status with reference to "reality," it is no wonder that composition teachers have had to fight for whatever recognition they have gained on college campuses. Derrida, however, begins to overturn this privileging; he points out that writing and speech are no more than separate instances of language in action. The belief that the signifier points to a referent outside language, as signifiers in an essay ostensibly describing a cat are assumed to lead the reader to a referential object—the animal itself—somewhere in the phenomenal world, suffers from the naïve acceptance, Derrida concludes, of what he calls "logo-centrism" or the "metaphysics of presence."

Responding to this metaphysics, Derrida argues that any given signifier leads us only to further signifiers, not to a signified. That is, when we think of "cat," we think in terms of other signifiers in order to define our belief as to what a cat may (and may not) be. These signifiers denote perceived (but not, as we soon shall see, actual) absences—as is easily seen in "not dog," "not human," "not mouse," and so on—even when the signifiers may seem to suggest a presence. Thus, "small" is formed through the apparent absence of "large" and the signifiers intervening between the two; "mammalian," through what we take to be the absence of "reptilian," "birdlike," and so on; and "fur-covered,'' through a seeming absence of ''scale-covered,'' ''feathered,'' and even ''featherless.'' A signifier cannot exist autonomously and have meaning. It is understood as being part of a chain or matrix of signification (in relationship to other signifiers) which never, according to Derrida, can be traced by human beings to an origin outside language, to what he calls the ''transcendental signified.'' Language, then, refers only to itself (signifiers refer only to signifiers). To assume otherwise is to believe that within the signifier exists the presence of a logos or conceptual (extralinguistic) meaning. This apparent error is to Western civilization, though, the truth of language. It is, then, for us inescapable. It is logocentric thought, the metaphysics of presence.

Because language has no definite, closing referent (no *telos*) beyond the signifier (beyond itself), no signifier—oral, written, or otherwise—can be granted a delimited origin of meaning. Any given signifier is defined not in and of itself but rather in its relationship to other signifiers. I have noted that a configuration of absences seems to result in meaning; ''absence,'' however, is a very problematic concept. If ''absence'' determines meaning, it determines ''presence.'' The distinction between the two must consequently break down; we can no longer consider them as being diametrically opposed. Absence enters into and becomes presence as, simultaneously, presence enters into and becomes absence. ''Whiteness,'' for example, which we understand as the absence of not only ''blackness'' but also the other colors, is constituted in actuality by ''blackness'' and every intervening color. Meaning emerges from the interplay—the absenting to become present—among the members of a chain of signification. No signifier has a clearly demarked meaning without this association with the other signifiers in the chain, which include, of course, the given signifier's opposite. Traces of these associated signifiers always already exist in any given signifier: ''blackness'' exists in, because it is part of, the meaning of ''whiteness''; and ''dog'' exists in, because it is part of, the meaning of ''cat.''

In Derridean or deconstructionist terms, language is inherently figurative, metonymic. I say ''metonymic'' because metonymy, a figure based on qualities shared by two objects being compared, is closer to the idea of interlocking chains of meaning than metaphor, which is based on differences seen between objects, differences that depend upon points of contrast, which are actually common ground between them. Looking at the syntax or diction of a text or even the etymology of a particular word, we must always take into account the infringement upon the signifier or signifiers of other members of the chain of signification. This infringement leads to the deferral of any final, closed meaning (any totalization) for the signifier or signifiers in question, a deferral which proceeds inexorably and which Derrida calls *differance*. One of the most important practical consequences of *differance* is that, in any text possessing an apparent authorial declaration or thesis, there will always exist a deconstructive description, an undercurrent of signification which undermines the declaration, making possible alternative and contradictory readings of the text in question. The description manifests itself at certain especially unstable points in the text; these points are, according to Derrida, characterized by a "hinge" or "*brisure*" (pp. 65–73—in French, *brisure* means literally "breaking point" as well as "hinge"). Exemplifying the tracing of the inherent figurative oscillation of language, Derrida shows that Rousseau's claim (in the *Essay on the Origin of Languages*) that, among other things, society evolved before language carries with it the attendant description that language must have preceded society. This reversal is not a simple contradiction but rather a normal function of Rousseau's language itself (see Derrida, pp. 265–68). Meaning, to Derrida, becomes not so much a matter of an "either/or" proposition, in which the semantic territory covered by a signifier is clearly demarked, as it does a "both/and" view, in which the semantic territory of a given signifier overlaps that of associated signifiers, thus compromising its univocality.

Another example of the action of the description against the declaration may be in order. Freshman composition students at the University of Kansas, where I teach, are required to write an adequate proficiency theme on a source essay in order to pass the first course in the required English sequence. At the time I am writing, the current crop of freshmen has completed a final essay based on Margaret Halsey's "What's Wrong with 'Me, Me, Me,'" originally published in *Newsweek* for 17 April 1978.[9] Halsey's thesis is that although the so-called me generation worships the self "with the strength and impetus of a new religion," its "narcissism . . . is all based on a false idea" that "inside every human being, however unprepossessing, there is a glorious, talented, overwhelmingly attractive personality" which "will be revealed in all its splendor if the individual just forgets about courtesy, cooperativeness, and consideration for others and proceeds to do exactly what he or she feels like doing" (p. 10). Strong words, to be sure. But they are immediately compromised by the single word following them, one given the dignity of a paragraph all to itself: "Nonsense" (p. 10). Herein, I suggest, lies the hinge: does the word "nonsense" comment upon the idea Halsey quotes, as she appears to declare, or does it refer to the notion that the idea is a "false idea"? Either interpretation is possible, and other hinges may be found.

Because I am merely suggesting a deconstructive reading, however, I will limit myself to a description based on only this element of Halsey's text.

Halsey accuses members of the "me generation" of searching for a "static," perfect selfhood, which, she claims, the "me generation" believes is to be found within the individual. "Being perfect," she comments ironically, "it does not need to change" (p. 11). Halsey urges her readers to aspire instead towards "honest knowledge of themselves—which with patience and courage could start them on the road to genuine development" (p. 10). Genuine development is a process that takes time, according to Halsey, and she asserts that the new narcissists believe they have no need to develop. Halsey's declaration, however, is undermined by her acknowledgment that such a thing as "a six-week course in self-expression" (p. 11) is undertaken and advocated by these narcissists. Apparently the narcissists believe, as does Halsey, that finding a perfect selfhood takes time and can be achieved through concentrating on other people (even a teacher—students must convince a teacher of their worth if they are to pass any class, even "a six-week course in self-expression") rather than the self. The distinction that she draws between narcissism and the process of development breaks down, consequently, and a description of her text avers that it is indeed "nonsense" to say that the idea underlying "the new narcissism" is "false" (p. 10), for the same idea underlies genuine self-development. To be adequate, I emphasize, my deconstructive reading of Halsey would have to be much expanded, to account for other features of the text. I offer here only an example of the sort of conclusions that deconstructive reading can lead one to.

In order to read well deconstructively, it is necessary to read well analytically. A composition teacher who encourages his or her students to read in such a manner the many essays drawn from the books of readings that are commonly used in writing classes should find the students reading much more closely, attentively, than they have before. This enhanced reading skill will not, as I have said, necessarily increase their ability to write well (the existence of a reading/writing connection is still not conclusively proven), but it will encourage inspiration and hence the invention of worthwhile essays. "The impulse to write," as Richard L. Larson stresses, "comes from the discovery of a comment worth making."[10] Writers are more likely to think that their comments are worth making if they *believe* those comments to be fresh, original, new (whether they really are or not is beside the point). The close reading that deconstruction demands—the closest sort presently achievable—is a fruitful means by which to come to fresh insights into a given text (of whatever sort). Hence, deconstruction is potentially (at least) a powerful aid to inspiration. The student who reads so closely has a greater chance of finding in an essay such as Halsey's the inspiration to write about some element of that text; she or he is likely to discover a new outlook worth exploring, worth considering, worth caring about. It is therefore likely, as I have suggested, that such a student will write an essay more noteworthy than will readers not trained in deconstruction.

The enrichment of reading ability that deconstruction is likely to lead to will no doubt encourage students to feel confident that their perspective on a text is valuable, but this is not the only contribution that deconstruction can make to inspiration. Following the deconstruction of a text enables one to gain a new pleasure from reading. This approach to the text overturns the tyranny of the logos and gives the interpreter the exhilarating freedom of tracing pathways of meaning as they emerge, through *differance*, from tangled forests of signification: "The deconstructive procedure . . . by playing on the play within language," notes Miller, may become "interpretation as joyful wisdom, the greatest joy in the midst of the greatest suffering, an inhabitation of that gaiety of language which is our seigneur."[11] Students who read deconstructively are thus trained to approach a text with freedom, to see the text as intertwining threads of signification that they are as free to unravel as anyone else (such readings cannot be arbitrary, of course—a deconstructive reading must begin with the univocal or logocentric interpretation, which it then proceeds to unravel by a more or less definable mechanism).

What forms might this unraveling take? Several, if one refers to essays from books of readings or even to topics of discourse.[12] John M. Bresnahan, Jr., for example, in his "Monday, March 5, 1770: Who Was to Blame?" (p. 40), emphasizes the gruesome details of the killings of the victims of the Boston Massacre. This emphasis undermines the author's attempt to exonerate the British soldiers accused of murder, indicating that he has at least unconsciously been influenced by the evaluation of them by American history books as "cold-blooded murderers" (p. 41). In "Who Killed the Bog Men of Denmark? And Why?" to point to another example, Maurice Shadbolt recounts a causal chain based on the writings of Tacitus, conjoined with an autopsy performed on a centuries-old male corpse (pp. 186–87). His insistence that the two point to the identities of the man's killers, however, is accompanied by associated signifiers affirming that we cannot solve any ancient mystery with complete certainty. Students in a deconstruction/composition classroom would be encouraged, perhaps, to go beyond readings of given texts. They may even dismantle, for instance, the opposition the "metaphysics of presence" posits between comparison and contrast, showing that two seemingly dissimilar objects must share similarity, must be linked in a chain of signification with each other (as are cat and dog, or outside and inside). Indeed, they may go so far as to relate comparison and contrast, with their concern for similarities and differences—presences and absences—to the process of signification itself. The tentative topics that I have suggested would all, if discovered by students, convince them that they have discovered fresh and original insights worth writing down, and several writers might then feel the desire to write them down. The sense of the playfulness of language that deconstruction engenders will thus stimulate inspiration, the first essential step of invention.

Adopting a deconstructive attitude will help students towards inspiration, to be sure, but it will also contribute to the breakdown of the picture of the composition-teacher/writing-student relationship advanced under the current-traditional paradigm. The current-traditional paradigm is logocentric: as Hairston notes, "it posits an unchanging reality which is independent of the writer" and hence of his or her language and (by extension) all language, "and which all writers are expected to describe in the same way regardless of the rhetorical situation" (p. 80). Language, in such a view, does no more than refer to a phenomenal world that is independent of it. The teacher, then, becomes the language master, who is more adept than his or her students at manipulating words as tools in order to build formally correct essays. Thus, the teacher's function under the old paradigm is as a guardian of privileged information, the esoteric knowledge of the logos. The student becomes an initiate, struggling to master the wisdom that the teacher is in the classroom/temple to impart.

Obviously, a deconstructive habit of mind changes things. If linguistic meaning is ever shifting, no single person, whatever her or his experience, can be said to have mastery over it. Every new reading becomes a narrative of the uncovering of new chains of signification. English teachers are not guardians of any sacred mirror or lamp, according to a deconstructive attitude; rather, they are the students' fellow explorers on the quest to read the oscillations in meaning which must occur in all language, inherently figurative as it is. Consequently, in the deconstruction/composition class, students may turn to their teachers for guidance in matters of form and style, because their teachers are competent judges of the expectations of society with regard to such things. But invention and inspiration become the shared province of teacher and student. This view of the equality of teacher and student before the potentiality of language will have fundamental significance for the composition instructor's aim to surmount the undervalued status of her or his discipline as a "skills course."

I shall return to this topic shortly, but in order to point to its wider implications, I must first suggest some of the ways in which deconstruction may be observed at work in not only texts traditionally considered to be language based but also those often considered to be only social or cultural phenomena. Derridean deconstruction leads to the belief that all so-called extralinguistic events are actually a language being read and hence subject to the play of *differance*.

Given the closure of language around only itself, Derrida follows Heidegger in arguing that all of human existence is construed in terms of language and is therefore figurative: "Entity and being are . . . *derivative*," Derrida writes, "with regard to difference; and with respect to . . . *differance*" (p. 23). All that we consider human being is derived from the play of figuration. In *Of Grammatology*, Derrida uses the term *writing* to refer not only to "writing in the vulgar sense"—by which he means a simple grapholect—but also to a type of protowriting or arche-speech, the process by which phenomena are distinguished, classified, and hence "understood." Through its action, we discern events and states of being; we name them. Only in naming them can we know they exist; therefore, writing in the Derridean sense constitutes them. This same procedure enables men and women to classify and define themselves. Hence it is that before writing can represent what is interpreted as a referential object, it must be "the condition of the *epistémè*" or the possibility of understanding our being itself (Derrida, p. 27). We determine existence and all of its facets by means of language. Consequently, our conception of "language," notes Paul de Man, "has to extend well beyond what is empirically understood as articulated verbal utterance and subsumes . . . what is traditionally referred to as perception."[13]

The deconstructive attitude leads to a perception of women and men as being fundamentally trapped and yet determined by the prison house of language; this view enables the deconstruction/composition teacher to bring under the heading of possible class topics all phenomena that are understood as being in existence. As Gayatri Chakravorty Spivak notes, it enables the deconstructive reader to move from literary texts to social texts.[14] Psychological states, such as that of Marilyn Katz's student who discovered that underlying her sense of beauty in nature was a fear of it, might be read in terms of a description undermining a declaration.[15] Similarly, one might interpret a homecoming parade—on the face of things an affirmation of a college football team's superiority over its opponent—as carrying with it an admission of potential inferiority in the simple insistence on its opposite; the same sort of pattern, no doubt, could be found within other academic/social conventions. A film such as George Romero's *Creepshow* almost begs the viewer to witness its deconstruction: it intermingles straightforward narrative—a medium that persists in affirming its referentiality to events in the "real world"—with devices that constantly call attention to the film's artificiality, including pans across apparent comic-book frames as transitional devices and garishly expressionistic lighting. Certainly, oscillations in meaning can be traced in films that are supposedly more realistic as well; a Nazi leader's ceremonial tribute to Hitler in the documentary *Triumph of the Will*, which avers that Germans will not know everything that Hitler means to them until their flag (and hence their nation) crumbles, is a suggestive example. (And of course, political texts—words and deeds—are notorious for their oscillations in meaning.) Once again, deconstructive reading, this time of nonacademic texts, leads potentially to original insights, insights likely to encourage inspiration and the better writing attendant upon it.

The possibilities I have just raised indicate the full extent of the new and vital role of the composition teacher in higher education, to which I have been alluding. Training in deconstruction provides for critical and probing analyses of texts in grapholect, in the mind, in culture, in society, in aesthetics, in politics, and so on. Those who learn to read with this attitude will almost certainly be led to adopt an actively inquisitive approach to all aspects of life, and the development of such an attitude in students is surely one of the most desired goals of the educational system. Introducing deconstruction into the composition classroom is likely to lead students to inspiration and invention, as I have noted. But deconstructive reading can also encourage students to attempt to unravel the inherent figuration of language and, because language speaks man, the intricacies of the human mind and human society. The teacher who helps to inculcate such an inquiring mind-set will be teaching more than a skill. He or she will be teaching a way of life. Thus, the deconstruction/inspiration instructor becomes more than an adjunct to the educational system; that is, she or he becomes an integral member of it who strives to meet one of its highest ambitions.

Deconstruction has potential immediate value for the teaching of invention in that its originality of approach encourages inspiration as well as leads to a central place for its advocate/teacher in the mission of education. I do not mean to suggest, however, by my admittedly polemical remarks, that we should jettison all existing modes of invention and replace them with an extended course in deconstructive reading. If I may step down from my theoretical soapbox for a moment, I wish to reiterate a statement I made near the outset of this essay: in the teaching of invention, the composition teacher should use whatever seems to produce results. If students write first-rate essays using Burke's Pentad, so be it. We know too little about the composing process to align ourselves blindly with one particular approach to invention. I am, in this essay, merely affirming my belief that deconstructive reading is a potentially powerful means for students to discover ideas they will be inspired to set down and argue for in writing.

Deconstruction is not a heuristic, but reading with such an attitude can aid in the application of heuristics. A person who reads deconstructively is not following a rule-governed procedure; rather, he or she is simply practicing, as Miller puts it, "analytic criticism as such"; nonetheless, it is the most rigorous such criticism currently being practiced.[16] Deconstructive theory, in addition, postulates that the text itself is what undergoes deconstruction—a deconstructive reading merely follows its progress. The inquiring frame of mind and insightful, joyful reading necessary for deconstructive criticism, though, are useful in the application of extant heuristics. Donald M. Murray's "rehearsal-for-writing" stage in his model of the invention process, for example, may be read as the period during which implications of a deconstructive reading are worked out; and the analogical thinking advocated by several theorists can be usefully related to a deconstructive awareness of chains of signification.[17] Although it certainly has value in conjunction with existing methods of invention (which I would prefer to call methods of development), deconstructive reading is worth introducing in writing classes not only as a tool of analysis but also as an attitude towards the texts surrounding us.

The shift from the current-traditional paradigm in the teaching of composition has meant that more and more attention is being paid to writing as process rather than as product. One offshoot of this shift has been a renewed interest among teachers in invention. I have argued in this essay that deconstructive literary theory and the mode of close reading it engenders provide powerful incentives to inspiration, the first essential step towards the invention of a fresh, insightful piece of writing. Deconstructive reading, be it of a literary text or of the world, is the most intensive kind being practiced today. But more importantly, accepting Derrida's position on the nature of language leads students to the cultivation of a sense of playful intellectual joy in interpretation and a competence in their ability to trace figuration. This attitude, combined with the confidence in their reading skills that deconstruction encourages, is more likely than are logocentric modes of interpretation to produce the conviction in students that their perspectives on topics—be they literary, social, academic, aesthetic, political, or whatever—are original and insightful. This conviction will probably inspire them to believe that their ideas are worth stating. Furthermore, ideas worth setting down in written form are worth caring about. "Put otherwise," as Sabrina Johnson notes, "students, like the rest of us, will care most about how they say something if they care about what it is that they are saying."[18] And this caring, which can be stimulated by the process of deconstruction/inspiration for which I have argued in this essay, will result, I am convinced, in improvement in writing.

NOTES

1. Maxine Hairston, "The Winds of Change: Thomas Kuhn and the Revolution in the Teaching of Writing," *College Composition and Communication* 33 (1982): 76–77. Further references to this essay will appear parenthetically in the text.

2. See also Marilyn Katz, "From Self-Analysis to Academic Analysis: An Approach to Expository Writing," *College English* 40 (1978): 288; and Sharon Crowley, "Of Gorgias and Grammatology," *College Composition and Communication* 30 (1979): 279.

3. W. Ross Winterowd, "Invention," in *Contemporary Rhetoric: A Conceptual Background with Readings*, ed. Winterowd (New York: Harcourt, 1975), p. 39 (hereinafter cited as *CR*).

4. Richard Young, "Invention: A Topographical Survey," in *Teaching Composition: Ten Bibliographical Essays*, ed. Gary Tate (Fort Worth: Texas Christian University Press, 1976), pp. 1–2.

5. Both Sabrina Thorne Johnson, in "The Ant and Grasshopper: Some Reflections on Prewriting," *College English* 43 (1981): 234; and Mary Scott Simpson, in "Teaching Writing: Beginning with the Word," *College English* 39 (1978): 937, emphasize the improvement in writing that often occurs when students believe they have something worthwhile to discuss.

6. J. Hillis Miller, "The Function of Rhetorical Study at the Present Time," in a special issue of the Sept.–Nov. *ADE Bulletin*, no. 62 (1979): 13.

7. I am indebted to Derrida's *Of Grammatology*, trans. Gayatri Chakravorty Spivak (Baltimore, Md., and London: Johns Hopkins University Press, 1976), pp. 6–73 (in particular), for most of the summary on the next three pages. Subsequent references to this work will appear parenthetically in the text.

8. Crowley, "Of Gorgias and Grammatology," p. 283. Further references to this work will appear parenthetically in the text.

9. Reprinted in *Composition and Literature* (Lawrence: University of Kansas, Department of English, 1982), pp. 10–11. Page references will be to the essay's reprinting and will appear parenthetically in the text.

10. Richard L. Larson, "Discovery through Questioning: A Plan for Teaching Rhetorical Invention," in Winterowd, ed., *CR*, p. 150.

11. Miller, "The Critic as Host," in Harold Bloom et al., *Deconstruction and Criticism* (New York: Seabury Press, 1979), pp. 230–31; see also pp. 250–53.

12. The source for the essays I will be working with is Laurie G. Kirszner and Stephen Mandell, *Patterns for College Writing: A Rhetorical Reader and Guide* (New York: St. Martin's Press, 1980), the standard reader used in composition courses at the University of Kansas. Page references will be to this book and will be given parenthetically in the text.

13. Paul de Man, *Allegories of Reading: Figural Language in Rousseau, Nietzsche, Rilke, and Proust* (New Haven, Conn.: Yale University Press, 1979), p. 234.

14. See Gayatri Chakravorty Spivak, "Reading the World: Literary Studies in the 80s," *College English* 43 (1981): 67–79, reprinted above in this volume.

15. Katz, "Self-Analysis to Academic Analysis," pp. 289–90.

16. Miller, "Critic as Host," p. 252.

17. Donald M. Murray, "Write before Writing," *College Composition and Communication* 29 (1978): 376–77. For examples of arguments in favor of analogical thinking as a link to invention see Robert de Beaugrande, "The Processes of Invention: Association and Recombination," *College Composition and Communication* 30 (1979): 260–67; and Linda S. Flower and John R. Hayes, "Problem-Solving Strategies and the Writing Process," *College English* 39 (1977): 454–55.

18. Johnson, "Ant and Grasshopper," p. 234.

A Release from
Weak Specifications:
Liberating the Student Reader

Nancy R. Comley

Why is the writerly our value? Because the goal of literary work (of literature as work) is to make the reader no longer a consumer, but a producer of the text.

—Roland Barthes, *S/Z*

Contemporary literary theory and criticism has not yet made much of an impression on the way in which literature is taught in our high schools and colleges. For example, witness the continuing popularity of textbooks and courses labeled "Writing about Literature." As the preposition makes clear, such texts are doggedly loyal to the old new critical approach to literature. In this artifactual approach, the text is kept at arm's length (the better to admire it) as one endeavors to label the similes, metaphors, and symbols that provide the keys to the hidden deeper meaning. My 1950 edition of Brooks and Warren's *Understanding Poetry* bears evidence of my own struggles with such explication: in the margin next to Blake's "The Sick Rose," I find carefully inscribed: "rose = girl; worm = death." My freshman-English professor had yielded up the keys to the secret lurking in the poem, and I suppose I was grateful for the information, having had no previous experience with either Blake or sick roses. What I do remember most clearly from that class was the feeling of being shut out from literature; that which had given me great pleasure had now been made mysterious, at times even inaccessible—unless the professor yielded up the secret.

Most of my freshman students have either been subjected to this mystery approach to literature or have had very little experience in reading at all, let alone reading interpretively or critically. Most of the reading that they do seriously is reading for information, the isolation of facts; too few of their courses ask them to think by writing about what they read. An informal poll taken last spring in our second-semester composition courses at Queens College showed that the overwhelming majority of the students wrote papers for English courses only. Evaluation in most of their other courses was by short-answer quizzes or short-essay examinations. Reading for objective tests such as these means extracting content by isolating it through underlining, highlighting, or note-taking.

For students who read in this way, language is considered to be transparent, revealing content that is to be accepted, not questioned; memorized, not interpreted. The content, figuratively speaking, is to be consumed and then regurgitated on an exam. The majority of students spend the majority of their lives as consumers in both the literal and figurative senses of the word. The majority of students are not attending college for aesthetic reasons; they have definite vocational goals in mind, and they expect to get their money's worth out of each course they take. They read as serious consumers, whether the text be a poem or a microeconomics textbook. As for literature, getting your money's worth means never reading the same text twice. The sure sign of the serious consumer is his use of the verb "to do" with regard to reading, as in "We *did The Great Gatsby* in senior English." Implicit in this remark is: "So it would be a fat waste of time for me to have to *do* it again." To have "done" a text means that the student had to memorize the plot and characters for the test on "what happened" in the story, play, or poem. Should the test ask for the meaning of what happened, the student is careful to parrot the instructor's interpretation of the work, and thus reading the literary text is concretized into a "this means this" approach, one that suits the exchange system dear to student consumers: "Tell me what you want, and I'll give it back to you." This mode of teaching and learning is deplored by Paulo Freire, who describes it as a " 'banking' concept of education, in which the scope of action allowed to the students extends only as far as receiving, filing, and storing the deposits."[1]

It is possible to change students' attitudes and approaches to texts in a course whose goal is to turn readers-as-consumers into readers-asproducers of their own readings of texts and of their own written texts. Students should be writing in, through, and upon texts and not simply "about" them. They need to see literature as writing, and they need to explore their own processes of reading and writing. In literature and composition courses they can be given writing assignments that take advantage of the reader's work by actualizing through writing the different roles they play as readers. It is important, too, for students to regard their written responses seriously, as part of the intertextual network of every literary text. They can best learn to do this if the instructor allots as much time to the discussion of student texts as she does to the discussion of "professional" texts. Let me turn now to three types of assignments that can best illustrate this reader-as-producer approach to literary texts.

WRITING WITHIN THE TEXT: GHOST CHAPTERS

In an introductory course, students should be encouraged to examine their reading processes, to confront what they bring to a text from their daily lives and from their schooling, and to consider how such emotional, cultural, and intellectual baggage effects the inferences they make when they read. Asking students to enter a text through the writing of what Umberto Eco has termed the "ghost chapter"[2] requires them to examine their baggage and also to examine those elements in the text that have encouraged certain inferences, as well as the textual evidence that such baggage has caused the reader to ignore or misread.

As readers, we construct ghost chapters whenever there is a gap in the text; that is, whenever events are missing at the level of discourse but are presumed to have taken place at the story level. The writer assumes that the reader will fill in the missing events, will infer that they have taken place. Sometimes this is a very straightforward operation, as when at the end of a paragraph, a character gets on a train in New Haven, and at the beginning of the next paragraph walks out of Penn Station in New York City. Nothing eventful, we assume, has taken place on that train ride. We know only that it took place and that the writer wanted us merely to infer that it did. At other times, we are given more work to do. In *Tristram Shandy*, for example, we are asked to infer frequently, because Laurence Sterne has put the reading and writing processes in the foreground. His ghost chapters are signaled by the asterisks with which he peppers his pages, and then there is the famous ghost chapter 38 of book 6, where we are given a blank page and a half on which to "paint" our conception of the Widow Wadman. And how are we to paint this concupiscible being?

> Sit down, Sir, paint her to your own mind—as like your mistress as you can—as unlike your wife as your conscience will let you—'tis all one to me—please but your own fancy in it.

At the end of the blank section, the narrator comments:

> —Was ever anything in Nature so sweet—so exquisite!
> —Then, dear Sir, how could my uncle Toby resist it?
> Thrice happy book! thou wilt have one page, at least, within thy covers, which MALICE will not blacken and which IGNORANCE cannot misrepresent.[3]

Sterne is of course playing games with us, insisting that we draw on our own conception of a desirable sensual female, but he is also directing us, making us imagine a woman who could be desired by my uncle Toby, and so we have to take this amiable character into account in our own construction of the Widow Wadman. Of course we must include what we know of the Widow herself, her burning curiosity about my uncle Toby's anatomy being her most obvious character trait. If you asked your students to write chapter 38, you would be asking them to enter into the process of the text, to actively play out the role assigned to them, that of being a competent reader of sensibility.

Most ghost chapters are not presented so obviously as they are in *Tristram Shandy*. But any passage of time that is unaccounted for at the discursive level of a text asks us to construct a ghost chapter. In James Joyce's "The Boarding House," such a chapter is signaled by a door that closes in our faces. This story has been described by some of its critics as "guileless," the least difficult of the stories that constitute *The Dubliners*.[4] On the level of story, "The Boarding House" is fairly simple: a thirty-four-year-old celibate Irish Catholic, who has a good job with a Dublin wine merchant, is trapped into marriage by his landlady and her flirtatious daughter. (Or you could say he allows himself to be trapped.) But "The Boarding House" is challenging to students who have no frame of reference, either intertextual or cultural, for what it meant to be an Irish Catholic in Dublin at the turn of the century. Other challenges to the reader are provided by shifts in time, notably in the use of flashbacks, and in the absence of a strong manipulative narrator. With the help of an instructor who is willing to fill in the cultural gaps, students can reconstruct the fictional world of "The Boarding House." A writing assignment arises quite naturally from a gap in the discourse which, in this text, is signaled by a space on the page, separating the time between Mr. Doran's descent of the stairs on his way to Mrs. Mooney's parlor to face her demands for "reparation" and the time when Mrs. Mooney calls Polly from her reverie: "Come down, dear. Mr. Doran wants to speak to you."

Asking students to write ghost chapters about the confrontation between Mr. Doran and Mrs. Mooney, the butcher's daughter who "deals with moral issues as a cleaver deals with meat," seems simple enough. We know from the text that Mrs. Mooney will accept only marriage as reparation for what she sees as the loss of her daughter's honor, and we know that Mr. Doran's "sense of honour told him that reparation must be made for such a sin." You might assume, as I did when I first tried this assignment, that the students would write fairly similar papers, presenting an overbearing Mrs. Mooney who is browbeating a contrite and miserable Mr. Doran. Though many did take this approach, an appreciable number did not, and this is when I started paying more attention to the codes and subcodes that students bring to their reading. Many students could not bear the idea of entrapment, even though they may have felt from the evidence in the text that Mr. Doran was surely trapped by his religion and by his landlady. Of these students, some picked up on his indecision about Polly: "He could not make up his mind whether to like her or despise her for what she had done. Of course, he had done it too." They allowed Mr. Doran to save face and announce to Mrs. Mooney that he was indeed in love with Polly and would gladly marry her. A very few others picked up on the voice of Doran's instinct: "Once you are married you are done for"; they took seriously his desire, as he descends the stairs, "to ascend through the roof and fly away to another country." These romantics allowed an indignant Mr. Doran to tell off Mrs. Mooney and to leave the boarding house forever—without Polly (and with no interference from that "hard case," Jack Mooney).

While this is a fairly structured assignment, it does allow for a good deal of improvisation and of freedom in the elaboration of form and content as students explore the possibilities of the structure. Writing in voices other than their own is a liberating experience for most students, since their own voices are as yet unsure and still very much in the training stage. They consider an assignment like this "creative" (a synonym for "fun"), and while it certainly is that, it is also one that requires close reading of a new kind. In order to create their own texts, students have to know the original from the inside. In class, it is their discussion of their own texts as part of an intertextual network that further opens up the original.

WRITING THROUGH THE TEXT:
POSSIBLE WORLDS

The next step after working within a text is to work through it, to consider the possibilities of interpretation that are being offered to the reader. This kind of assignment is more challenging than the ghost chapter because it calls for the evaluation of the whole text in order to construct a new one. Possible worlds, in Eco's terms, are "sketches for another story, the story the actual one could have been had things gone differently. . . . they are worlds imagined, believed, wished."[5] The fictional text is itself a possible world because it is constructed of a possible set of events chosen by the writer. The reader's construction of possible worlds occurs most frequently in open-ended texts, or in texts in which we have become deeply involved with the characters and want their stories to go on or have wished that their stories had turned out more happily (if only Scarlett had married Ashley Wilkes—). It is natural for us to wonder what happens to Nora after the door slams at the end of *A Doll's House*. To ask students to create a possible world for Nora—or for Torvald Helmer, for that matter—beyond Ibsen's text is to ask for a close assessment of those characters as they are presented to us in the play. Of course, Nora's or Torvald's success in a possible world is dependent on the reader's reactions to them, and these may be influenced by such variables as one's feelings about mothers who walk out on their children (for whatever reason), or about men who treat their wives as possessions.

In a play the characters present themselves through their speech and actions, but in an enigmatic text such as Hawthorne's "Wakefield," the reader has more work to do (unless, of course, we are willing to accept without question what the narrator tells us). It is natural for us to wonder what sort of reception Wakefield will receive after perversely staying away from his wife for twenty years. And because we have been instructed in voyeurism from following Wakefield and putting up with the moralizing of the omniscient (and therefore equally voyeuristic) narrator, we can with impunity defy this narrator who says, "We will not follow our friend across the threshold." Of course we will; we're curious and perhaps even outraged by Wakefield's behavior, and we can now give voices to characters whose thoughts and actions have merely been described to us by this moralizing narrator. Through writing, we can explore some of the enigmas of this curious tale.

A more challenging text, because of its moral and ideological issues, is Ursula Le Guin's "The Ones Who Walk Away from Omelas." It invites the reader to enter into the fabulous construction of a utopia and then sets forth the conditions that make its happiness and prosperity more ''believable'': that a child must suffer abuse in isolation to ensure the happiness of everyone else. The reader, like the inhabitants of Omelas, must accept these conditions by rationalizing the child's situation, or like other inhabitants, he or she will reject this utopia and leave. The question that the text ends with is where do they go, the ones who walk away from Omelas? We are told: ''The place they go towards is a place even less imaginable to most of us than the city of happiness. I can not describe it at all. It is possible it does not exist. But they seem to know where they are going, the ones who walk away from Omelas.'' To create a possible world beyond this text, readers must consider why they would leave as well as where they would go. The world that they create should be logically dependent on the text, but there is an additional problem here: can readers reject the possible world that they have helped to construct within the text? Having drawn on their encyclopedias of imaginable pleasures, what is left for a ''less imaginable'' world? Further, we are drawn inevitably into comparing Omelas with the only society we know—our own. And when we try to answer the questions What are we walking away from? and Where do we think we're going? the experience is both unnerving and valuable as we examine the cultural codes and ideological biases that block our attempts to create a whole new world. Many readers accept the conditions of Omelas as ''the way things are.'' To those who are not so willing to accept such conditions comes the realization that the only possible world we can construct may be a reconstruction of the one that we already have.

THE PROBLEMATIC TEXT AND THE QUESTION OF AUTHORITY

In working with a text like ''The Ones Who Walk Away from Omelas,'' readers are required to draw on and to reexamine their codes of reference. Now we go a step further: we consider a text that not only defies most readers' codes of reference but that also thrusts upon the reader an authority of a most unsettling kind—namely, Henry James's *The Turn of the Screw.* Just as the absent master of Bly vests the governess with ''supreme authority'' with the injunction to ''meet all questions herself,'' so readers are vested by James with the authority of supplying the ''specifications'' of evil and meeting the questions of interpretation. In the introductory frame we have been warned by Douglas, the keeper of the governess's manuscript, that ''the story *won't* tell . . . not in any literal vulgar way.'' James, reflecting on his story in the Preface to the New York edition, describes his model readers as ''those not easily caught . . . the jaded, the disillusioned, the fastidious."⁶ Readers who are presumably jaded and disillusioned by the usual ghost story and its weak specifications are to be led into the trap of supplying the same sort of specifications that they so dislike because of their vulgar literalness. The text encourages readers to construct ghost chapters that it does not necessarily validate and that it will in fact encourage the reader to deconstruct. For example, Miles's dismissal from school has, according to the governess, "but one meaning . . . that he's an injury to others" (p. 11). However, Mrs. Grose reads "injury" as merely being "naughty," whereas the governess reads it as "to contaminate." Readers are left to infer what they will from this discussion and, having done so, will be forced almost immediately to revise their inferences. In the next chapter, to *see* Miles, as the governess does, with his "fragrance of purity," his "sweetness of innocence" (p. 13), is to guiltily question one's (possibly) prurient inferences regarding his schoolboy adventures. This missing chapter of Miles's career at school will be revised and revised again, and even when Miles finally confesses to having "said things" (pp. 86–87), the story will never tell what those "things" are.

As Shoshana Felman has pointed out, it is our forced participation in this "scandalous story" that has generated such heated criticism over the years.

> [T]he reader's innocence cannot remain intact: there is no such thing as an innocent reader of this text. In other words, the scandal is not simply *in* the text, it resides in *our relation to the text*, in the text's *effect on us*, its readers: what is outrageous in the text is not simply that *of which* the text is speaking, but that which makes it speak to us.⁷

With introductory-level students, the effect of the text is one of anxiety, which manifests itself in a desire to fix the meaning. In class discussion, students assume the traditional battle lines: the governess is a reliable narrator (the ghosts, therefore, are "real"), or the governess is unreliable (because she is mad, possessed, etc., and may be projecting the ghosts). But when they start to work out their positions in writing, problems arise. Unlike the earlier critics of *The Turn of the Screw*, for whom evil was more than an abstraction and for some of whom the ghosts were "real," as references to psychic phenomena attest, present-day students do not have such frames of reference to draw upon (with one exception: one of my students claimed to have lived in a haunted house). Even if students find enough textual evidence to substantiate the reality of the ghosts, they have great difficulty in accepting them as agents. In the solitary intimacy of reading, it is far more threatening to actualize a ghost—to make it come alive, as it were—than to deal with cinematic horrors. We can more easily leave movie ghosts behind us when we walk out of the theater or turn off the television set. We haven't made those ghosts our own; they are the products of someone else's imagination, not ours. And in a theater we share our temporary thrills with others. Reading *The Turn of the Screw*, however, leaves us on our own, with ghosts of our own making.

Thus the possibility of a hallucinating governess becomes very attractive as a release from anxiety about ghosts. The instructor had best be prepared to come to the governess's defense (consider her very detailed description of Quint, for example), and then go on to examine very carefully the difficulty of pinning down much of what she reports (consider her very vague description of Miss Jessel). The instructor must resist the role of authority (the keeper of meaning) and assume that of reader, leading discussion toward the experience of reading rather than toward the fixing of meaning. I require students to record in their journals their experience of reading. Their entries serve as a record of themselves as readers, and the journal serves as a site in which they can examine their likes and dislikes of required reading without penalty. For the purposes of this particular text, it is important for them to have their own readings recorded before we move on to examine another group of authorities: the critics of *The Turn of the Screw*.

We use the Norton Critical Edition of the text, which contains a representative range of the criticism from 1898 to 1966 and which I supplement with more recent readings. Both Shoshana Felman (1977) and Christine Brooke-Rose (1981)[8] have done thorough studies of the criticism, Felman from a psychoanalytic point of view and Brooke-Rose from a more eclectic standpoint, and both show how the critics act out the conflicts in the text. Brooke-Rose provides a compendium of the "non-methodology" of critics of *The Turn of the Screw*, in which she demonstrates how "the text invites the critics unconsciously to 'act out' the governess's dilemma" (p. 128). One of the results of this "acting out" is that "the critics reproduce the very tendencies they so often note in the governess: omissions; assertion; elaboration; lying even (or, when the critics do so, let us call it error)" (p. 132). Very few of those who read *The Turn of the Screw* before 1966 can see (or admit?) that the text may be indeterminate. They wish to fix meaning (or in many cases, to fix the blame for Miles's death either on the ghosts or on the governess). For students, the critics' battles with each other provide lively reading, and the critics' misreadings prove most instructive. If nothing else, the "authorities" provide object lessons in the dangers of trying to fix language. Students can see the professionals committing some of the same errors in logic that they have been called to task for in their own papers. As the professionals lose their mystique of authority, students see their own readings as worthy of joining the large intertextual network surrounding *The Turn of the Screw*.

Certainly, James's little *amusette* provides a valuable lesson in reading, but there's one other bonus I've overlooked: it provides pleasure. I will let one of my freshman students have the last word on that:

> By reading the views of the Freudian critics, I was able to understand the story better. But my question still remains—did Henry James want his story interpreted this way? I believe not, because the mystery which surrounds the story is the aspect which made the book enjoyable to me. Thus, I feel that the mystery is the component of the story which needs no explanation, for if there were, it could only lessen one's enjoyment of reading it.[9]

NOTES

1. Paolo Freire, *Pedagogy of the Oppressed*, trans. Myra Bergman Ramos (New York: Continuum, 1982), p. 58.

2. Umberto Eco, *The Role of the Reader* (Bloomington: Indiana University Press, 1979), pp. 214–15.

3. Laurence Sterne, *Tristram Shandy*, ed. James A. Work (Indianapolis, Ind.: Bobbs-Merrill, 1940), bk. 6, chap. 38.

4. William Tindall, quoted by Nathan Halper in his essay "The Boarding House," in *James Joyce's "Dubliners,"* ed. Clive Hart (New York: Viking Press, 1969), p. 72. In Halper's opinion, "This is not a difficult story."

5. Eco, *Role of the Reader*, p. 217.

6. Henry James, *The Turn of the Screw*, Norton Critical Edition, ed. Robert Kimbrough (New York: Norton, 1966), p. 120.

7. Shoshana Felman, "Turning the Screw of Interpretation," *Yale French Studies* 55/56 (1977): 97.

8. Christine Brooke-Rose, *The Rhetoric of the Unreal* (Cambridge: Cambridge University Press, 1981).

9. John Egleston, "Freudian Views on *The Turn of the Screw*" (unpublished paper, 1980).

3

DECONSTRUCTION AND THE TEACHING OF LITERATURE

Teaching Deconstructively

Barbara Johnson

Teaching literature is teaching how to read. How to notice things in a text that a speed-reading culture is trained to disregard, overcome, edit out, or explain away; how to read what the language is doing, not guess what the author was thinking; how to take in evidence from a page, not seek a reality to substitute for it.[1] This is the only teaching that can properly be called literary; anything else is history of ideas, biography, psychology, ethics, or bad philosophy. Anything else does not measure up to the rigorous perversity and seductiveness of literary language.

Deconstruction has sometimes been seen as a terroristic belief in meaninglessness. It is commonly opposed to humanism, which is then an imperialistic belief in meaningfulness. Another way to distinguish between the two is to say that deconstruction is a reading strategy that carefully follows both the meanings and the suspensions and displacements of meaning in a text, while humanism is a strategy to stop reading when the text stops saying what it ought to have said. Deconstruction, then, has a lot to teach teachers of literature to the extent that they see themselves as teachers of reading.

What, then, is a deconstructive reading, and how can its strategies be translated into classroom procedures? Deconstruction is not a form of textual vandalism or generalized skepticism designed to prove that meaning is impossible. Nor is it an a priori assumption that every text is self-reflexive, that every text consists only in a play of signifiers, or that every text is about the relation between speech and writing. Rather, it is a careful teasing out of the conflicting forces of signification that are at work within the text itself. If anything is destroyed in a deconstructive reading, it is not meaning per se but the claim to unequivocal domination of one mode of signifying over another. This implies that a text signifies in more than one way, that it can signify something more, something less, or something other than it claims to, or that it signifies to different degrees of explicitness, effectiveness, or coherence. A deconstructive reading makes evident the ways in which a text works out its complex disagreements with itself. As Paul de Man puts it: "The deconstruction is not something we have added to the text but it constituted the text in the first place. A literary text simultaneously asserts and denies the authority of its own rhetorical mode, and by reading the text as we did we were only trying to come closer to being as rigorous a reader as the author had to be in order to write the [text] in the first place."[2] Because deconstruction is first and foremost a way of paying attention to what a text is doing—*how* it means not just *what* it means—it can lend itself very easily to an open-discussion format in a literature seminar. And because it enables students to respond to what is there before them on the page, it can teach them how to work out the logic of a reading on their own rather than passively deferring to the authority of superior learning.

What kinds of signifying conflict, then, are articulated in, and constitutive of, the literary text? And what sorts of reading do they demand? I will begin by listing quickly a number of examples and then go on to develop three readings more fully, though by no means completely. These cases are designed to stand as examples of the type of challenge to reading that a text might provide—and that deconstructive attention might further—in a classroom.

1. *Ambiguous words.* Derrida's readings often focus on a double-edged word as a condensed articulation of conflicting levels of assertion in a text. In Plato's *Phaedrus*, for example, the word *pharmakon* can mean both "remedy" and "poison."[3] In referring to writing itself as a *pharmakon*, Plato is therefore not making a *simple* value judgment. Yet translators, by choosing to render the word sometimes by "remedy" and sometimes by "poison," have consistently decided what in Plato remains undecidable, and thus have influenced the course of the history of readings of Plato. When one recalls the means of Socrates' death, one can see that the undecidability between poison and remedy is not a trivial matter. Far from posing confined, local interpretive problems, ambiguities can stand as the hinge of an entire discourse.

2. *Undecidable syntax.* One of the most condensed examples of syntax as the locus of a suspension of the text's claim structures between two often incompatible possibilities is the rhetorical question. As Paul de

Man suggests,[4] a reading of Yeats's poem "Among School Children" is drastically changed if one admits the possibility that its terminal question—"How can we know the dancer from the dance?"—is *not* rhetorical. Or the question with which Baudelaire ends his celebration of a woman's hair in "La Chevelure"—"Are you not the gourd from which I drink the wine of memory?"—suspends the energy of the poem not only between self and other but between the success and the failure of the attempt to rewrite the other as a container for the self.

3. *Incompatibilities between what a text says and what it does.* An obvious example would be the figure known as *praeteritio*, in which a text elaborates itself by detailing at length what it says it will *not* speak about. Variants upon this structure pervade all literature, as when an author devotes much more space to what he wants to eliminate than to what he wants to instate, or when a text in one way or another protests too much. Another rather simple example of the discrepancy between saying and doing occurs in the last line of Archibald MacLeish's "Ars Poetica": "A poem should not mean but be." The line itself does not obey its own prescription: it means—*intends* being—rather than simply being, thus revealing that it is more complicated than it first appears to be for a poem to assert what the relations between meaning and being are.

4. *Incompatibilities between the literal and the figurative.* In Lamartine's poem "L'Isolement," the speaker, who is lamenting the death of his beloved, cries, "There is nothing in common between the earth and me." He then goes on: "I am like the withered leaf." In a poem that is entirely devoted to the question of the mode of aliveness of one whose heart is in another world, this suspended stance between earthliness and unearthliness reveals that the problem of mourning has something to do with the opposition between the figural and the literal, and vice versa.

5. *Incompatibilities between explicitly foregrounded assertions and illustrative examples or less explicitly asserted supporting material.* Derrida points this out in the discrepancy between Saussure's explicit assertion that linguistics should study speech, not writing, and his repeated recourse to linguistic properties that are derivable from writing, not speech. A more literary example can be found in Wordsworth's "Intimations Ode." The poem begins by asserting the fact of loss:

> There was a time when meadow, grove, and stream,
> The earth, and every common sight,
> > To me did seem
> Apparelled in celestial light,

> The glory and the freshness of a dream.
> It is not now as it hath been of yore;—
>   Turn wheresoe'er I may,
>   By night or day,
> The things which I have seen I now can see no more.

This sense of loss expands mythically, phylogenetically, and ontogenetically to include the common experience of all mankind:

> Our birth is but a sleep and a forgetting;
> The soul that rises with us, our life's star,
>   Hath had elsewhere its setting,
>   And cometh from afar:
>   Not in entire forgetfulness,
>   And not in utter nakedness,
> But trailing clouds of glory do we come
>   From God, who is our home:
> Heaven lies about us in our infancy!
> Shades of the prison-house begin to close
>   Upon the growing boy,
> But he beholds the light, and whence it flows,
>   He sees it in his joy;
> The youth, who daily farther from the east
>   Must travel, still is Nature's priest,
>   And by the vision splendid
>   Is on his way attended;
> At length the man perceives it die away,
> And fade into the light of common day.

But in the supporting invocation to the little child, Wordsworth cuts the ground out from under this narrative of loss:

> Thou, whose exterior semblance doth belie
>   Thy soul's immensity;
> Thou best philosopher, who yet dost keep
> Thy heritage, thou eye among the blind,
> That, deaf and silent, readst the eternal deep,
> Haunted for ever by the eternal mind,—
>   Mighty prophet! Seer blest!
>   On whom those truths do rest,
> Which we are toiling all our lives to find,
> In darkness lost, the darkness of the grave;
> Thou, over whom thy immortality
> Broods like the day, a master o'er a slave,
> A presence which is not to be put by;
> Thou little child, yet glorious in the might
> Of heaven-born freedom on thy being's height,

Why with such earnest pains dost thou provoke
The years to bring the inevitable yoke,
Thus blindly with thy blessedness at strife?

The little child, the seer of the light, here turns out to be blind to his very ability to see. The experience of blessed sight, the loss of which Wordsworth began by lamenting, seems never to have existed in the first place as a lived experience. The loss of *something* is a story retrospectively told in order to explain the *sense* of loss. What we have lost by the end of the poem is precisely loss itself.

6. *Obscurity.* A student's first encounter with the work of a poet such as Mallarmé can be profoundly disconcerting. If one attempts to smooth over the difficulties and make the poem add up to a meaning, the student might well ask, "Ce n'est donc que ça?—Why couldn't he have said it in plain, comprehensible language?" One would have to answer that "it" isn't something his language is *saying* but something his language is *doing*.

A look at the sonnet "La chevelure vol d'une flamme à l'extreme occident de désirs" reveals that although one can't make sense of it, it contains an interesting collection of highly charged images and concepts: man and woman, life and death, doubt and joy, truth and mockery, tenderness and defamation, nakedness and jewelry, outward exploits and inner fires, weather, geography, and education. The entire complexity of the world seems to be condensed down to a microchip. This is what Mallarmé called "simplifying the world." But the text itself is far from simple.

What does one do? One starts to ask questions. Does the word "vol" mean "theft" or "flight"? Is the word "or" a noun or a conjunction? Is "continue" a verb, transitive or intransitive, or an adjective? Why is the "I" in parentheses? Discussion of these questions and the attempt to follow out the consequences of each possibility *and* the consequences of their simultaneousness can go on for a long time, but something inevitably gets worked out in this process of asking what each element is doing with respect to other elements in the poem, rather than asking point blank what it *means*. What happens in reading Mallarmé is that one talks one's way into the poem by describing the specificity of one's difficulties. Rather than remain stuck before an obstacle or paralyzed before a forking path, the reader must say: "My reading is blocked here because I can't tell whether this is theft or flight, literal or figurative, noun or verb, statement or question, masculine or feminine, and so forth. But that uncertainty may be precisely what the poem is talking about." The reader can then track down each thread of all possibilities and ask the significance of their coexistence. Eventually, the narrating of one's frustrations and difficulties begins to fill in for, and to partake of, the missing thematic coherence in the poem. The poem is not *about* something *separate* from the activity required to decipher it. Simplification, doubt, distance, and desire—all are acted out by the reading process as well as stated in the poem.

With Mallarmé, in other words, the student can learn to see the *search* for meaning as being illuminating and meaningful in itself. One's struggles with ambiguity and obscurity cease to be obstacles to reading: they become the very *experience* of reading. Meaning is not something "out there" or "in there," to be run after or dug up. It inhabits the very activity of the search. And what better training for "living as and where we live" (as Stevens puts it) than to learn to direct our attention to what we experience *now* rather than to those answers that lie somewhere up the road; to take indecision, frustration, and ambivalence, not as mere obstacles and incapacities, but as the very richness and instructiveness of the reading process? This is what Mallarmé's poetry has to teach, not by *telling* us this, but by making us go through it, interminably, for ourselves.

7. *Fictional self-interpretation*. Sometimes the challenge posed by a text is not excessive obscurity but, rather, some form of excessive clarity. Many literary texts appear to comment upon themselves, to solve the enigmas they set up. A common student response to texts in which such self-interpretations are explicit is to protest that the author has taken all the fun away by doing the work the reader ought to do. Deconstruction, with its insistence on interpretation itself as a fiction-making activity, enables one to read such metalinguistic moments as allegories of reading, as comments on the interpretive process itself, in a sort of inside-out version of the involvement the student engages in with Mallarmé.

I would like to conclude with a somewhat more extended version of what can come out of a discussion of textual self-interpretation. For this, I will comment on two inversely symmetrical thematizations of textuality itself: Hawthorne's "The Minister's Black Veil," in which a character named Reverend Hooper mysteriously and without warning dons a piece of black crepe, which he refuses to remove even on his deathbed, and Hans Christian Andersen's "The Emperor's New Clothes," in which two imposters weave nonexistent clothes for the emperor, telling him that their cloth has the property of being invisible to those who are either simpletons or unfit for their offices. The two stories are thus both woven around a textile: in "The Minister's Black Veil" the textile is opaque and obscure; in "The Emperor's New Clothes" it is self-evidently transparent. In foregrounding the textuality of a text, both stories also situate the activities of writing and reading, and in both cases an explicit reading is offered as definitive. Both stories indeed end with that reading as a sort of punch line. In "The Minister's Black Veil" the meaning of the enigmatic symbol is given by its "author" as follows:

> "Why do you tremble at me alone?" cried he, turning his veiled face round the circle of pale spectators. "Tremble also at each other! Have men avoided me, and women shown no pity, and children screamed and fled, only for my black veil? What, but the mystery which it obscurely typifies, has made this piece of crape so awful? When the friend shows his inmost heart to his friend; the lover to his best beloved; when man does not vainly shrink from the eye of his Creator, loathsomely treasuring up the secret of his sin; then deem me a monster, for the symbol beneath which I have lived, and die! I look around me, and, lo! on every visage a Black Veil!"[5]

And at the end of the "Emperor's New Clothes," the child in the crowd exclaims, "But the Emperor has nothing at all on!" and the crowd repeats the exclamation as the truth.

In the "Minister," then, the definitive reading involves an exposure of universally denied concealment. In the "Emperor," it involves the exposure of universally denied exposure. In the first case, the figure of the veil reveals the nonliterality of meaning, the darkness that prevents any encounter from being literally face-to-face. In the second case, the nakedness of the emperor reveals literality *as* meaning. In the first case, the final reader is the veiled author. In the second, the reader is a child. The truth propounded by the first is the inescapability of the figural. The truth propounded by the second is the inescapability of the literal. Yet in both cases, the solving of the obvious textual enigma only serves to resituate the real mystery elsewhere. For in both cases, what remains to be explained is how the apparently inescapable is so apparently escaped. Both texts consist in the putting in question of their own, apparently definitive, self-interpretations.

The first thing one notices about each text is that the major part of its energy is devoted to the description of acts of reading. The minister's congregation is obsessed with the question, "What does the veil mean?" By ending the tale with an apparent answer to that question, Hawthorne seems to be usurping the interpretive activity that the reader may feel is rightly hers. But this is so only as long as the reader believes that the *veil* is the text's enigma. By presenting a solution to that enigma, Hawthorne is substituting interpretation itself as a new enigma, as the object of *his* reader's interpretive activity. By putting *en abyme* the question, "What does the veil mean?" Hawthorne substitutes a new question: "What does it mean to ask what the veil means? What do people actually do when they try to determine meaning?" The first thing they do, in both the "Minister" and the "Emperor," is to deny literality. The minister's parishioners cannot believe that the veil is simply a piece of black crepe. The barrier to communication cannot be seen as meaningless. If this is so, then meaningfulness would seem to inhere in what blocks or veils communication. Yet in the "Emperor" it is the very lack of such a blockage that needs to be interpreted. Again, literality cannot be seen as such.

The denial of literality takes place, in both stories, in an intersubjective context in which meaning is tied to a figure of authority. The minister and the emperor are, for their subjects, the guarantors of a meaningful social world. Participation in that world entails the acceptance of official ways of denying literality. Hence the child's literal reading is an asocial reading, a reading that, though correct, is outside the system in which social meanings are agreed upon. The minister's veil and the emperor's clothes are tests of their readers' suitability for membership in the society of which they are a part. The reading activity thus consists of a nervousness of self-examination. Faced with the text, the reader's search for meaning is an examination of *his own* credentials. The emperor's ministers deny simple literality in order to deny the possibility that they themselves are simple. The minister's hidden face forces the parishioners to confront their own hiddenness. In their desire to deny their own hiddenness, they read hiddenness in the other as a sign that he is hiding whatever they are hiding. In revealing on his deathbed that the veil concealed nothing but, rather, that it revealed the fact of concealment, the minister situates the meaning of his symbol, not within it or within his own intentions, but within the readers' blindness to their own misreading—their blindness to their own blindness. Yet the minister cannot face his own veiled image in the mirror, for if his veil's message is the revelation of the universality of concealment, how can the meaning of the veil escape the self-blindness that it says is universal? In living a life that stands as a figure for misreading, the minister, in his triumphant attempt to proclaim obscurity clearly, ends up being the only person who has not read his own figure *correctly*.

The emperor's subjects thus veil from themselves the literality of the invisibility of what they see, while members of the minister's congregation, projecting their own concealments behind the veil, are blind to the possibility that nothing is being concealed—or that concealment is what is being revealed. Both stories dramatize the intrusion—indeed, the inescapability—of allegorical structures in the conduct of "real" life. Socialization is training in allegorical interpretation. But an allegory that reveals that the act of reading consists in a blindness both to literality and to the fact that one is allegorically denying literality puts *us* in a difficult position. If the blindness of the emperor's subjects and of the minister's parishioners is a forgetting of literality through the act of reading *themselves* into the text, then aren't we, by reading the texts as allegories of reading, suffering from the same blindness to the second degree? Yet could we have chosen to read literally? Or is the act of reading always, in a sense, an act of resistance to the letter?

At the beginning of this paper I defined deconstruction as a reading strategy that carefully follows both the meanings and the suspensions and displacements of meaning in a text, while humanism was a strategy to stop reading when the text stops saying what it ought to have said. What the deconstructive reading of Hawthorne and Andersen has shown, however, is that no matter how rigorously a deconstructor might follow the letter of the text, the text will end up showing the reading process as a *resistance* to the letter. The deconstructor thus comes face-to-face with her own humanism. This is small comfort, of course, since the text has shown humanism to consist in the blindness of self-projection. But then, in the final analysis, it is perhaps precisely as an apprenticeship in the repeated and inescapable oscillation between humanism and deconstruction that literature works its most rigorous and inexhaustible seductions.

NOTES

1. This is not meant to imply that nothing should be read outside the text at hand, or that a text is unconnected to any discourse outside itself. The "inside" of the text is no more a "given" than the "outside," and what is inside the text is not necessarily accessible to the reader without philological, historical, biographical, etc., research. But it does imply that history, philology, biography, the "spirit of the age," and the "material conditions of production" are not less problematic—or less textual and interpretively constructed—than the literary text they would come to explain. Training in reading must also be training in evaluating the relevance and authority of external resources as well as internal ones.

2. Paul de Man, *Allegories of Reading* (New Haven, Conn.: Yale University Press, 1979), p. 17.

3. See Derrida, "Plato's Pharmacy," in *Dissemination* (Chicago: University of Chicago Press, 1981).

4. In the opening essay of *Allegories of Reading*.

5. Nathaniel Hawthorne, "The Minister's Black Veil," in *The Celestial Railroad and Other Stories* (New York: Signet, 1963), p. 114.

Understanding Criticism

Geoffrey H. Hartman

What difference does reading make? Is it perhaps, like traveling, a fool's paradise? "We owe to our first journeys," writes Emerson, "the discovery that place is nothing. At home I dream that at Naples, at Rome, I can be intoxicated with beauty, and lose my sadness. I pack my trunk, embrace my friends, embark on the sea, and at last wake up in Naples, and there beside me is the stern Fact, the sad Self, unrelenting, identical, that I fled from. I seek the Vatican, and the palaces. I affect to be intoxicated with sights and suggestions, but I am not intoxicated. My giant goes with me wherever I go."

Emerson is urging us to self-reliance; yet the more we read him, the more *he* is the giant, seductive or overwhelming, who stands in the way of a liberation he commends. There is no getting around him: we must think him through, allow him to invade our prose.

The difference that reading makes is, most generally, writing. The thinking through, the "working through" (the metaphor of work applied to psychic process being Freudian, yet appropriate in this context) is hard to imagine without writing. Certain poets, like Mallarmé, even seek a type of writing that would end reading as tourism or as merely a reflection on a prior and exotic fact.

The division of literary activity into writers and readers, though it may appear to be commonsensical, is neither fortunate nor absolute. It is crass to think of two specialties, one called *reading* and one *writing*; and

This is a chapter from *Criticism in the Wilderness: The Study of Literature Today* (New Haven, Conn.: Yale University Press, 1980).

149

then to view criticism as a particularly specialized type of reading which uses writing as an "incidental" aid. Lately, therefore, forms of critical commentary have emerged that challenge the dichotomy of reading and writing. Besides the involutions of Nabokov's *Pale Fire* (1962) and the essays of Borges, there are such experiments as Norman O. Brown's *Closing Time* (1973), Harold Bloom's *The Anxiety of Influence* (1973), Maurice Blanchot's *Le Pas au-delà* (1973), Jacques Derrida's *Glas* (1974), and Roland Barthes's *A Lover's Discourse* (1977). They are literary texts in their own right as well as commentary. They belong to the realm of "letters" rather than to purely "critical" writing, and they make us realize that we have narrowed the concept of literature.

Even when its form is less spectacular, such criticism puts a demand on the reader that may cause perplexity and resentment. For it does not see itself as subordinated in any simple way to the books on which it comments. It can be pedagogic, of course, but it is free *not* to be so. It is aware that in philosophy there is less of a distinction between primary and secondary literature: ask a philosopher what he does, and he will answer "philosophy." It could be argued, in the same spirit, that what a literary critic does is literature.

Yet the reader-critic's claim to parity is continually chastened by the fact that he remains addicted to reading, to traveling through those "realms of gold" in the hope of being instructed and surprised. His supposed self-reliance is undermined by a famous Miltonic axiom, Satan's boast to the angels in *Paradise Lost* (4.830): "Not to know mee argues yourselves unknown." That is the seductive boast of every book. We are tempted to enter an unknown or forbidden realm.

The spectacle of the critic's mind disoriented, bewildered, caught in some "wild surmise" about the text and struggling to adjust—is not that one of the interests that critical writing has for us? In more casual acts of reading, this bewilderment can be muted, for there is always the hint of a resolution further on, or an enticement to enter for its own sake the author's world. However, in *containing* this bewilderment, formal critical commentary is not very different from fiction itself. Fiction also carries within it a hermeneutic perplexity: there is a shifting of focus, or a changeable perspective, or a Jamesian effort to discern the "felt meaning." It is not Dr. Johnson alone who has his troubles with *King Lear*: on reading the exchange between Lear and a Gloucester whose eyes have been put out—

> *Lear.* Your eyes are in a heavy case, your purse in a light; yet you see
> how this world goes.
> *Gloucester.* I see it feelingly.

—we can only echo Gloucester's own words in accepting so appalling a mixture of pathos and pun.

The critic, then, is one who makes us formally aware of the bewildering character of fiction. Books are our second Fall, the reenactment of a seduction that is also a coming to knowledge. The innermost hope they inspire may be the one Heinrich von Kleist expressed: only by eating a second time of the tree of knowledge will we regain paradise. Consider, in this light, Yeats's "Leda and the Swan."

> A sudden blow: the great wings beating still
> Above the staggering girl, her thighs caressed
> By the dark webs, her nape caught in his bill,
> He holds her helpless breast upon his breast.
>
> How can those terrified vague fingers push
> The feathered glory from her loosening thighs?
> And how can body, laid in that white rush,
> But feel the strange heart beating where it lies?
>
> A shudder in the loins engenders there
> The broken wall, the burning roof and tower
> And Agamemnon dead.
>   Being so caught up,
> So mastered by the brute blood of the air,
> Did she put on his knowledge with his power
> Before the indifferent beak could let her drop?

It comes like a voice from nowhere, catching us too offguard. "A sudden blow: the great wings beating still. . . ." Where got Yeats that truth? Part of the magic to be resisted is the poet's imperious assumption of a visionary mode, as if it were self-justifying. His exotic and erotic subject matter displaces the question of authority. For Yeats may be a voyeur rather than a visionary: we do not know where he is standing, or how ancient his eyes are, or if they glitter. Though we grant him, provisionally, the authority of his poem, we note that his empathy runs parallel to Leda's and focuses on the unspoken promise of an initiatory or "strange" knowledge—in fact, on the first temptation, which Genesis spells out: "Ye shall be as gods, knowing good and evil." Leda, surprised by the swan-god, cannot but "feel the strange heart beating where it lies."

So fiction imposes on us, by a subtle or blatant seduction. We are always surprised or running to catch up or wishing to be more fully in its coils. This may explain why the detective novel, with its mock catharsis of false leads and inconclusive speculations, is a favorite of intellectual readers. Literary commentary is comparable to the detective novel:

confronted by a bewildering text, it acts out a solution, trying various defenses, various interpretations, then pretending that it has come to an authoritative stance—when, in truth, it has simply purged itself of complexities never fully mastered.

Seduction, then, in fiction or life, seems to contain the promise of mastery or, paradoxically, of joining oneself to an overwhelming intent even at the cost of being subdued. In more innocent language, seduction is called *persuasion*; and rhetoric, or the art of persuasion, has always been criticized by competing arts, such as logic and dialectic, which assert a higher truth without being less vulnerable to the charge of seeking a powerful epiphany, or all-clarifying solution. Rhetoric, in any case, is to language what science is to the language of nature—a technique that can be mastered, perhaps for the purpose of further mastery. Yet it is also true that the verbal acuities of poetry or fiction challenge the rhetoric they use, as in the subtle, questioning progress of Yeats's poem. Rhetoric is the will doing the work of imagination, Yeats said.

At first we feel mainly the poet's rhetoric, his power in depicting an action that has power as its very subject. An episode that spans centuries is condensed in the representational space of a sonnet. The mimetic faculty is stirred by rhythmic effects (the additional beat in "great wings beating still," the caesural pause between "terrified" and "vague"), while inner bonding through repetition and alliteration ("beating . . . beating," "He holds her helpless . . .") tightens Yeats's verse as if to prevent *its* rupture. The energy of the event seems to produce its own *enargeia*, as rhetoricians call the picturing potential of words. The eyes are led along an axis that is sharper than ordinary sight: does "there" in "A shudder in the loins engenders there" refer to the place of vision as well as conception, to what is right *there* before the poet's eyes? He sees into the loins as into the heart. "Wisdom begins in images," Yeats remarked; rhetorical skill, the formal magic that recreates Leda, has made an image come alive.

Yet rhetoric in the service of mimesis, rhetoric as imaging power, is far from being *imitative* in the sense of reflecting a preexistent reality. Mimesis becomes poesis, imitation becomes making, by giving form and pressure to a presumed reality, to "Leda." The traditional theme, by being repeated, is endowed with a past that may never have been present. Leda is not even named within the poem; and the strongest images in the poem are not images at all but periphrases, like "feathered glory" and "brute blood of the air." These non-naming figures have the structure of riddles as well as of descriptions. Even the images in lines 10–12, stark metonymies, are a periphrastic riddle or charade for "The Destruction of Troy."

152

The last of these non-naming figures, "brute blood of the air," may be the most intriguing. Viewed in itself, detached from the representational frame of Yeats's lyric, it conveys a sense of internal generation, almost self-generation—something engendered from what is barely seen or grasped, that does not recall natural process so much as supernatural agency, not formation but transformation. It evokes the imminence of the visible in the invisible, an absence that can turn into a devastating presence. We are again projected beyond natural sight: air, as in omens, thickens, becomes concrete, theriomorphic, auguring; and to air there corresponds the airy womb of imagination, which also thickens here into an ominous historical projection, a catastrophe creation of which "Leda" is but the legendary medium.

Less an image, then, than a phantasm is represented. More precisely: is it an image, or is it a phantasm? By phantasm I mean an image with hallucinatory effect: "out of nothing it came" (see Yeats's "Fragments"). It cannot be explained or grounded by the coordinates of ordinary perception, by stable space-time categories. Does the poem revive a classic myth whose psychic truth is being honored ("to ground mythology in the earth" is one of Yeats's programmatic statements), or does it express a phantasm which that myth holds fast and stabilizes, so that mind can be mind and question it? Second quatrain and last tercet are questioning in form: one function of this form is to hold and elaborate what is happening.

I don't think I exaggerate the image/phantasm indeterminacy. Until we come to the one proper name, "Agamemnon," we are kept in the aura of an action whose reference is not fixed. Though a famous legend is presupposed, the poem effects a displacement from "Leda" and "Troy" to a nonproper, that is, unlocalized event that cannot be given a name or one name. The situating reference to "Agamemnon," the locking up of the action into the known if legendary context, is just that, a locking up; it does not resolve the indeterminacy; we continue to feel the imaginary within the reference myth, something that exceeds the latter like a riddle its solution, or periphrasis and metaphor the undisplaced word. As "Agamemnon" hovers between sonant matter and meaning, so the myth hovers between phantasm and legend-laden image.

We cannot, in short, neglect the airy pretension of a poem that fills the vacancy of prehistory with a paradigmatic primal scene. What space or time are we in? Is the poet standing in his own mind? Or in the third heaven of a domestic séance? Is what he communicates a vision or the variant of a traditional theme or his re-creation of a particular painting on that theme? Is he stationing a phantasm or framing something that even if it is an image is so nuclear in lines 10–12 that it could be detached from the poem and seen as Greek epigram or sybilline utterance?

These questions add up to a *hermeneutic perplexity*. Yeats's rhetorical skill has led us beyond or beneath firm knowledge, and we become unsure of the poem's real frame of reference. Who is (the) "Being so caught up"? Correlatively, we become unsure of the poet's authority: is he seer or subjective thinker or superstitious crank? It may be, of course, that it is we who think *against* the poem, who wonder why we were willing to suspend our disbelief and to accept this fiction. We could then follow our own suspensive or "negative" thinking, make it part of the subject matter. But in any significant act of reading, there must be (1) a text that steals our consent and (2) a question about the text's value at a very basic level: are we in the presence of a forged or an authentic experience?

There is an alternative to this last question, but it leads to a further uncertainty. For to raise the question of authenticity could be to mistake the mode-of-being of poetry—to make a category mistake about it—by seeing poetry as potentially a revelation, a disclosure of previously unapprehended truth. Should not the very concept of fiction, and of the poet as image maker, avert that perspective with the help precisely of a poet like Yeats, who is a maker of images and has no further claim? But what are images, then, and fictive images in particular?

Philosophy from Husserl to Bachelard and Merleau-Ponty, and theoretically oriented reflection on art from I. A. Richards and John Dewey to Wolfgang Iser and Murray Krieger, have worked closely with the assumption that aesthetic experience is related to perception (or perceptibility, *Anschauung*, the sighting of insight); further, that this relation is what is expressed by the centrality the word "image" has won. The "image" is the point where the received and the productive meet. Our ideational response to the work of art tends to analyze itself in terms that favor the "image." Even without seeking to explain this turn of events, we would find it hard to give up the by now historical liaison between image and formal values in art or between image and any model poetics—despite the counterthrust of semiotic theory and deconstructionist mediation. Perceptibility—that all things can be made as perceptible as the eye suggests—may itself be the great *classic* phantasm, the mediterranean fantasy, continued even by Romantic or Modernist artists who are aware that the image is also a resonance, a musical as well as visual phenomenon:

> Ces nymphes, je les veux perpétuer.
>
> Si clair
>
> Leur incarnat léger . . . .[1]

What images are, then, is a question that involves the make-up of our minds, or at least of our terms, our very language.

I have suggested that the image of Yeats's poem serves to stabilize a phantasm or to frame a fantasy. It is tempting to guess at an equation: the more image, the more fantasy. The phantasmic material is brought into a discourse that it keeps motivating and unsettling. I have not identified, however, the phantasm or the fantasy; to do so would be to intrude a frame of reference of my own. I am not unwilling as critic or interpreter to do this: to suggest, for example, that the swan-god fantasy potentiates feelings of touch that at once stimulate and unrealize the eyes. A taboo may be breached that involves the relation we have to our own body-image, or the way we organize its capacities into a hierarchy of senses, higher and lower, animal, human, divine. Ordinarily I would have no choice but to develop the poem in this manner. All the more so if the taking-by-surprise so affectively rendered here is not simply a man's version of a woman's presumed desire for "divine rape" but goes behind that doubtful cliché to the question of how ideas of sight exceed sight and elicit monsters or masques. For the moment, however, I want to turn from a particular poem and explore critical thinking generally.

Critical thinking respects heterogeneity. Like good scholarship it keeps in mind the peculiarity or strangeness of what is studied. By "keeping in mind" I mean it does not make art stranger or less strange than it is. But what is strange about art? The word may point to the phantasm in the image. It may also point to historical otherness, to assumptions or conventions we have difficulty appreciating. Are we, however, talking about the strange or the other, or both? Strangeness involves a sense that the strange is really the familiar, estranged; otherness (alterity) precludes any assumption about this matter, or it demands of understanding an extraordinary, even self-altering, effort. Something more than empathy; something that carries empathy beyond itself to the point where, as Rimbaud declared, "I is an other."

In Biblical hermeneutics there was often a conflict between regarding Scripture as *analogical*, or written in the language of men, accommodated to human understanding; and *anagogical*, or taking the mind out of itself, inspiring it until it appeared "beside itself." The question is whether we must insist on the one or the other: on the resolvable strangeness or the unresolvable otherness. Could we not say there must be a willingness to receive figurative language? To receive is not to accept; between these, as between active and passive, critical thinking takes place, makes its place. We cannot solve, a priori, the issue of strange *or* other; we can only deal with it in the mode of "resonance" that writing is. We rewrite the figure, in commentary or fiction, we elaborate it in a revisionary way.

That writing is a calculus that jealously broods on strange figures, on imaginative otherness, has been made clear by poets and artists rather than by the critics. The latter are scared to do anything except convert as quickly as possible the imaginative into a mode of the ordinary—where the ordinary can be the historically unfamiliar familiarized. But a poem like "Leda and the Swan" is not, or not only, a virtuoso staging of ancient myth, a re-presentation that gives it verisimilitude. Yeats sustains or fulfills a figure: myth is used to disclose the shape of history, and history (as we shall see) the truth of myth. Between Yeats's vision and the received myth a *typological* relation forms itself. Even though the figures can be given their ancient names (Agamemnon, etc.), they stand in a complex *contemporaneity* to the poet.

This remains true even when the question of time is not raised as dramatically as in "Leda and the Swan." Where there is imaginative impact, and where that impact is worked out in art, a hermeneutic patience appears that can circumvent the desire for advent—or event—but cannot ignore it. In Yeats that patience is a contrary state of soul achieved despite the apocalyptic pressure of an era—his own time—with which he identifies. To abide or not to abide one's time, that is the question. Wordsworth, too, is under pressure, but the way he broods on "a sudden blow" is quite different. However disparate the experiences depicted in "Leda and the Swan" and "I wandered lonely as a cloud," they deal with strong and sudden images. Wordsworth's poem is well known, but I quote it for convenience.

> I wandered lonely as a cloud
> That floats on high o'er vales and hills,
> When all at once I saw a crowd,
> A host, of golden daffodils;
> Beside the lake, beneath the trees,
> Fluttering and dancing in the breeze.
>
> Continuous as the stars that shine
> And twinkle on the milky way,
> They stretched in never-ending line
> Along the margin of a bay:
> Ten thousand saw I at a glance,
> Tossing their heads in sprightly dance.
>
> The waves beside them danced; but they
> Out-did the sparkling waves in glee:
> A poet could not but be gay,
> In such a jocund company:

I gazed—and gazed—but little thought
What wealth the show to me had brought:

For oft, when on my couch I lie
In vacant or in pensive mood,
They flash upon that inward eye
Which is the bliss of solitude;
And then my heart with pleasure fills,
And dances with the daffodils.

Why did Wordsworth refuse to classify "I wandered lonely as a cloud," with its picture of daffodils seen "all at once," as a "Poem of the Imagination"? Because, he said, the impact of the daffodils on his "ocular spectrum" had been too strong. His lyric moves in two directions, therefore: it respects the near-hallucinatory effect of daffodils that flash even on his inner eye long after they were seen (this reintroduces the coordinate of time), and it shows the receptive mind trying to regain the initiative, to be imaginative vis-à-vis a psychedelic image.

An instinctive phenomenologist, Wordsworth analyzed the insidious role of accident or surprise in stimulating the imagination. The problem, as he saw it, was one of separating essential from contingent in such incidents, and to arrive at a view of imagination that would deliver it from novelty or sensationalism—from the accusation that it depended on these quasiliterary drugs, on the need for an induced strangeness. Taken by surprise the mind might react with superstitious fantasies, or learn to forestall them by trivialized ideas of the supernatural, like the personified spirits in the inane and gaudy poetry around him, or the frantic marvels of the Gothic novel. The true strangeness of nature should be honored, as childhood had seeded it; images and sounds had their own life, their own agency, even if their impact on the mind derived also from the mind. For Wordsworth insisted that the "images" were not all on the side of nature; mind always blended with nature, even when imagination was involuntarily aroused; but this curious balance or harmony of image and idea—this "indeterminacy" in the act of imaginative perception—was precarious because the image tended to become a phantasm and so overbalance mind.

The pressure on mind or imagination, then, came from supernatural fantasies. Yet these did not work in a vacuum. Wordsworth was one of the first to talk of sensory shock in relation to the Industrial Revolution: the crowding into cities of people and experiences, the explosion of "news" in the Napoleonic era, that kind of daily assault on the senses. The natural rhythms, he felt, were faltering, eroding; life in rural nature was becoming a memory, and could not buffer conscious-ness as before. The health of the pressured mind depended, therefore, on preventing an alliance of supernatural fantasies with political fears and the siege of daily events. New images had to be liberated from within, or old ones cleansed and renewed; and we can watch this happening in another typical poem, "Resolution and Independence," where there is also a sudden appearance: an old leech gatherer (leeches were used for medicinal blood letting) surprises the poet in a desolate region on the border between England and Scotland. Though the scene is totally realistic, and there is ultimately no question that the old man is of flesh and blood (even if meagerly, almost skeletally so), the poet's mind under the pressure of the strange becomes strange to itself, and the line between imagination and reality begins to waver. The image is also the phantasm. To be surprised by daffodils or by the apparition of this Ancient of Days is curiously similar: behind the startlement lurks a potential phantasm. Strange fits of passion had he known.

These fits are not innocent, even if associated by Wordsworth with "wise passiveness." They are marks of the reception of otherness, but they are equally signs of an exhausting mental struggle ending in a nearly vacant or inert state of being. Wordsworth's complacency is, at times, not far from Dr. Johnson's classicism: "Wonder is novelty impinging on ignorance." There is nothing new under the sun, and the principle of uniformity consolidates this disenchantment in the name of Nature or Reason. Or the struggle ends in too thorough an enchant-ment, an escape from the vacillation that enthusiasm brings. Sunk too deep or mounted too high, the soul finds its permanent support within, as in mysticism, psychosis, or the continuous allegory of gnostic fantasy. From so absent-minded a mode of being, one can expect at most "a flash of mild surprise."

Let me return a moment to Wordsworth's "Resolution and Inde-pendence." It depicts as significant a temptation as "Leda and the Swan." Is this old leech gatherer, met by chance, a decrepit vagabond, or is he an omen, a more-than-natural intimation of a more-than-natural way of sustaining one's life? May he be a kind of phantom: image and *image of voice* working so strangely on the poet that he loses his bearing and sees heaven in a leech gatherer and infinity in a handful of leeches?

We are certainly close to something crazy in this poem, as Words-worth's laughter, at the end, suggests: "I could have laughed myself to scorn to find / In that decrepit man so firm a mind." Wordsworth interprets his laughter morally and invents an exit—a Chaucerian "sentence"—to a perplexity which really has no end. The situation is intrinsically a hermeneutic one and focuses on Wordsworth's awareness of his quirky imagination, one that acts up with transformative zeal. The poet's choice lies, essentially, between a preemptive Gnosticism that sees not only a tale but an allegory in everything, and so must dull the sharpness of accidents, even of life in time itself; and a religious mania that exults in accidents and in the cathectic power of imagination to view them as magnalia rather than trivia. A third choice is the one actually made, but is coincident with *timing*: the poem's rhythm, a resonant writing-thinking, a revisionary elaboration that does not end or begin except formally.

The strangeness of fiction, then, does not issue from its objective character, so that when that object-quality is carefully honored by explication, the fiction is understood. On the contrary, objectification may be a way of neutralizing the experience, by boxing it, labeling it "A Vision," and so forgetting the question of, for example, where Yeats is speaking from, and by what authority. It credits the rhetorical character of the enterprise too much or accepts the figurative language too readily. Hermeneutics is bypassed.

Hermeneutics has always inquired into the scandal of figurative language, when that was extraordinary or transgressive. Maimonides devotes an entire book to explaining the anthropomorphisms in the Hebrew Bible. Christ's language is often a stumbling block, and even today some of his parables appear harsh or obscure. The older hermeneutics, however, tended to be incorporative or reconciling, like Donne's "spider love that transsubstantiates all." The Bible and Greek culture, a faith and a philosophy, differing reports of a significant event (as in the case of the Gospels or contradictory traditions), even legends whose colorful features seemed to mask a basic structure: these might be brought into harmony with each other and become fables of identity. German idealism in its major phase, particularly the "identity philosophy" of Schelling, extended this reconciling perspective over the entire sphere of human knowledge, secular and sacred.

Criticism, however, a newer kind of hermeneutics, "affirms" the power of negative thinking.[2] How to define negative thinking, without converting it into a positivistic and dogmatic instrument, is of course very problematic. Not only a philosophy like that of Hegel, whose dialectic is a mode of negative thinking, struggles with this question: Keats's "negative capability" and Wallace Stevens's wish to ablute or withhold the name of the sun—to see it "in the difficulty of what it is to be"—are instances of a parallel concern.

Criticism as a kind of hermeneutics is disconcerting; like logic, but without the latter's motive of absolute internal consistency, it reveals contradictions and equivocations, and so makes fiction interpretable by making it less readable. The fluency of the reader is affected by a kind of stutter: the critic's response becomes deliberately hesitant. It is as if we could not tell in advance where a writer's rhetoric might undermine itself or where the reader might be trapped into perplexity. For the older hermeneutics the choice was clear: Yeats's supernaturalism would be blasphemous, competitive with a dominant faith, and so beneath interpretation; or it would be harmonized with that faith and absorbed. The heterogeneity of poem or original text by no means disappears in the older hermeneutics, but it appears only by way of the daring interpretation that is startling and even liberating in its very drive for harmony. Everyone knows the many marvelous acts of exegesis that try to launder the Song of Songs, that see it as a pious poem.

Modern critical exegesis faces a different situation. It must both suspend its disbelief in the scandalous figure and refuse to accept this figure as mere machinery, as only ''poetic.'' It is not sufficient to resolve this dilemma by claiming that no one really takes Yeats's supernatural theme in a literal way. There it is, after all. How are we to think of it? Do we try to resolve ''Leda and the Swan'' into an ''allegory'' or a ''symbol'' or even a ''philosophy of symbols''? But that would simply defer the entire question of how this visionary kind of writing can survive: perhaps *the* question when it comes to understanding poetry.

Some might say, at this point, that the survival of visionary or extravagant fictional modes—of nonrealism in fiction—is a matter for time to decide in conjunction with literature as an institution. But this is to forget how often the visionary strain is kindled by scholarship itself: by revivals that include the more learned critics. These ''extraliterary'' forces are part of the institution of literature. The recovery of pagan forms of rhetoric and myth in the Renaissance, the revival of Celtic and Northern mythology in the eighteenth and nineteenth centuries, the more recent explosion of interest in the matter of Araby and Polynesia, even the continuing presence of Classical themes and figures—these are unthinkable without the devoted, worried, ingenious researches and reconstructions of a host of scholars and critics.

''The commentary has entered the text,'' Sainte-Beuve remarked of Ballanche, whose *Orphée*, a prose epic, was an imaginative rehearsal of Vico's philological speculations on Roman law and literature. Philology is made flesh and provides a new art form as well as a new science. It is hard to conceive of Joyce's later work without Vico. It is hard, also, to consider twentieth-century modernism without recognizing the importance of the Cambridge Anthropologists (Frazer, Harrison, Murray, etc.), who inaugurated a new revival of the Classics on a broader—

an Orientalist and anthropological—base. Nietzsche too started as classicist and philologist. Picasso tells us that the old Musée de l'Homme in Paris (Trocadéro), its collection of masks and fetishes, played a crucial role in his own development and so in that of modern painting and sculpture. As if reading were inevitably a journeying East—and often a resistance to that drift—the Leda phantasm or similar "dark italics" (Wallace Stevens) have underwritten all significant movements of our time, both in art and philology. Leda—or Sheba, Edda, Roma, Gradiva, Orienda—is also part of the hoard of scholarship.

Understanding Art and Understanding Criticism are, even historically considered, cognate activities. Yet while poets and novelists often borrow from each other and seem to communicate across national lines, critics and scholars find it much harder to do the same. The Yeats scholar may skirmish with the Wordsworth scholar, but only the rankest amateur will venture a triangulation of these major writers with Hölderlin. The survival of "supernatural song"—or the difficulty of interpreting visionary trends and their modern persistence—has been central to German hermeneutic scholarship, yet in the Anglo-American domain it all continues to be explained by the term *secularization*, which is not reflected on (as in Max Weber) but is accepted as an explanatory concept. Nothing is involved save an admirable technical achievement, a calm transfer of properties from one area (the supernatural) to another (the natural).

There is, of course, some truth to this honoring of technique. Technique is a modern and demystified form of magic. In Yeats, as in Goethe, art itself is the magic: it naturalizes mystery by creating so clear an image of it. Yeats's poem grounds an exotic mythology in common psychic experience: the seduction of strangeness and our childish yet persistent interest in the instant of conception. Both types of experience, of course, haunt us because they master or determine us. An active imagination must strike back, repeatedly, at this passivity. The swan-god's supernatural nature encourages in us thoughts of *our* natural supernature.

Yet only the former, supernatural nature, is evident in "Leda and the Swan." While the god is both swan and god, Leda remains Leda. Her humanity is problematized, not redeemed or exalted. Though the assault of the divine on human consciousness is less disturbing here than in other lyrics by Yeats—the bewilderment is Leda's rather than explicitly the poet's—the scene that Yeats now projects, now meditates on, builds up masterfully a contrast between mastery and mystery, divine power and human knowledge. "Did she [Leda] put on his knowledge with his power . . . ?"

Through this question Yeats tries to imagine Leda as a person rather than as a medium (persona) through which the god acts. The question implies a further question: if Leda, knowing what the god knows, seeing what the god sees, still has a face, how do we envisage it? Is it gay, mad, or transfigured: does it "see" in the ordinary sense of the word? The idea insinuated is the insufferable one of a human being having to foresee all that consequence. The sudden blow entails an "elision of the richly human middle term" (Thomas Whitaker), a divine disregard cruelly apparent in the first tercet:

> A shudder in the loins engenders there
> The broken wall, the burning roof and tower
> And Agamemnon dead.

The ultimate indeterminacy, then, centers on this face that cannot be imagined. Face or mask, human or inhuman stare: the indistinctness cannot be resolved, and is roused by no more than an intonation, a questioning and quasimusical statement. "Agamemnon," similarly, is more and less than a name. It is a sound-shape with a curious hum and a recursive inner structure. The *m*'s and *n*'s bunch together, so that "Agamemnon dead" is the climactic "And" writ large. The consequence leaves the cause behind, for who could bear that visionary knowledge, that AND? Only a nonperson, a god, or a woman metamorphosed into divine impassibility. Or the poet, who has here, in this very poem, become impersonal and painted himself out of the picture.

Is the poet, then, the last of Leda's brood, the last of these births that are also vastations? The depersonalization of Leda is brought into contact with a poetics of impersonality. The poet *is* present, but as part of this myth, even as an unnamed, unacknowledged deity. Yeats's final question, to which no answer can be given, is undecidable only as it brings us close to the unthinkable. If Leda did put on the god's knowledge, what then? We begin to understand the reserve of that question, and that Yeats wants us to intuit the psychic reality of crazies like Cassandra or mythic figures vastated by seeing too much and who are mad, divine, or both. A myth of origins is made to yield a clue to the origins of myth.

I have used "Leda and the Swan" as a fable for the hermeneutic situation. Yeats's lyric is, in genre, a prophecy after the event (*ex eventu*) and recreates the psychic milieu from which such myths of annunciation come. This psychic grounding is interesting, but it intensifies rather than resolves the problem. A discontinuity remains between natural and supernatural, between the mortal psyche and elated states of mind. In a famous notebook passage (13 June 1852), Emerson talks of "Miss B—, a mantua-maker in Concord, [who] became a 'Medium,' and gave up her old trade for this new one; and is to charge a pistareen a spasm, and nine dollars for a fit. This is the Rat-revelation, the gospel that comes by taps in the wall, and thumps in the table-drawer." In *A Vision*, Yeats inserts "Leda and the Swan" into a section given the byline of "Capri"; but "Capri" could also have been "Naples" or "Cuma" or other sibylline places. The impersonality theory that T. S. Eliot and the New Critics furthered (it has links also to Henry James), though less magical or mystical, is no less a form of mystery management.

A critic aware of the survival in art of the *language* of mystery and myth is in a case exactly parallel to Yeats's. What offends cultural standards may still attract us because of its imaginative daring and peculiar organization. Like an observer of alien rites, the critic is often caught between acknowledging the consistency or attractive horror of what he sees and rejecting it in the name of his own enlightened customs. The split may tear him apart, even at a distance.[3] And if, like Kurtz in Conrad's *Heart of Darkness*, or the spy at Bacchic orgies, the critic then immerses himself in the destructive element, he still creates, as it were, the writer who has gone in search of him. The critic is always a survivor or someone who comes late. So the *character* or *role* of being a critic is implicated in this conflict between mastery and mystery, or rhetoric and hermeneutic hesitation.

The theological writings of the young Hegel are instructive in this regard. Hegel wishes to understand the triumph of Christianity over paganism without vulgar apologetics, without denying the integrity of previous life forms and even their present intelligibility. He shows "critical" respect for that which once was and which cannot be entirely superseded. To understand Christianity in its concrete historical life, alien or archaic religious forms must be recalled by the dialectical consciousness of the critic who sees them as stages in the march of reason toward an absolute form. "The heathen too had intellects," Hegel writes. "In everything great, beautiful, noble and free they are so far our superiors that we can hardly make them our examples but must rather look up to them as a different species at whose achievements we can only marvel." A religion, he continues, "particularly an imaginative religion, cannot be torn from the heart, especially from the whole life and heart of a people, by cold syllogisms constructed in the study." The supersession of paganism by Christianity, therefore, can only be explained by a process far more inward, specific, and dialectical than the model of Providence offered by Christian apologists.

For Hegel the very mobility of human consciousness at once uncovers and resolves contradictions in the forms of life it continues to institute. If there is Providence, it must be understood as the totalizing process which we call history and which the philosopher reads as he runes. The pattern of the Gothic novel of Hegel's time, which introduced a strange or uncanny event gradually resolved into the familiar and rational (Kleist's *Marquise of O*— endows this *surnaturel expliqué* with its finest psychological shading), is modified in the direction of modern social anthropology. The strange is construed rather than explained; hermeneutic hesitation leads to a more positive awareness of otherness; and if a teleological rationalism wins the day, that day is as long as history itself and includes mysteries denser and more detailed than are found in the Nine Nights of Blake's *Vala*.

It would be foolish not to claim Hegel as a hermeneutic thinker just because the patience of the negative moment in his system is structural, and the ruins of time are always transcended by an eagle-eyed dialectic. Though Hegel remains a master builder, he recalls a capacity we feared was lost: the power of the mind to keep interpreting despite evidences of death, to build on and by means of negation. As this "questionable shape" he confronts Jacques Derrida: "What remains today, for us, here and now, of a Hegel?" Composed of explicit or inner quotations, of verbal debris, *Glas* (whose opening sentence I have just quoted) labors in Hegel's shadow to remove his absoluteness and create a negative or deeply critical work of *philosophic* art.

This philosophic work of art was, of course, an aspiration of German Romantic thinkers. Friedrich Schlegel's *Athenaeum* fragments foresee a synthesizing criticism that would combine art and philosophy. Whether the desired work would be more like art or more like philosophy was an intriguing question that was never quite answered. Nor is it answered at the present time. Even should Plato's curse be lifted, and poetry be admitted once more into the Republic, "can philosophy become literature and still know itself?"[4]

What is required is a work of power in which philosophy recognizes poetry. Yet a happy ending, as in a comedy of reconciliations, cannot be assured. The recognition scene may lead to tragic or uncertain vistas. After so long a separation, there may not be a shared language anymore. Heidegger fears that, yet he tries to recover a simulacrum of the original, unified language. And literary studies that compare, for instance, Hegel's *Phenomenology* to a Bildungsroman or to the elaborate passage work of a Gothic tale, one that never quite purges from its enlightened scheme a dark and daemonic idea, are important, not because they colonize philosophy or subject it to the claims of literature, but because they raise the question of whether that philosophical work of art is possible even as a heuristic idea.

But the philosophic work of art can also be understood from the side of art. In that spirit I want to conclude: to show how effectively Kleist's *Marquise of O—* rouses the reader from the dogmatic dream that everything can be resolved. Kleist makes us into charmed and bewildered readers who feel that hermeneutic hesitation is the essential quality of philosophical art.

Despite its formal resolution (closure) Kleist's novella unsettles, and keeps unsettled, the relation of the human imagination to the sphere in which it moves. The story begins with a startling solecism. A highborn widow announces in the local newspapers that she is with child and asks the father to come forward so that she may marry him. The story then gives the background to this scandalous act and tells how a father is found. Yet we cannot be sure that this "foundling" is the father. Not to accept him as that would mean, however, to abandon the search for "natural" truth and to entertain one of two positions: that there is a supernatural cause for the marquise's "unconscious conception," or that a positive identification of the father is less important than his acceptance of that role, demanded by the institution of marriage. A natural relation may prove to be fictional or self-covenanted.

Kleist's story leaves us in this bind, which is perhaps the only thing that ties it, and us, together. He suggests that natural bonding in human life is so fragile that even when it is strengthened by an etiquette he so beautifully renders, only the violence (war, rape, haste, scandal) breaking that bond is memorable, or else the bind—perplexity of mind—itself.

Now in Hegel also the riddle of historical existence involves a rift between man and nature. Man leaves the path of natural being, betrays his bond, and continually projects his own self-alienation. This riddle is intensified rather than explained by the Hegelian dialectic, which binds all the violent repetitions we call history together. What is strange in Hegel's story is not so much the "dark" past in relation to the "enlightened" present, but the repeated—if dialectically repeated—link between self-alienation and self-realization. "Man's life is thought," Yeats wrote in "Meru"; he cannot cease "ravening, raging, and uprooting that he may come / Into the desolation of reality." The violence of the spirit vis-à-vis the natural world (Yeats's philosophy of history is explicitly centered on it, as in *A Vision's* "Dove or Swan" which is preceded by "Leda and the Swan") is modified only by a laborious and patient mode of negativity—something like philosophical analysis, or a hermeneutic hesitation that construes rather than explains spirituality.

There is a rift, then, between the human imagination and the natural or social sphere, one which no supernatural thought, no violence of spirit, can repair. Spirituality, in fact, in its very violence—even the violence of its drive for harmony and reconciliation—is simply a supreme form of the negative. *The Marquise of O—* is full of this violence of spirit, but it meets us initially as a form of writing: as the scandal of advertising, a magnificent, subversive act of womanly abasement with (in that society) the force of graffiti. When she advertises for a husband, the marquise is no less spiritual, no less *protestant*, than when she insisted on her immaculate state. But now she calls for the demon lover to appear, to take on human form, and so to deny the possibility of an immaculate or purely ideal conception. What is negated by the story is also sublated, to use Hegel's terms: the force of a woman's voice, or of the child's voice in the woman, the voice of someone who gives up without giving up a deeply imagined possibility.

The critical spirit, to conclude, does not automatically place itself on the side of reason, enlightenment, or demystification. Since the Enlightenment, in fact, it has sought to develop a style of discourse of its own which could respect the difference, perhaps discontinuity, between "ordinary" and "extraordinary" language. In England, the problem of "poetic diction" which arose after Milton—whether that kind of diction contains, residually, an archaic but still important understanding of religious mystery, or is a mystery only in the sense of "craft"—is a symptom of the general problem of diction, in criticism as well as in poetry. The temptation for criticism to become a type of science, with its own axioms and formal principles, would have been even stronger if this division of language (often simplified into one that opposes prose to poetry) had not continued to challenge the systematizers in several ways. (1) Can literature heal the division in language; or is it as divisive as it is reconciling? (2) Is a comprehensive theory of verbal artifacts, comprising prose and poetry, ordinary and extraordinary language, possible? (3) What should the verbal style of the critic be: how "ordinary," how "prosaic"?

One thing we have learned: whatever style of critical inquiry may be evolving today, criticism cannot be identified as a branch of science or as a branch of fiction. Science is strongest when it pursues a fixed paradigm or point of reference, however subtly modified, however self-transformed. Fiction is strongest as paraprophetic discourse, as prophecy after the event—an event constituted or reconstituted by it, and haunted by the idea of traumatic causation ("A sudden blow," "A shudder in the loins"). But contemporary criticism aims at a hermeneutics of indeterminacy. It proposes a type of analysis that has renounced the ambition to master or demystify its subject (text, psyche) by technocratic, predictive, or authoritarian formulas.

This criticism without a name cannot be called a movement. It is too widespread, miscellaneous, and without a program. Its only program is a revaluation of criticism itself: holding open the possibility that philosophy and the study of art can join forces once more, that a "philosophical criticism" might evolve leading to the mutual recognition of these separated institutions. A corpus of works with some commonality of purpose is already in evidence, but it would be a mistake to identify what is happening with tendencies that have been surfacing during the last ten or twenty years. My examples from Yeats, Wordsworth, Hegel, and Kleist are meant to point to a longer-range view in which the problem of how to understand visionary or archaic figuration—perhaps figuration as such—draws criticism constantly back into the sphere of hermeneutics through the persistence of the Ancient Classics and Scripture: a language of myth and mystery that has not grown old and continues to be explosive, in art as in politics.

NOTES

1. Mallarmé, "L'Après-midi d'un faune." We have no word corresponding to "image" that would express the ideational surge of internal *sound* or *speech*. I sometimes use "sound-shape" (Elizabeth Sewell) or "image of voice" (Horace's periphrasis for echo); and "resonance" can be called on to modify "reflection." Poetics has barely begun to struggle with this issue, to take back its own from music, and to bring "clarity" into conjunction with "indeterminacy" via a more sensitive, more poetically centered, theory of meaning. George Steiner sees this challenge in historical terms: he has remarkable comments on the surfacing of inner speech between the seventeenth century and the present. Mallarmé's poetry, he suggests, or the subtle density of diction in his period, still managed to keep the "membrane between inner and outer speech" intact, while allowing the chiaroscuro of self-colloquy to filter through. That membrane is then pierced by psychoanalysis and other soundings. See "A Remark on Language and Psychoanalysis" and "The Distribution of Discourse," in *On Difficulty and Other Essays* (New York: Oxford University Press, 1978).
2. For one influential view of negative thinking see Herbert Marcuse, especially *Reason and Revolution* (1941) and a "Note on Dialectic," prefaced to the 1960 reissue. Also Theodor Adorno, equally dependent on but less appreciative of Hegel, whose *Negative Dialectic* (1966) rejects any thinking about history that results in more than an "ever-new Mene Tekel, residing in the smallest things, in debris hewn by decay itself." Hegel's most famous statement on negative thinking is in the preface to the *Phenomenology of Spirit*, which speaks of "the

seriousness, the suffering, the patience and the labor of the Negative." The presence of Sartre as writer and philosopher was, till recently, the dominant one in England and America: his dialectic too can be characterized as counteraffirmative and, while remaining deeply engaged with Hegel, is used to purge false totalizations from art and history. The Anglo-American tradition approaches "understanding" from the obverse side of "belief" or "provisional assent": see, for example, Eliot's essay on Dante (1929), or such recent statements as Wayne Booth's *Modern Dogma and the Rhetoric of Assent* (Chicago: University of Chicago Press, 1974).

3. Cf. Clifford Geertz, "Found in Translation: On the Social History of the Moral Imagination," *Georgia Review* 31 (1977): 788–810; and Ludwig Wittgenstein, "Remarks on Frazer's 'Golden Bough,'" *The Human World* 3 (1971): 18–41. See also Richard H. Bell, "Understanding the Fire-Festivals: Wittgenstein and Theories of Religion," *Religious Studies* 14 (1978): 113–24.

4. I quote the ending of Stanley Cavell's *The Claim of Reason* (New York: Oxford University Press, 1979).

New Criticism and Deconstruction: Two Attitudes in Teaching Poetry

Andrew P. Debicki

When teaching literature, it is easy to think of diverse critical approaches as neatly separable "methods," each of which will produce different results. Such a view is useful in differentiating analytic criticism in general from other kinds of literary study. An analytic critic, examining a work, uses methods that show how its language functions and what effects it achieves; a historian of ideas, dealing with the same work, employs different methods, which examine it in a philosophical context. Seeing such distinctions, we try to use a similar process to define various kinds of analytic criticism, and we seek specific differences in method between New Critical studies, on the one hand, and poststructuralist and deconstructivist criticism on the other.

These differences, however, are more elusive. It is hard to define exactly what makes J. Hillis Miller's analysis of a section of *Troilus and Cressida* deconstructive but makes Cleanth Brooks's comments on "The Rape of the Lock" quintessentially New Critical.[1] We discern a preference for terms such as "irony" and "paradox" on the part of Brooks, and "anacoluthon" or "chiasmus" on the part of Miller; we observe Brooks's efforts to find patterns of resolution that contrast with Miller's view of the irreducibility of the text. Such distinctions, however, do not define separate methodologies, do not give direct answers to the student who wants to "practice" New Critical and deconstructive methods and to describe the differences between them. The actual commentaries on texts by deconstructive critics often extend out of

169

previous traditions of close reading. Where the deconstructivists do differ from the New Critics is in matters of attitude rather than of specific techniques and methods. By looking at several poetic texts and by exploring some of these differences in attitude, as well as their practical consequences for the commentary on these texts, I will try to shed light on some implications that deconstructive criticism has for the teaching of poetry. Attention to these broader differences in attitude should also keep from limiting the discussion to narrow classroom strategies or teaching tools.

Before exploring the distinctions in attitude between a New Critic and a deconstructivist, one should take into account a more general difference in the attitude toward a literary work that is taken by analytic critics steeped in New Criticism, on the one hand, and that taken by all those critics within the structuralist and poststructuralist tradition on the other (deconstruction being, of course, a facet of the latter). At the risk of simplifying, we could say that while the main concern of the New Critics was explicating what they took to be the central meanings of a given work, structuralist and poststructuralist critics strive to investigate, in a variety of ways, diverse structures to be found in literary texts. The very distinction between "work" as a static repository of set meanings and "text" as a system of signs, the value of which can be open to question, makes clear this difference in attitude. In a classic New Critical formulation, Cleanth Brooks wrote about a literary work as a "pattern of resolved stresses," which offers its reader a unique yet coherent vision; in a basic structuralist statement, Roland Barthes discussed interpretation as the discovery of textual pluralities rather than as an attempt to define central meanings.[2]

To then distinguish between a structuralist and a deconstructive perspective, we could say that the latter strives to examine critically the project of the former and to study the ways in which the structures and pluralities of the text are, in the words of Jonathan Culler, "subverted by the workings of the texts themselves."[3] The deconstructive critic is very much aware that each sign and set of signs "signifies" in more than one fashion, that all of them play off against each other in a variety of ways, and that successive readings of a single text will tease out of it new insights and perspectives.

The differences between a New Critic and a deconstructive critic will lead the latter to ask different questions and seek different goals than would the former. Skeptical of the possibility of discovering finite meanings, the deconstructive critic will explore, in tentative fashion, a variety of possible readings; more oriented to the text as a system of signs that are open to being subverted, he or she will develop that variety of readings by looking at ways in which the parts of the text modify and undercut each other. By delaying any attempt to discover meaning, by suspending final judgments, and by treating all interpretations as subject to constant reversal, such a critic will, as Geoffrey Hartman suggests, take into account the constantly unfolding nature of the text.[4]

The implications of all this for the study of a text, and especially for its study in the context of a classroom experience, become clear as we look at the ways in which a New Critic and a deconstructivist might handle a poem. My first example, untitled, is a work by Pedro Salinas, which I first analyzed many years ago and which I have recently taught to a group of students influenced by deconstruction:

> Sand: sleeping on the beach today
> and tomorrow caressed
> in the bosom of the sea:
> the sun's today, water's prize tomorrow.
> Softly you yield
> to the hand that presses you
> and go away with the first
> courting wind that appears.
> Pure and fickle sand,
> changing and clear beloved,
> I wanted you for my own,
> and held you against my chest and soul.
> But you escaped with the waves, the wind, the sun,
> and I remained without a beloved,
> my face turned to the wind which robbed her,
> and my eyes to the far-off sea in which she had
> green loves in a green shelter.[5]

My original study of this poem, written very much in the New Critical tradition, focused on the unusual personification of sand and beloved and on the metaphorical pattern that it engendered.[6] In the first part of the work, the physical elusiveness of sand (which slips through one's hand, flies with the wind, moves from shore to sea) evokes a coquettish woman, yielding to her lover and then escaping, running off with a personified wind, moving from one being to another. Watching these images, the reader gradually forgets that the poem is metaphorically describing sand and becomes taken up by the unusual correspondences with the figure of a flirting woman. When in the last part of the poem the speaker laments his loss, the reader is drawn into his lament for a fickle lover who has abandoned him.

171

Continuing a traditional analysis of this poem, we would conclude that its unusual personification/metaphor takes us beyond a literal level and leads us to a wider vision. The true subject of this poem is not sand, nor is it a flirt who tricks a man. The comparison between sand and woman, however, has made us feel the elusiveness of both, as well as the effect that this elusiveness has had on the speaker, who is left sadly contemplating it at the end of the poem. The poem has used its main image to embody a general vision of fleetingness and its effects.

My analysis, as developed thus far, is representative of a New Critical study. It focuses on the text and its central image, it describes a tension produced within the text, and it suggests a way in which this tension is resolved so as to move the poem beyond its literal level. In keeping with the tenets of traditional analytic criticism, it shows how the poem conveys a meaning that is far richer than its plot or any possible conceptual message. But while it is careful not to reduce the poem to a simple idea or to an equivalent of its prose summary, it does attempt to work all of its elements into a single interpretation which would satisfy every reader. It is thus highly "logocentric": it makes all of the poem's meanings reside in its verbal structures, and it suggests that those meanings can be discovered and combined into a single cohesive vision as we systematically analyze those structures.

By attempting to find a pattern that will incorporate and resolve the poem's tensions, however, this reading leaves some loose ends, which I noticed even in my New Critical perspective—and which I found difficult to explain. To see the poem as the discovery of the theme of fleetingness by an insightful speaker, we have to ignore the fanciful nature of the comparison, the whimsical attitude to reality that it suggests, and the excessively serious lament of the speaker, which is difficult to take at face value—he laments the loss of *sand* with the excessive emotion of a romantic lover! The last lines, with their evocation of the beloved/sand in an archetypal kingdom of the sea, ring a bit hollow. Once we notice all of this, we see the speaker as being somehow unreliable in his strong response to the situation. He tries too hard to equate the loss of sand with the loss of love, he paints himself as too much of a romantic, and he loses our assent when we realize that his rather cliché declarations are not very fitting. Once we become aware of the speaker's limitations, our perspective about the poem changes: we come to see its "meaning" as centered, not on the theme of fleetingness as such, but on a portrayal of the speaker's exaggerated efforts to embody this theme in the image of sand.

For the traditional New Critic, this would pose a dilemma. The reading of the poem as a serious embodiment of the theme of evanescence is undercut by an awareness of the speaker's unreliability. One can account for the conflict between readings, to some extent, by speaking of the poem's use of irony and by seeing a tension between the theme of evanescence and the speaker's excessive concern with an imaginary beloved (which blinds him to the larger issues presented by the poem). That still leaves unresolved, however, the poem's final meaning and effect. In class discussions, in fact, a debate between those students who asserted that the importance of the poem lay in its engendering the theme of fleetingness and those who noted the absurdity of the speaker often ended in an agreement that this was a "problem poem" which never resolved or integrated its "stresses" and its double vision. This mirrored the opinions of several critics of Salinas's poetry, who have emphasized the unresolved nature of much of his early work and have accused the poet of a playful intellectualism that made his work less impressive, for example, than that of Jorge Guillén or Federico García Lorca. Such attitudes make clear a very important premise of the New Critical approach—its assumption that a single orderly resolution of a work's meanings is a positive standard of its value.

The deconstructive critic, however, would not be disturbed by a lack of resolution in the meanings of the poem and would use the conflict between interpretations as the starting point for further study. Noting that the view of evanescence produced by the poem's central metaphor is undercut by the speaker's unreliability, the deconstructive critic would explore the play of signification that the undercutting engenders. Calling into question the attempt to neatly define evanescence, on the one hand, and the speaker's excessive romanticism on the other, the poem would represent, for this critic, a creative confrontation of irresoluble visions. The image of the sand as woman, as well as the portrayal of the speaker, would represent a sort of "seam" in the text, an area of indeterminacy that would open the way to further readings.[7] This image lets us see the speaker as a sentimental poet, attempting unsuccessfully to define evanescence by means of a novel metaphor but getting trapped in the theme of lost love, which he himself has engendered; it makes us think of the inadequacy of language, of the ways in which metaphorical expression and the clichés of a love lament can undercut each other.

Once we adopt such a deconstructivist perspective, we will find in the text details that will carry forward our reading. The speaker's statement that he held "her" against his "chest and his soul" underlines the conflict in his perspective: it juggles a literal perspective (he rubs sand against himself) and a metaphorical one (he reaches for his beloved), but it cannot fully combine them— "soul" is ludicrously inappropriate in reference to the former. The reader, noting the inappropriateness, has to pay attention to the inadequacy of language as used here. All in all, by engendering a conflict between various levels and perspectives, the poem makes us feel the incompleteness of any one reading, the way in which each one is a "misreading" (not because it is wrong, but because it is incomplete), and the creative lack of closure in the poem. By not being subject to closure, in fact, this text becomes all the more exciting: its view of the possibilities and limitations of metaphor, language, and perspective seems more valuable than any static portrayal of "evanescence."

The analyses I have offered of this poem exemplify the different classroom approaches that would be taken by a stereotypical New Critic, on the one hand, and a deconstructive critic on the other. Imbued with the desire to come to an overview of the literary work, the former will attempt to resolve its tensions (and probably remain unsatisfied with the poem). Skeptical of such a possibility and of the very existence of a definable "work," the latter will focus on the tensions that can be found in the text as vehicles for multiple readings. Given his or her attitude to the text, the deconstructive critic will not worry about going beyond its "limits" (which really do not exist). This will allow, of course, for more speculative readings; it will also lead to a discussion of ways in which the text can be extended and "cured" in successive readings, to the fact that it reflects on the process of its own creation, and to ways in which it will relate to other texts.[8]

The differences that I have suggested between a New Critical and a deconstructive reading are less a matter of technique than of attitude; they come down to a different vision of language and of reality. Even those differences which seem most specific—between the poem as a portrayal of fleetingness, via its central metaphor, and the poem as an embodiment and a demonstration of the possibilities and limits of language, carried out by the tension between image and tone—are the result of the larger difference between a logocentric attitude on the part of the New Critic, on the one hand, and a more open attitude on the part of the deconstructivist, on the other. This difference is what accounts for the very different process followed in class discussion. And it suggests that the New Critic, much as he/she may take into account all the nuances of the work, ultimately seeks what that work communicates, while the deconstructivist examines what it does to and with language.

We can explore this difference further by contrasting the view of metaphor taken by critics in the New Critical tradition with one developed by Paul de Man, which is based on a deconstructive attitude.

The former is illustrated by Philip Wheelwright's definition of metaphor as a juxtaposition of two planes for the purpose of creating a new meaning, which draws on both the similarities and the differences between planes.[9] In a critical study, Pedro Salinas offers a similar view when he speaks of metaphor as being the creation of a "third reality, raised on the ruins of the two elements compared, which fade or die to give way to the new poetic object."[10] For Wheelwright and Salinas, metaphor culminates in the transcendence of the two objects that are being juxtaposed; in very New Critical fashion, they place stress on the organic set of meanings that remains when the metaphor has done its job.

De Man, on the other hand, places emphasis on the way in which metaphor suspends meaning and "freezes hypothesis, or fiction, into fact."[11] Using an example from Rousseau, he suggests that a primitive man's use of the term "giant" for a fear-inspiring being merely objectifies his own attitude. Thus "metaphor is error because it believes or feigns to believe its own referential meaning. This belief is legitimate only within the limits of a given text." In contrast with the New Critical perspective, de Man's stresses the ways in which metaphor breaks the rules of literal reality in order to engender perspective play, to open up a process of reading and misreading without seeking the closure that is engendered by the production of the definitive meaning that Wheelwright and Salinas are seeking.

This difference in the view of metaphor underlies the interpretations of the Salinas poem already discussed. The hypothetical New Critic, who saw in the metaphor of sand as woman a means of embodying the theme of fleetingness, was seeking closure; the deconstructivist, who viewed it as a "seam" and an invitation to explore diverse implications that were engendered by it, was providing for the openness and the multiple possibilities of the text.

The implications of these two very different attitudes to metaphor become even clearer when we envision New Critical and deconstructive readings of another poem by Salinas, titled "35 Watts." Here a light is presented as a princess/beloved:

> Yes. I will release her
> when I so wish. She is imprisoned
> here on high, invisible.
> I see her in her clear
> glass castle, watched over by
> —one hundred thousand lances—the rays
> —one hundred thousand rays—of the sun.

But at night,
with windows closed
so that the stars—winking spies—
do not see her,
I will release her. (Push a button.)
Her whole being will fall from above
to kiss me, to envelop me
with blessings, clarity, love—all pure.
In the room she and I alone, eternal
lovers, she my illuminating
sweet muse, against
the massed secrets of the night outside
will decipher light forms, signs,
pursued in seas of whiteness
by me, by her, artificial princess,
electric beloved.[12]

A traditional analytic critic would focus on the unusual image of electric light as princess and beloved, noting that it contradicts our usual perspective, in which modern artifacts belong in a realm completely different from that of romance. The poem, in contrast, insistently underlies the connection between the two, supporting it with very specific bridges between modern life and romance: the light's presence within the bulb's glass is a princess's imprisonment in a castle; the flow of light is a kiss; closed windows are protection from the enemy. It uses several words that acquire double meanings, depending on the plane to which they refer: "envelop" and "illuminating" can be fitted both into the literal realm of the light bulb and into the figurative one of the princess. The speaker's insistence upon all of these connections stresses even more the far-fetched nature of the image, which is further emphasized by the opposition between the stock fairy-tale elements of one plane (the princess imprisoned in a castle) and the literal reality of the other.

Following Wheelwright's vision of metaphor, a New Critic would focus on the way in which this image, by creating tension between its two planes, leads us to a whole new perception of reality. Suddenly we have to come to the realization that modern life and chivalric romance are not totally separate from each other, that in the former we can find, if we so wish, elements of the latter. Transcending its two specific planes, the poem conveys the possibility of finding beauty and romance in the midst of the modern objects that surround us. This becomes its "true meaning," the pattern that emerges from the tensions and stresses that are produced by the juxtaposition of princess and light bulb.

A critic who is influenced by deconstruction would focus on the same metaphor; his/her method of analysis would not be radically distinct from that of the New Critic. But instead of using this metaphor to determine the poem's ultimate meaning, he/she would explore the differences that it engenders. Following de Man's view of metaphor as "error," he/she would question the implications that it has regarding the speaker's perspective. By making the light resemble a princess, this speaker is asserting something that is untrue outside the poem's context. He is also revealing his superior attitude toward both women and light: both respond to his arbitrary control, both are at once idealized and made submissive and lacking in initiative. The reader, on the other hand, notes the difference between them; the reader stands back from the speaker and tends to reject the speaker's perspective, in which the woman is made submissive like the light. The very far-fetched nature of the metaphor makes the reader even more inclined to adopt a skeptical posture and to refuse to accept the speaker's equation.

Once we have questioned the poem's central figure and the speaker's perspective which has engendered it, we notice that a whole series of specific conflicts is present in the text. The speaker's fantasy, at the end, in which he sees the beloved as joining him in an active quest against darkness, undermines and is undermined by the submissiveness with which she was previously endowed. The phrase "electric beloved" stresses this conflict in the speaker's attitude and seems to incorporate its tensions and differences. "Electric," on the one hand, suggests something vital and, on the other, refers to the passivity of the light, which is controlled by the speaker; "beloved" both evokes the woman's descending actively upon the speaker in the poem's second part and conjures up the image of the dependent princess in the tower. Together with the companion phrase "artificial princess," "electric beloved" reinforces the conflicts in the speaker's attitude and renders his whole vision less integrated.[13]

The conflicts that are present within these phrases undercut not only the speaker but also any consistent perspective on the light/princess. We have no clues that would help us resolve the speaker's contradictions, and we cannot simply call those the view of an unreliable narrator which the reader can transcend. The lack of resolution with respect to the poem's main image undercuts its ending, which asserts a triumphant battle against darkness on the part of the speaker and of the light/princess. Given the poem's enigmas, any triumph seems hollow. The use of the phrase "decipher light forms, signs" supports this reading: while it does suggest a striving for resolution, it also underlines the enigmatic nature of the reality that is present and makes the speaker's task more one of a detective's futile seeking after clues than one of a confident discovery. And even this striving to decipher is set out as a future hypothesis and is located in "seas of whiteness," which suggest further enigmas. Once we begin to perceive the conflicts in the speaker's attitude toward his main image, everything in the poem begins to unravel, creating a play of differences which put into question what to the New Critic seemed a confident vision of romance in a modern setting.

It is important to note that the comments that I have made as part of a deconstructive reading were not based on analytic techniques different from those that a New Critic might use. The observation of contradictions in the speaker's attitude, the discussion of double meanings in the phrase "electric beloved," and the analysis of "decipher" could all be parts of a traditional close reading. What was different was my attitude toward the text: instead of seeking a resolution to the stresses that are present within the poem's main metaphor, I used those stresses to explore the play of differences engendered. My reading, in fact, does not even reject the New Critic's analysis of the metaphor as a means of finding beauty amid the modern; it merely calls it into question, finding the seams within it and confronting it with its opposites, leading the reader beyond any resolution and to an awareness of the enigmatic openness of the text and of the reality to which it alludes. It does reject (or transcend) the New Critical attitude that makes cohesiveness of structure and meaning a value in itself.

The significance of a deconstructive reading, in contrast with a New Critical one, becomes clear when we place the poems that I have examined in the context of Pedro Salinas's work and of the criticism written about that work. Both texts are taken from his early work: the first poem from the book *Presages*, published in 1924, and the second from *Certain Chance*, which came out in 1929. Salinas's early poetry has traditionally been seen as intellectual, playful, and yet not very significant; one of the best-known histories of contemporary Spanish literature speaks of it as limiting itself to "the echoes of sensations" and revealing an "incomplete organization of chaotic elements."[14] Even one of the most important critics of Salinas's poetry finds in *Presages* and in *Certain Chance* an avoidance of sensorial meaning and a concentration on the play of ideas, which, he suggests, make these volumes less significant than Salinas's later work.[15] Such criticism reveals an unconscious New Critical emphasis on a resolved and integrated vision of things. This emphasis also may account for a tendency to consider one of the dominant themes of Salinas's early poetry—namely, the enigmatic nature of modern objects—as less important than those of Guillén and

García Lorca and to judge Salinas's transformations of mechanical items as interesting but lacking in depth.

A perspective influenced by deconstruction would lead us to different conclusions. Noting how Salinas personifies inanimate modern objects, transforms them in strange ways, and finds magic in them (a characteristic that was noted but not explored by earlier critics), we see in his poetry a way of combating neatly resolved views of reality, as well as an invitation to the reader to join in the exploration of life's enigmas. Salinas's transformations fulfill perfectly de Man's notion of metaphor as being the production of creative misreadings. This is illustrated in "35 Watts" and underlies much of the poet's early work. In "Underwood Girls," for example, typewriter keys are personified as nymphs, whom the speaker invites to write something more creative than a dictated text; the image engenders a conflict between a realistic and a fanciful and almost mad vision of the subject, offers no resolution, and leaves the reader witnessing a stretching of reality beyond its normal limits. (Salinas's use of an English title intensifies the playful vision.) Likewise, in "Spring, April, Model," Salinas juxtaposes an ideal spring with a Paris model/mannikin and plays on the double meaning of "model" (archetype on the one hand, petty exhibitor of clothes on the other) to yoke together two opposite perspectives which undercut each other.[16] A deconstructivist perspective leads to a major reappraisal of Salinas's early poetry.

The way in which this poetry calls apparently clear meanings into question is illustrated in "Distant Sea"; without using modern mechanical images, this poem first evokes and then undercuts and transforms its supposed subject:

> But it is not the sea, it is its image,
> its imprint, upside down, in the sky.
> . . . .
> But it is not the sea, it is its name
> in a lipless language,
> a peopleless one,
> with no word other than this one:
> sea.
>
> But it is not the sea, it is an idea of it
> fiery, incomprehensible, clean;
> and I,
> burning, drowning in it.[17]

The very first line begins to undercut the subject named in the title, a process that continues right on to the end. A traditional reading might suggest that the sea is never denied, that it is merely defined, in paradoxical fashion, as distant, indirect, reflected in the sky and abstracted beyond its realistic image. But a reading that is infused by a deconstructive perspective goes further (and seems to be far more interesting). It would note that the poem's title introduces not so much a subject as a sign, the word "sea"; the speaker, by continuously denying the *object* "sea," is calling this sign into question, is making us feel the absence of any clear referent for it. By focusing on the fact that it is a name in an abstracted language, he removes it from the realm of concrete things. At the end of the poem, the idea and the sign "sea" constitute an enigma combining the normally opposite concepts of "incomprehensible" and "clean." "Sea" contains within itself the opposite characteristics of fire and water, at once drowning and burning the speaker. As the speaker has explored the sign, he has left further and further behind any ordinary perspective of the object sea and has immersed us in the enigmas of a term whose meanings fan out in diverse directions and end up overwhelming him in contradictory ways. The sign, in effect, has come to mark an absence rather than a presence.[18] Seen this way, the poem, far from being a description of an enigmatic sea, is a study of the ways in which a sign does and does not name a reality.

Several perceptive critics of Salinas's work, most notably Concha Zardoya, have examined the poet's ways of seeking "transrealities," of always reaching beyond the surface view of things and denying common formulations in a quest for different visions.[19] Having adopted a deconstructive perspective and having explored the play of difference in Salinas's poems, we can see the importance of this quest in a new way— not because it might lead to the discovery of answers (which it clearly does not), but because it constitutes a way of putting into question reality and the naming of reality. Suddenly Salinas's work becomes enormously significant and ahead of its time.

This new view of Salinas's poetry emerged very strongly when I studied it with a class that had been reading deconstructive criticism. The play of difference in some of the poems that I have mentioned produced animated discussion; the lack of resolutions among the perspectives that were engendered evoked great interest, and several students came to consider Salinas as the most compelling poet of his era. The mere fact that the class had read some deconstructive criticism would not account, in my opinion, for such enthusiasm. Rather, I suspect that both deconstructive criticism and Salinas's poetry, with its constant play of differences, appealed to the students' inclination to perceive the open-endedness of meaning, to their awareness of the limitations of linguistic expression, and to their sense that literature is composed, not of works with resolved meanings, but of constantly evolving texts that undermine their own meanings.

The discussions that took place in this course were also founded on a vision of criticism different from those which underlie a traditional analytic approach. Once the class was conscious of the ways in which a play of differences is produced within a text, it by necessity came to see its task, not as the arrival at definitive interpretations, but as the extension of the text's possibilities. This reorientation of goals led, in turn, to a revaluation of many of the works that were being studied; those that offered the richest play of differences and that provided the greatest opportunity for such extension attracted the most interest. (It is worth noting that the mere presence of tensions and double meanings does not make a text susceptible to such play; in many cases, dualities invite a search for paradox and an effort at resolution. Salinas's poems drew attention because they did not set up such oppositions but instead put into question the very nature of their signs and the referents to which these might or might not allude.)

These discussions also made me aware of a difference in attitude between a teacher and a class immersed in New Criticism, on the one hand, and a teacher and a class infused by deconstruction on the other. The former group, operating under a tacit assumption of the work's permanent meaning, will be more likely to expect an authoritative solution to all of its problems on the part of the teacher; if none such is forthcoming, it will probably attempt to invent an authoritative solution itself, and then smugly move on to the next problem and poem. The latter group will be more likely to indulge in a freewheeling discussion, in the awareness that any interpretation that is offered can be subverted. As a result, whereas the teacher of a New Critical class has to expend effort to keep the process of analysis open, the teacher of deconstructors will, in all probability, have to keep discussion from ranging so widely as to disintegrate into total relativism. (One should note, if only in passing, that while a deconstructive perspective assumes the validity of different readings, it does not accept *any* reading as valid but demands textual relevance in an interpretation.)[20] A deconstructive perspective will make the students work harder at developing their own readings and at confronting other readings creatively; it will help them to transcend simplistic visions of literary texts, of other systems of signs, of the world around them.

We can come back, in concluding, to a crucial distinction in attitude between a New Critic and a deconstructivist, which I have already explored—that between a search for an integral view of the work, on the one hand, and an exploratory quest for the possible ramifications and extensions of a text on the other. This distinction does affect, in certain fashion, the techniques used by the critic: a deconstructivist would be less likely than a New Critic to attribute major importance to paradox, which suggests a resolution of contradictions, and would be especially attentive to figures that leave open the possibilities of a text and what Barbara Johnson refers to as "the teasing out of the warring forces of signification."[21] He or she would also define basic figures differently, as we saw exemplified in the ways in which Wheelwright and de Man interpreted metaphor. But any such specific differences seem secondary, mere results of a larger difference in attitude. Both the New Critic and the deconstructivist operate within the tradition of close reading, which started under the auspices of the former; but whereas the New Critic looks for and invites the student to seek resolutions and unification, the deconstructivist asks the student to join in a process of questioning, undermining, and extending the text—and *all* texts.

NOTES

1. See Miller, "Ariachne's Broken Woof," *Georgia Review* 31 (1977): 44–60; and Brooks, *The Well Wrought Urn* (New York: Harcourt, Brace, 1947), chap. 5.

2. See Brooks, *Urn*, pp. 202–10; and Barthes, "From Work to Text," in *Textual Strategies*, ed. Josué V. Harari (Ithaca, N.Y.: Cornell University Press, 1979), pp. 73–81. For a deconstructive view of New Criticism see Paul de Man, *Blindness and Insight* (New York: Oxford University Press, 1971), pp. 17–30.

3. Culler, *On Deconstruction: Theory and Criticism after Structuralism* (Ithaca, N.Y.: Cornell University Press, 1982), p. 22; pp. 85–109 and 180–225 offer an excellent assessment of the critical consequences of a deconstructive perspective.

4. See Hartman, *Criticism in the Wilderness* (New Haven, Conn.: Yale University Press, 1980), pp. 265–72; see also pp. 19–41, reprinted above.

5. The poem, untitled, is from the book *Presagios*, originally published in 1924. I take the text from Salinas, *Poesías completas*, ed. Juan Marichal (Madrid: Aguilar, 1955), p. 25, in my translation, which I have attempted to make as literally close to the original as possible. The Spanish originals of this and other poems quoted appear in the Appendix.

6. See Debicki, *Estudios sobre poesía española contemporánea* (1968), 2d ed. (Madrid: Gredos, 1981), pp. 72–73.

7. Deconstructive critics, following Derrida, have used the term "navel" to refer to those signs and places within a text which mark its unraveling; see Carol de Dobay Rifelj, "Los artífices de la deconstrucción," *Explicación de textos literarios* 8 (1979/80): 6; and Douglas Atkins, *Reading Deconstruction/Deconstructive Reading* (Lexington: University Press of Kentucky, 1983), pp. 24–25; pp. 15–33 of the latter offer an excellent overview of the deconstructive perspective.

8. In "Stevens' Rock and Criticism as Cure, II," *Georgia Review* 30 (1976): 131, J. Hillis Miller writes: "The critical text prolongs, extends, reveals, covers,

in short, cures, the literary text in the same way that the literary text attempts to cure the ground." The essay gives a good overview of Miller's vision of deconstruction.

9. Wheelwright, *Metaphor and Reality* (Bloomington: Indiana University Press, 1962), pp. 72–91.

10. Salinas, *Ensayos de literatura hispánica*, 2d ed. (Madrid: Aguilar, 1961), p. 362.

11. *Allegories of Reading* (New Haven, Conn.: Yale University Press, 1979), pp. 150–52. For a discussion of the contemporary visions of metaphor see Jonathan Culler, *The Pursuit of Signs* (Ithaca, N.Y.: Cornell University Press, 1981), chap. 10.

12. Salinas, *Poesías completas*, p. 71. It might be worth noting that in the 1920s a 35-watt bulb would have been considered powerful.

13. These phrases provide an excellent example of the way in which a text can set up a "network of differences" which bring forth conflicting "forces of signification." I take these terms and concepts from Barbara Johnson, whose book *The Critical Difference* (Baltimore, Md.: Johns Hopkins University Press, 1980) gives superb examples of deconstructive readings. See especially pp. x, 4–5, 23–29.

14. See Angel Valbuena Prat, *Historia de la literatura española*, vol. 3 (Barcelona: Ed. Gustavo Gili, 1953), pp. 646–49.

15. Julian Palley, *La luz no usada: La poesía de Pedro Salinas* (Mexico: Ed. De Andrea, 1966), pp. 31–45.

16. See Salinas, *Poesías completas*, pp. 120 and 98, respectively. Both poems come from *Fábula y signo* (Fable and Sign), originally published in 1931.

17. Ibid., p. 97; this poem also comes from *Fábula y signo*.

18. See Atkins, *Reading*, p. 17; Johnson, *Critical Difference*, pp. 45–48; and Rifelj, "Artifices," pp. 6–7.

19. Zardoya, "La 'otra' realidad de Pedro Salinas," in *Pedro Salinas*, ed. Debicki (Madrid: Taurus, 1976), pp. 63–84.

20. On this issue see Jonathan Culler, *On Deconstruction*, pp. 133ff.; and J. Hillis Miller, "The Critic as Host," in Harold Bloom et al., *Deconstruction and Criticism* (New York: Seabury Press, 1979), pp. 230–32, 249–52.

21. Johnson, *Critical Difference*, p. 5.

APPENDIX
Spanish Texts of the Poems Quoted

1.

Arena: hoy dormida en la playa
y mañana cobijada
en los senos del mar:
hoy del sol y mañana del agua.
A la mano que te oprime
le cedes blanda
y te vas con el primer viento
galán que pasa.

Arena pura y casquivana,
novia versátil y clara, te quise por mía
y te estreché contra el pecho y el alma.
Pero con olas y brisas y soles te fuiste
y me quedé sin amada,
con la frente dada al viento que me la robaba,
y la vista al mar lejano donde ella tenía
verdes amores en verde posada.

2.
35 bujías

Sí. Cuando quiera yo
la soltaré. Está presa
aquí arriba, invisible.
Yo la veo en su claro
castillo de cristal, y la vigilan
—cien mil lanzas—los rayos
—cien mil rayos—del sol. Pero de noche,
cerradas las ventanas
para que no la vean
—guiñadoras espías—las estrellas,
la soltaré. (Apretar un botón.)
Caerá toda de arriba
a besarme, a envolverme
de bendición, de claro, de amor, pura.
En el cuarto ella y yo no más, amantes
eternos, ella mi iluminadora
musa dócil en contra
de secretos en masa de la noche
—afuera—
descifraremos formas leves, signos,
perseguidos en mares de blancura
por mí, por ella, artificial princesa,
amada eléctrica.

3.
Mar distante

Si no es el mar, si es su imagen,
su estampa, vuelta, en el cielo.

. . . .
Si no es el mar, si es su nombre
en un idioma sin labios,
sin pueblo,
sin más palabra que ésta:
mar.

Si no es el mar, si es su idea
de fuego, insondable, limpia;
y yo,
ardiendo, ahogándome en ella.

Plot, Character, or Theme?
Lear and the Teacher

Jasper Neel

PROPHECIES

"When Priests are more in word than matter;
When brewers mar their malt with water;
When nobles are their tailors' tutors,
No heretics burn'd, but wenches' suitors;
When every case in law is right,
No squire in debt nor no poor knight;
When slanders do not live in tongues,
Nor cutpurses come not to throngs;
When usurers tell their gold i'th'field,
And bawds and whores do churches build:
Then shall the realm of Albion
Come to great confusion.
Then comes the time, who live to see't,
That going shall be us'd with feet.

This prophecy Merlin shall make, for I live before his time."[1]

    A prophecy, a making, the words of a fool, and a rupture in the very middle of our greatest poet's greatest work. Word after word, scene after scene, we are swept from king's palace to earl's castle to duke's palace to heath to other part of heath as we follow Lear and Gloucester on their downward (upward?) spiral toward death. Then, suddenly, this rupture in the fabric. The other tears we could ignore. This one the play itself falls into, carrying us willy-nilly into the abyss.

Homer nods, and Shakespeare too. What a stupid goof. If only Shakespeare had revised more carefully, even at his noddiest he would not have had the Fool quote the prophet who will live after him. And therein lie the questions. Who comes after whom? Who wrote what? Where does the play begin? Where does it end? And the supreme question: What does it mean? Questions that we cannot ask if an end to questions is our point. Questions that, once asked, forever ask themselves in different places and in different ways. There is a gaping hole in the middle of the play: no way to the other side (to the end!) without crossing it; no way of crossing it without falling in. Once in, forever in.

If we trace the exposed loose strands that lead into the rupture, we follow them back and forth forever. The entire passage, for example, is absent from the early quartos (a rupture of a different sort?). Whoever prepared those quartos apparently thought the passage not a part of the play. It appears first in the Folio. Heminge and Condell apparently thought the passage was a part of the play. Ribner and Kittredge say, "Most critics regard the passage as an interpolation."[2] Muir says, "*Some* have thought it to be an interpolation" (italics mine).[3] Most other editors make no mention of a possible interpolator.[4] Are these lines part of the play or not? And how could we ever know for sure? Did Shakespeare write them? If not, does that mean they are not part of the play? Why do they appear in every modern edition? Do consensus and tradition mean they are part of the play, whether or not Shakespeare held the pen that wrote them? And what are we to make of recent theories that Shakespeare wrote *two* versions of *Lear*, one with the passage and one without?

The very existence of the word *Merlin* in the text blurs the boundary of the text itself. By uttering it, the Fool carries the text into a future where it cannot possibly go. By having him utter it, the author (interpolator?) reaches back into a past (primitive English history), forward through that past into a future (Arthurian England), and forward through that (for the writer) already past future to the present future (Renaissance Britain) to a well-known epigram, "Merlin's Prophecy," which these lines parody. Yet the strand does not end here, for "Merlin's Prophecy" was, throughout the Renaissance, ascribed to Chaucer, an ascription universally denied by our own Chaucer scholars and termed "absurd" by Kittredge.[5] Our greatest poet (or his cipher) parodies his greatest predecessor, who already is not there. Past things (the Fool's words in Lear's primitive court) become future things (Merlin's words in Arthur's not-yet-existing court), which in turn become future fictional things (Merlin never spoke the words but was given them by a, for Merlin, future poet).

Once in, forever in. The urge, the need, however, is to get out. The effort to get out has continued for centuries, and it has been enormous. But the result of the effort, as anyone who reviews the record can plainly see, is not escape, or even movement toward it. The result is an ever-deeper fall through the rupture into the abyss. The standard ways of attempting to escape are by way of plot, character, or theme, those objects of analysis that have constituted American literary pedagogy for fifty years. Each term, however, tangles the interpreter so hopelessly that it becomes in itself a catachresis—the name for a procedure that is no procedure at all. When one talks about the plot or characterization or theme of *Lear*, what ends up being talked about is something not there or something there in more than one way. The famous triad of terms names nothing but the traces of an already-absent mode of escaping the text. The result for a reader who attempts to use these terms as keys for "analysis" is a frustration so intense that in anger the reader finds a way to annihilate the text and its endless play of signification.

PLOT

"Report is changeable."[6]

When one names "the plot" of *Lear*, already there is a rupture, a split. In fact, there are several. For example, according to the plot, is Cordelia alive or dead at the end? And for whom? Does Lear die in ecstasy, thinking she is alive? Or is he merely mad again? And if, though mad, he believes her alive and dies from joy, does it truly matter whether her corporal being has a pulse? More problematically, is Lear himself dead at the end? For slightly more than half *Lear*'s three-century stage history since the reopening of the theaters at the Restoration, Lear was alive, as were Cordelia, Gloucester, and Kent. Indeed, Cordelia and Edgar got married, and the play ended with a couplet spoken by the to-be-king, Edgar: "Whatever Storms of Fortune are decreed / That Truth and Vertue shall at last succeed."[7] Everyone who saw the play for 142 years (1681–1823) saw this version. Garrick, Kemble, and Kean all acted it, and the full Shakespearean text was not restored until Macready did so in 1838.

What were audiences watching during that 157-year period? Nahum Tate answers in the seventeenth century by saying that in watching his extensively revised version, audiences had the opportunity to see Shakespeare's unstrung, unpolished heap of jewels after it had been strung and polished. In the eighteenth century, Dr. Johnson answers that the public is right in preferring the Tate version because all reasonable beings wish to see justice rewarded and because the death of Cordelia is simply too shocking to endure. Lamb, however, answers in the nineteenth century that giving the play a happy ending is an example of misunderstanding all of the plot leading up to that ending. Shortly afterward, Hazlitt answers in a similar way, and in 1823 the plot changes![8]

Or does it? In this century, for example, Susan Snyder agrees with Lamb that the tragic ending is necessary, not, however, as Lamb had argued, because the whole plot leads up to it, but because the whole plot leads away from it. Even more confusingly, R. W. Chambers contends that six generations of British playgoers (and especially Dr. Johnson) did not know a happy ending when they saw one. Tate's ending, says Chambers, is not happy at all; but the tragic one is. To Chambers, "Thou'lt come no more, / Never, never, never, never, never" is a speech of joyous beatification, a triumphant celebration.[9]

And if we broaden the view to include more than just the ending, "plot" becomes less describable than ever. The harder we look at it, the less we see. Bradley, for example, offers a catalog of gross, plot-marring improbabilities, contends that the double plot is a "principal structural weakness," and accuses Shakespeare of shamelessly manipulating our expectations in order to deal them "a sudden and crushing blow." Eight decades later, Theodore Weiss agrees that Bradley's list of improbabilities is plausible and then turns this admission on its head, saying these improbabilities "confirm the play's plausibility." In other words, the implausible plot that makes *Lear* a dramatic failure in 1904 is the same implausible plot that makes it a success in 1981, and in 1981 the implausibilities are what make it so plausible![10]

Between Bradley and Weiss, the interpretation of plot is so over-determined by readers that for all practical purposes it vanishes. Maynard Mack, for example, agrees with Bradley that the plot is improbable. He even adds new items to Bradley's already copious list of improbabilities and then explains that almost every production of *Lear* ever mounted foundered because the director did not know better than to attempt to make the plot "reasonable." Mack advises future directors not to rationalize the irrational, regularize the irregular, or unify what cannot be unified, the clear implication being that the plot of *Lear* is irrational, irregular, and ununified—something that there is far from universal agreement about. For Wilson Knight, Kenneth Muir, and Larry Champion, the plot is one of the main strengths of the play. Muir finds it whole at every level. For Knight and Champion, the double plot works beautifully, reflecting, emphasizing, and exaggerating "all the percurrent qualities of the Lear-theme'' and serving as the ''single most important structural element'' in the play. G. B. Harrison agrees that the plot works: it is a magnificent and compelling force, carrying the reader effortlessly toward the end of the play. Instead of the two plots, so troublesome for Bradley and Mack, however, Harrison finds three (Edmund's machinations as a high roller provide the third), with all three being dexterously managed.[11]

The more one looks, the less one sees. The more one struggles, the farther one falls. D. G. James says the plot is not improbable because Shakespeare was not trying to write a probable plot but rather ''moral ideas or states, imaginatively apprehended.'' Thus, those who quibble about plot have yet to see the play. Kenneth Myrick says the plot is not improbable because it fits precisely with Renaissance conceptions of special providence. What modern readers see as sudden, unbelievable twists of plot were ''in the Elizabethan frame of reference . . . quiet but solemn reminders of a divine order.'' Because the plot is comic, says Susan Snyder, complaining about improbabilities is like complaining about fairies in *A Midsummer Night's Dream* or coincidence in *The Comedy of Errors*.[12]

The question raised by all of this becomes not ''What is the plot of *Lear*?'' but rather ''What is plot at all?'' In association with the *Lear* text milieu, at least, it is at best a catachresis, a term, yet no term, that names only if one never demands to know what is named. In the *Lear* text milieu, plot ''means'': Cordelia is alive and she is dead; the story line leads up to the end and away from it; the events reinforce each other and detract from each other; the play ends happily and tragically; the play ends happily only if it ends tragically because it would be tragic for it to end happily; the audience's preferences should govern the ending and they should not; because Shakespeare was unconcerned about plot, plot is a nonissue; and so on.

CHARACTER

Lear. Who is it can tell me who I am?
Fool. Lear's shadow.

Character in *Lear* is no less a problem than plot. At least about *Lear* one could justly say that definitive explications are at hand in inverse proportion to the amount of previous explication. The more a perceived problem is criticized, the more it is a problem and the further it moves from resolution.

Analyses of Cordelia and Edgar are good examples. (There are so many analyses of Lear that any sort of summary would be exceedingly tedious.)[13] Gervinus accuses Cordelia of making a tragic error in using a foreign army to save her father. Coleridge gently chides her for being proud and willful in the first scene. If she had not been so intransigent, most of the tragic results of her expulsion from England could have been avoided. James Kirsch says she is unwilling to be diplomatic because it would compromise the purity of her unquantifiable love. Roy Battenhouse compares her to the prodigal son's unforgiving elder brother and faults her for not knowing true Christian love at the beginning of the play. If she had, she could have used a little hypocrisy to save a world of suffering. Instead, she behaves much like her father. At the end of the play, Nicholas Brooke finds, not patience, but "a barely restrained impatience," almost as if Cordelia were making an effort not to excoriate her father for being so stupid. Brooke sees her as having to make a conscious effort not to show contempt when she says, "No cause, no cause."[14]

Bertrand Evans finds Edgar's effect in the play centrifugal, almost destructive. Edgar is neither integral nor real; he diverts rather than concentrates, dissipates rather than focuses our final view. We know him only through a spectacular series of disguises. We do not care that he wins his fight with Edmund: "We know Edgar not at all; Edgar is a non-entity, whose original dim image has been obliterated by his successive roles."[15]

Clearly, then, Cordelia deserves at least some of the blame for the horrors that befall England, and Edgar has been so much the chameleon throughout the play that by the end he is an unimportant blank. Well, not quite. The more frequently stated view of Cordelia and Edgar is that they are redeemers, though redemptionists hotly dispute whether they are Christian redeemers or merely exceptionally virtuous people in a pagan world. D. G. James, though resolutely arguing that they are in no way Christian, says they are the answer to Hamlet's "Who would fardels bear?" They are "patient merit" incarnate, transcending with detachment and disinterest the problems of living, death, and the power of evil. For Virgil Whitaker, Cordelia is the primary agent who restores order to a suffering world. For Paul Siegel, she is Christ offering Lear a miracle, his redemption for heaven. G. B. Harrison defends her against those who attack her behavior in the first scene. Her love, he argues, is so deep and inexpressible that she cannot exhibit it before a gaping court. She is like an innocent youth who cannot speak in the face of such shocking greed. Thomas McFarland sees her in mythic, if not Christian, terms. She saves her reborn father, like "the eternal mother brooding over the infant's crib."[16]

Whereas Evans sees Edgar's mad talk as jibberish in which we lose interest, Roy Battenhouse sees the same talk as "shrewdly relevant," allowing for surrealist commentary, a choric function, and even a spiritual kinship with the mad Lear. For Larry Champion, Edgar is the spokesman "for disinterested self-knowledge vital to man's successful completion of his journey through this tainted society"; for R. W. Chambers, Edgar is a Christian gentleman, whom Shakespeare likes and approves; for Wilson Knight, he is the very "voice of the *Lear* philosophy," its "high priest"; and for McFarland, Edgar, like Cordelia, is the good-child parental tutor, leading his father to the salvation of the family as a haven.[17]

In other words, a study of character leads to the conclusion that Edgar is a detracting nonentity in whom we have no interest, or that he is the high priest of the play's theme. At the end of Act IV, Cordelia hides impatience and contempt for her father, or she is the stoic-heroine/Christ/world-mother, filling the stage with tenderness and mercy.

The record of *Lear* criticism shows that we can use a term such as *character* and believe in what it reveals only as long as we do not look at what is revealed by its use, for each character is a rupture. The harder we look, the harder it is to see anything clearly or singly. Everything not only doubles itself but also contradicts itself. Edgar can, in fact, vanish before our very eyes even as he speaks the *Lear* theme. Indeed any sort of survey of the explications of any "character" leads to multiple "characters" so overdetermined, so minutely described, that again what is put in question is not the "characters" in *Lear* but character as a name for anything at all. We despise Cordelia for being the favorite spoiled child who will not condescend to slather on a few words for her father (or do we love and respect her for this?), and we love her for her tenderness toward her mad father (or do we find her impatient, even ludicrous, as she pretends to be happy in an imbecilically absurd world?). The very moment we see any "character," we see another. The redoubling is so violent that it finally reveals a gap, an absence. Neither Cordelia nor Edgar (and certainly not Lear, Gloucester, or Edmund) can be reduced to a meaning. There is no founding meaning that the signifying chain leads back to. There was always a redoubling, a covering over again of the absence of the base meaning from which each "character's" "character" suggests derivation.[18] Even the word *char-acter* is already a hiding of its ancient past. Traced back far enough, *character* becomes *kharakter*, then *kharassein*, the ancient Greek verb meaning "to inscribe."[19] Each "character" already was an inscription, a sign in a system, a representation with the thing represented always already absent.

THEME

"O, these eclipses do portend these divisions."

Everything in *Lear* divides; every division subdivides. The play is a record of eclipses—things that cannot be seen and yet call attention to their invisibility precisely because they have always appeared before. What makes an eclipse remarkable is that one can no longer see what one has always seen. The standard, the source, the light is obscured. *Lear* is a catalog of divisions in plot—tellings, retellings, and changed tellings—but the first telling is an absence, always going back one step further from *Lear* to *Leir* to Spenser to Holinshed to Higgins to Geoffrey of Monmouth to the Cinderella teller; always going sideways to Sidney or to the popular Elizabethan story of Sir Brian Annesley, whose daughters, Christian and Lady Wildgoose, tried to take his estate and whose daughter Cordell (!) intervened and saved him; even going forward to the anonymous publishers of the two early quartos, to Heminge and Condell, or to whichever edition is currently in vogue. *Lear*'s characters (*kharassein*) are themselves eclipses and divisions. We recognize them by what is not there (there is light in an eclipse, but its origin is gone). There are always divisions, for we always feel at least two ways about them.[20] Only through theme, however, do we see the size of the rupture in the play.

The number of loose strands running into the rupture is astonishing, even to someone accustomed to reading twentieth-century Anglo-American literary interpretation. *Lear*, one discovers, is a Christian play (Battenhouse, Bickersteth, Campbell, Craig, Duthie, Holloway, Kirsch, Myrick, Siegel). Reading *Lear* as a Christian play can cause misinterpretation (Barnet). *Lear* is entirely pagan (Elton, Everett, James, Muir, Snyder). *Lear* is agnostic (Knight) or at best a Christian play about an agnostic world (Maxwell). And this is just the beginning. *Lear* is about love (Chambers, Knight, Knights, Muir); it is not about love in any meaningful way at all (Holloway). It is a grandiose Morality play (Campbell, Whitaker); it is not a Morality play (McFarland, Everett); it is sort of a Morality play (Mack). Lear is educated about his sin (Champion, Knight); he is incapable of understanding his sin (Whitaker). Gloucester's suicide is so prepared and performed that we find it reasonable (Bradley); it is pitifully absurd (Kott). The play's theme is so powerful that it is unactable (Bradley); it is particularly actable (Goldman). And so on.[21]

In general, one can say, interpreters of *Lear*'s theme fall into two groups, redemptionist and nihilist, though the two finally blur together; and there is no significant agreement in either general group about the reasons for finding *Lear* redemptionist or nihilist. Quite the contrary, each reading is a fully closed system that obviates all the others.

The redemptionists, for example, all see Lear as redeemed or saved at the end. But the mode of his redemption depends on the critic. *Lear* could, says Bradley, be renamed *The Redemption of King Lear*, because the theme leads to renunciation and hatred of the world. Lear and Cordelia are "rather set free from life than deprived of it"; Lear's death "is not one of pain but of ecstasy"; and actors who do not play Lear's last speech with "an unbearable *joy*" are "false to the text." John Danby agrees that the play is redemptive but explains Lear's last speech differently. For him, it is merely another lapse into madness. And L. C. Knights, after anguishing over all the suffering, concludes that "the mind, the imagination so revealed is directed towards affirmation in spite of everything."[22]

Lear has been described as a tragedy of redemption: because both Gloucester and Lear find the family as haven and are reborn under the loving tutelage of their good children; or because the play's poetry is so exhilaratingly joyous that a transfiguring celebration "is expressed, not in things or possessions, but, as he [Lear] is broken open to a larger world and its creatures, in an expansion of himself, a participating in others beyond that self"; or because Lear learns to be open to feeling and vulnerability, to recognize that no one is everything.[23]

All of these redemptionists are, of course, redemptionists; they are not, however, *Christian* redemptionists. And there is a difference. A host of interpreters see *Lear* as an unmistakably Christian play, even though Shakespeare carefully set it in pre-Christian Britain and scrupulously avoided any mention of Christ or anything else Biblical. The case gets made in a variety of ways, from Hardin Craig's argument that Lear's sanity is coextensive with his religious faith to John Holloway's argument that a fall into chaos fitted Elizabethan expectations of the divinely planned route to salvation as did the Christian ending of "being brought back to rectitude."[24] And there is more. Cordelia is a Christ type who harrows hell and is, like Christ, hanged.[25] The entire focus of the play is on Lear's redemption into a sort of nontheological Christian stoicism.[26] Though *Lear* is apparently pagan, it is pervaded by a Christian feeling.[27] Because it "is a Christian play," Lear and Gloucester "die in a state of spiritual health."[28] *Lear* is "a Christian play about a pagan world."[29] It is "a story of sin and redemption" in which Lear is "saved" and "received by the angels of heaven."[30] Though it is a Jungian journey toward contact with the unconscious, *Lear* follows a clearly Christian pattern.[31] *Lear* is Shakespeare's *Divine Comedy*, informed by the pattern of fall, crucifixion, and last judgment; moreover, it is an object lesson on what would happen to England if it ever turned from Christianity.[32]

If the redemptionists are divided among themselves, as obviously they are, they are even farther divided from the nihilists, who extend at least as far back as Swinburne, for whom Gloucester's cry against the gods, "They kill us for their sport," was "the keynote of the poem."[33] (One could fairly assume that the nihilists extend back to Tate, for there would have been no need to change the ending had it not seemed nihilistic and therefore unacceptable.) Nihilism has found many adherents in the twentieth century: for example, through Cordelia's death is revealed an "invincible and unassailable" malevolence.[34] The end of the play leaves nothing but a "blind and bloody shambles," with no vestige of a moral order.[35] "The core of the play is an absurdity, an indignity, an incongruity."[36] *Lear* calls into question providential goverance, asks "What then?" and makes irrelevant the existence of just gods or a just afterlife.[37] Because in 1606 most Englishmen saw the world as a dissolute, stinking stew of corruption, *Lear* is a vision of stark, unrelieved pessimism, and "the pessimism is in Shakespeare himself . . . not in the story of *Lear*."[38] The true meaning of *Lear* is the revelation of "an imbecile universe" where the hero "dies unreconciled and indifferent to society," penance is impossible, and charity, resilience, harmony, and God are delusions.[39] *Lear* undoes not only order but also the possibility of order; its greatness "is in the perfect completeness of its negation," which requires "our adjusting to a state of universal disorder."[40] *Lear* is an anticipation of Beckett, Ionesco, and Dürrenmatt in that it is about the absurdity of life in which there is no Christian heaven, no happiness, no rational view of history, no god, no good nature—nothing but an empty, bleeding earth where a king, a fool, a blind man, and a madman carry on a "distracted dialogue."[41] Because Lear fits precisely the Renaissance idea of a skeptic, there is absolutely no possibility of a Christian or redemptive reading; at the end, there is no angelic chant or Faustian struggle with devils, just "a perplexing silence."[42] Those left standing on the heath at the end of *Lear* can reconstitute and recompose society, but having experienced its underlying void, they are greatly diminished and have no hope of joy, grandeur, or certainty.[43]

Not surprisingly, given the heat of the debate over salvation and damnation, there are those who equivocate before giving in to the need to escape the text and the concomitant necessity to join one group or the other. Wilson Knight, for example, has it both ways by writing back-to-back essays which come to different and mutually exclusive conclusions, one absurdist, the other redemptive. Knight neither makes an effort to reconcile the two nor admits they differ. Barbara Everett sees nothing redemptive or optimistic in the play itself, but she argues that since the great suffering of which humanity is capable can be captured in art, through art that suffering can at least be mastered. Maynard Mack calls the redemptionists "too simple" and the nihilists too trendy. Then he offers his own darkly redemptive reading, based on the fact that audiences do not commit suicide at the end of the play: "If our moral and religious systems can survive this [the terrors of the modern world], and the record suggests that for many good men they do and can, then clearly they will have no trouble in surviving the figure of Lear as he bends in his agony, or in his joy, above Cordelia." Susan Snyder, like Mack, says *Lear* is neither *The Divine Comedy* nor *Endgame*; rather, it is the constant juxtaposition of comic structure and character set against a tragic result. The effect of the play is so wrenching because we are invited constantly to expect resolution only to have it snatched away. Whereas Mack is darkly redemptive, Snyder is comically nihilistic, concluding that Lear on the heath and Gloucester at Dover frustrate our comic-redemptive hopes to the point that the entire idea of redemption is negated.[44]

What, then, *is* the theme of *Lear*? As with plot and character, the problem lies not in the answers but in the question. The record reveals that the word *theme* in fact names nothing, or at least it names so many contradictory, irreconcilable things that the things named are overdetermined into nothingness. Anyone can see how *Lear* might be interpreted as nihilistic, as a darkly pessimistic Renaissance *Endgame*, just as anyone can see how *Lear* might be interpreted as a play of redemption, even of Christian redemption. Most find one or the other view harder to imagine, but almost no one can honestly say that either is impossible to imagine. What is put in question is not the meaning of *Lear*; what is put in question is the mode of reading that implies that there is *a* meaning of *Lear*. A discussion, whether in the classroom or in the standard twenty-page essay, of the "theme" of *Lear* turns out to be no discussion at all, because the strategies for case making and the rules for evidence in such a discussion require the death of the text and an end to the experience of reading (dialogue and explication are mutually exclusive phenomena).[45] Before the interpreter can tell the text what it says, the text must be silenced and the reader freed from the "labyrinth of linkages" that extends farther than the most patient reader can ever go.[46] The very word *theme* implies an original place, a discernible thing on and around which the text was built. The critic in search of "theme" must work backward through the signifying chain to the original place. But there is no such place. There never was an "ideal Jacobean interpreter" whose response we can describe and imitate.[47] Even the word *theme* turns out not to be a place as we trace it back to the Greek word *tithenai*, which means "to place," with the *thing* being placed already absent.[48]

THE TEXT

> *Gloucester*. What paper were you reading?
> *Edmund*. Nothing, my lord.

What, then, is left? Take away plot, character, and theme, and the result is professorial stutter. What is left is less, actually, than might appear. Without plot, character, and theme to obscure it, the abyss that is the text looms large, for the problem of the text itself can no longer be ignored. What, after all, *is* the text called *Lear*? The standard answer has been that it is the text published by Heminge and Condell. But there are serious problems with that answer. To begin with, three hundred lines that have been universally accepted as part of the play do not appear in the Folio (including one entire scene [IV, iii] and a major section of another [III, vi, 17–55]). And there is considerable question about the provenience of the Folio. The orthodox theory is that the Folio is a correction of the first quarto, with the prompt book serving as the guide for corrections. Since 1978, however, even that has been put in question by theories, first, that the quarto holds provenience over the Folio and, second, "that there may be no single 'ideal play' of *King Lear* (all of 'what Shakespeare wrote'), that there may never have been one, and that what we create by conflating both texts is merely an invention of editors and scholars." This second theory leads to the belief that "editions of the complete works should include both texts" because Shakespeare, in effect, wrote two plays, somewhat in the same way that Wordsworth wrote two *Preludes*.[49] A method that evaluates plot and character or defines theme depends absolutely on a fixed text, something there never has been for *Lear*. Everything about the play is a back and forth, a question preceded by other questions. Wherever one looks, what was to be found there is gone.

Where does the text begin? Where does it end? And what does it include? For the modern reader it is almost impossible to find a copy without an Introduction, extensive glosses, and a set of equivocations about the editorial process. Are these part of the play?[50] The experience for almost every beginning reader of Shakespeare is that the plays come encapsulated—front and back, top and bottom, left and right—with other texts. For the experienced reader, these encapsulations have become part of the text. In other words, even if the words of the text itself were certainly Shakespeare's, where is the line of demarcation separating everything that is *Lear* from everything that is not? There is probably no living reader whose experience with *Lear* has not included several layers of encapsulation.

In fact, the experience of reading *Lear* is a continuous passage from text to text, a passage so intertwined with the play that play and milieu are no longer separable. Introductions always discuss the sources (the texts from which Shakespeare made his now-unavailable text). New readers are always shocked by Shakespeare's "plagiarism." Notes point out his borrowings and explicate his meanings. New readers are always annoyed by these notes, but out of guilt and insecurity they can never resist looking. And editors explain their attempts to retrieve the now-lost Shakespeare text and, intentionally or not, point out the ruptures in the fabric of words. Just as Shakespeare moved among many texts (the old *Leir, Arcadia, Declaration of Egregious Popish Impostures, A Mirror for Magistrates, Albion's England, The Faerie Queene*), the modern reader moves among many texts until the experience of reading *Lear* becomes a diegesis—a story retold, retelling itself. It is the playing out of repetition, forever the same and forever new. *Lear* is, through repetition, part of the old *Leir*, the Paphlagonian king, and myriad other tellings. In it something is both found and lost as the story is told even in the moment of retelling itself.

THE TEACHER

"When madmen lead the blind."

Hillis Miller's unfortunate term for the nature of the text is "unreadable." What he means by that often misunderstood (sometimes, one suspects, intentionally misunderstood) term is more precisely "unstoppable" or even "un-unreadable." For he does not mean that *Lear* cannot be read; rather, he means that once the reading starts, it never stops and that the unstoppability goes in multiple directions.[51] If, for example, one asks before reading *Lear*, "What did Shakespeare write?" the series of questions generated by that first question extends backwards forever, with the pristine text receding ever more rapidly than the attempts to catch it. Or if one wonders, "How original was Shakespeare?" the search for what he may have used retraces an endless web of strands that make up the play, with each strand in the web generating new strands. What, for instance, do we know once we know that the names of Edgar's devils almost certainly came from Harsnett's *Egregious Popish Impostures*?

Unreadability means the existence of self-including opposites, of clues for multiple and contradictory readings. Thus "Thou'lt come no more'' is a clue both for a reading in which the *Lear* world and our world are absurd and for a reading in which Lear is redeemed and sets a pattern for our own redemption. Unreadability means the lure of the promise of final resolution. The thing that we desire most from the text is to master it, close it, and encompass it. The greatest danger, however, is to give in to that desire, for all readers who have ''read'' the text have fallen victim to the desire for final resolution and have forced a stopping place.[52]

Lear is, in fact, unreadable in any sort of permanent way. The pedagogy of the twentieth century, however, is founded on the assumption of permanent readings. Students know intuitively that such readings are forced on the text. Their response is normal: ''That's the teacher's opinion. My opinion is just as good, but I need the grade.'' Or, ''There is no way Shakespeare could have known all the stuff the critics say.'' Their experience with *Lear* is nothing like what the formal explications say. But then neither was the experience of the explicators, for the formal explications can begin only after the text has been silenced and changed into a collocation of data which is to be used in describing what once was a text.

The actual process of reading *Lear* is a diegesis, not an encounter with univocal meaning. Indeed, Lear's story itself is a diegesis, a split in multiple directions. In one way it is the retelling of an ancient folk tale about a misunderstood daughter; in another, the retelling of Elizabethan histories of Britain; in yet another, a retelling of itself as the Lear story mirrors and is mirrored by the Gloucester story. None of these retellings is ''plot'' distinct from the system of plots through which it exists. The Lear story and the Gloucester story, which is itself a retelling of the Paphlagonian king, are split-apart tellings, forever inseparable from each other. Indeed, all of *Lear* exists as a split that was before and continues after. Before the play begins, Lear himself was a split. He appeared as an integrated person exactly to the extent that his person remained unrevealed (''he hath ever but slenderly known himself,'' ''The best and soundest of his time hath been but rash,'' ''All this done / Upon the gad?'' ''O Lear, Lear, Lear! / Beat at this gate, that let thy folly in / And thy dear judgment out!''). Scene 1 is itself an act of splitting: father from daughter, sister from sisters, king from kingdom, ruler from loyal subject, language from feeling, symbol from power, past from future. Scene 2—itself a splitting from scene 1, from Lear family to Gloucester family, from palace to castle—is a retelling of the already told: father from son, brother from brother, earl from earldom, language from meaning, and so on. Throughout the play, Lear and Cordelia, Gloucester and Edgar, Kent and Albany struggle to regain the point of wholeness, to get back before the original division, where the rupture can be prevented. Their struggle, which becomes our struggle, is so intense and so very, very painful that we refuse to know that there always already was the split. The historical place where all was whole, where univocal truth bound up the rupture, never existed. The play begins:

> Kent. I thought the King had more affected the Duke of Albany than
>   Cornwall.
> Gloucester. It did always seem so to us; but now in the division of the
>   kingdom, it appears not which of the Dukes he values most . . . .

The moment of the beginning is a division, but a division that is preceded by the preexisting division in Lear's affections for his sons-in-law.

Each of the first two scenes focuses on an even-more-fundamental rupture—the origin of origins. In scene 1, Cordelia answers Lear's demand for a love speech:

> Cordelia. Nothing, my lord.
> Lear. Nothing?
> Cordelia. Nothing.
> Lear. Nothing will come of nothing, speak again.[53]

Lear demands that wealth be linked to tropes. Because Cordelia denies him tropes, he denies her wealth. Throughout the rest of the play, however, the everlasting split between physical things and words becomes increasingly apparent. Kent becomes Caius; self-mutilation becomes a battle wound; join stools become daughters; a madman (who in a different sort of split is not mad at all) and a fool (who in another split is the least foolish person in the play) become judges; a flat place becomes a steep hill and then a precipice; prison becomes freedom; hearts burst smilingly from conflicting passions of joy and grief; life becomes death; and death, life. Cordelia's "Nothing, my lord" does not lead to nothing, unless, of course, one's reading of the play is so utterly nihilistic that at the end there is *absolutely* nothing. And even then, what occurs between "Nothing, my lord" and "we that are young / Shall never see so much, nor live so long" is far from nothing.

Scene 2 introduces a different split, which is yet the same as the split of scene 1: What is the origin of origins? The origin of the division in the Gloucester household comes absolutely from nothing, from Edmund's letter, which is not a letter at all but the absence of a letter.[54] Then again, it comes from something, from a previous split in Gloucester's affection for two women, one of whom will in later time become "the dark and vicious place" that "cost him his eyes." The splits between father and son, son and father, brother and brother that are the business of the play already existed before the play in the split of legitimacy and bastardy, of fidelity and adultery, of loyalty and perfidy. And neither can exist without the other: no legitimate children without bastards, no faithful husbands without adultery, no loyal siblings without perfidious ones. The origin of origins is that they always already were, and the point at which they already were is itself a split.

> *Gloucester.* What paper were you reading?
> *Edmund.* Nothing, my lord.
> *Gloucester.* No? What needed then that terrible dispatch of it into your
>   pocket? The quality of nothing hath not such need to hide itself.
>   Let's see. Come, if it be nothing, I shall not need spectacles.

The paper needed to be hidden with dispatch precisely because it was nothing. The mode in which its nothingness is hidden is the same mode through which its nothingness becomes a somethingness over which Gloucester would "unstate" himself to be in "resolution." Thus the scene in which an honest man becomes dishonest; a dishonest man, honest; a nonletter, a letter; two nonreaders, readers; a sighted man, blind; and an earl, a beggar is a metaphor for the criticism of *Lear.* Our desire is to be "in a due resolution." If that resolution costs us the play, so be it.

Every scene in the play carries undecidable opposites. We loathe Edmund yet cannot help being attracted to his frank self-evaluation and villainy. We detest Goneril and Regan but abhor Lear's behavior in the first two acts ("Call France. Who stirs?"; "Better thou / Hadst not been born than not t' have pleas'd me better"; "Let me not stay a jot for dinner, go get it ready") and cannot help feeling that his daughters have some cause to complain about his behavior and that of his knights.[55] We do and do not believe that Lear is more sinned against than sinning, that man is nothing but a "poor, bare, fork'd animal," that justice is merely a dog in office, or that a pure face presages vicious lust. We can feel both the absurdity and the poignance of Gloucester on the plain, just as we ache from the splitting end as we watch Lear die in utter despair or in absolute bliss. And all of the openings, the splits, and the ruptures do not become unified at any level, no matter how abstract. There is constant oscillation of feeling more than one way, of hearing more than one story, of envisioning contradictory and mutually exclusive resolutions.

Lear had never known himself before the play begins. After the irreconcilable rupture of the first scene, the remainder of the play is a record of his attempt to regain the whole self that never was. In Act I:

> . . . Only we shall retain
> The name, and all th' addition to a king;
> The sway, revenue, execution of the rest,
> Beloved sons, be yours, which to confirm,
> This coronet part between you.

And later in the act, "Who is it that can tell me who I am?" In Act II: "O Fool, I shall go mad!" In Act III: "this tempest in my mind / Doth from my senses take all feeling else." In Act IV: "they told me I was every thing. 'Tis a lie, I am not ague-proof"; "Give me an ounce of civet; good apothecary, / Sweeten my imagination"; "Let me have surgeons, / I am cut to th' brains"; "Would I were assur'd / Of my condition"; and "I fear I am not in my perfect mind." In Act V: "I am old now, / And these same crosses spoil me"; and "Look on her! Look her lips, / Look there, look there." The desires to escape the rupture, to satisfy the demands of the text, and then to put it aside are enormous, as powerful in *Lear* as in any work in the language. Just as Lear wants so desperately to get back to the place where things were right, we want to achieve the closure of a complete reading. For Lear, however, the place where things were right, the place where he was "himself," never was. For us, closure never comes.

"IS THIS THE PROMIS'D END?"

A prophecy, a making, a rupture. It is not possible to say where *Lear* begins. And once the reader is in the text, escape from the tracing and retracing, the telling and retelling, is impossible. The Fool (who is himself split off from normalcy and finally, inexplicably, split off from the play) quotes Merlin (who himself is also split off from normalcy and surely split off from this play). Lines that cannot be placed, meanings that recede ever faster than they are sought, speakers who know what they cannot know—these constitute the experience of *Lear*.

Plot implies beginning and ending. It implies the possibility of extracting a thing called *Lear* from a text milieu that extends backward to prehistory and forward to infinity. It implies a one-time telling, a closed system leading to a closed interpretation. Character implies an integrated being, a wholeness about which permanent conclusions can be reached. Theme implies a place where resolution exists. Reading *Lear* in all its unreadability is none of these things. Students expect the *Lear* of plot, character, and theme. As these terms are deconstructed, a process of reading literature is deconstructed also. More than that, a way of reading life is deconstructed, for without plot, character, and theme to obscure the forever rereading that is reading, students are forced into a labyrinth of linkages where they give up the expectation of origins and endings and enter the realm of the signifier where fools quote the wizards who will live after them.

NOTES

1. William Shakespeare (or Anonymous), *The Tragedy of King Lear*, in *The Complete Works of Shakespeare*, ed. Irving Ribner and George Lyman Kittredge (New York: John Wiley & Sons, 1971), p. 1228. No one is certain about the arrangement of these verses. Kenneth Muir, *The Arden Edition of the Works of William Shakespeare: "King Lear,"* rev. 9th ed. (London: Methuen, 1972), p. 105, also follows the Folio text in placing lines 91–92 (3.2) where Ribner and Kittredge do, but Blakemore Evans, *The Riverside Shakespeare* (Boston: Houghton Mifflin, 1974), p. 1275; and David Bevington, *The Complete Works of Shakespeare*, 3d ed. (Glenview, Ill.: Scott, Foresman, 1980), p. 1194, follow Warburton's suggestion that the lines belong after line 84.

2. P. 1229, note to line 79.

3. Pp. 104–5, note to line 80.

4. Neither Evans nor Bevington mentions the possibility of an interpolator.

5. P. 1229, note to line 79.

6. This and all quotes from *Lear* below are from *The Riverside Shakespeare*.

7. Nahum Tate, *The History of King Lear*, ed. James Black (Lincoln: University of Nebraska Press, 1975).

8. Tate's description of his redaction appears in a letter to Boteler, cited in Maynard Mack, *King Lear in Our Time* (Berkeley: University of California Press, 1965), p. 10. Charles Lamb, "On the Tragedies of Shakespeare . . . ," in *The Works of Charles Lamb* (New York: Harper & Brothers, 1838); William Hazlitt, *Characters of Shakespeare's Plays* (London: C. H. Reynall, 1817).

9. Susan Snyder, *The Comic Matrix of Shakespeare's Tragedies* (Princeton, N.J.: Princeton University Press, 1979), especially pp. 140–41; R. W. Chambers, "King Lear," in *His Infinite Variety*, ed. Paul N. Siegel (1940; reprint, New York: Lippincott, 1964), pp. 367–69.

10. Andrew C. Bradley, *Shakespearean Tragedy* (London: Macmillan, 1904), pp. 252–58; Theodore Weiss, "'As the Wind Sits: The Poetics of *King Lear*," in *On "King Lear,"* ed. Lawrence Danson (Princeton, N.J.: Princeton University Press, 1981), pp. 62–67.

11. Mack, *"King Lear" in Our Time*, pp. 3–4 and 25–41; Kenneth Muir, *Shakespeare's Tragic Sequence* (London: Hutchinson University Library, 1972), pp. 119–23; Wilson Knight, *The Wheel of Fire* (London: Methuen, 1949), pp. 168–71; Larry Champion, *Shakespeare's Tragic Perspective* (Athens: University of Georgia Press, 1976), pp. 156–60; G. B. Harrison, *Shakespeare's Tragedies* (New York: Oxford University Press, 1952), p. 165.

12. D. G. James, *The Dream of Learning* (Oxford: Clarendon Press, 1951), pp. 116–21; Kenneth Myrick, "Christian Pessimism in *King Lear*," in *Shakespeare 1564–1964*, ed. Edward A. Bloom (Providence, R.I.: Brown University Press, 1964), pp. 56–70; Snyder, *Comic Matrix*, pp. 140–41 and 156–57.

13. A useful point of entry into the labyrinth of *Lear* character analyses is Norman Holland's "Psychoanalysis and the Works: *King Lear*," in *Psychoanalysis and Shakespeare* (New York: McGraw-Hill, 1964), pp. 214–19. Holland summarizes several studies of Lear's personality, which, if followed up, lead on forever.

14. Gervinus is cited in Snyder, *Comic Matrix*, p. 56 n.30. Samuel Taylor Coleridge, "Lear," in *Literary Remains*, ed. H. N. Coleridge (London, 1839; reprint, New York: AMS Press, 1967), vol. 2, pp. 185–201; James Kirsch, *Shakespeare's Royal Self* (New York: G. P. Putnam's Sons, 1966), pp. 191–93; Roy Battenhouse, "King Lear and the Prodigal Son," *Shakespeare Quarterly* 17 (1966): 361–69, and *Shakespearean Tragedy* (Bloomington: Indiana University Press, 1969), pp. 282–88; Nicholas Brooke, "The Ending of *King Lear*," in *Shakespeare 1564–1964*, p. 81.

15. Bertrand Evans, *Shakespeare's Tragic Practice* (Oxford: Clarendon Press, 1979), p. 180.

16. James, *Dream of Learning*, pp. 16–21; Virgil Whitaker, *The Mirror up to Nature* (San Marino, Calif.: Huntington Library, 1965), p. 212; Paul Siegel, *Shakespearean Tragedy and the Elizabethan Compromise* (New York: New York University Press, 1957), pp. 161–88; Harrison, *Shakespeare's Tragedies*, p. 165; Thomas McFarland, "The Image of the Family in King Lear," in *On "King Lear,"* pp. 106–13.

17. Battenhouse, *Shakespearean Tragedy*, pp. 299–300; Champion, *Shakespeare's Tragic Perspective*, p. 155; Chambers, "King Lear," pp. 360–61; Knight, *Wheel of Fire*, pp. 191–97; McFarland, "Image of the Family," pp. 116–18.

18. My idea of character as split, gap, or absence comes from the writing of Jacques Lacan. For an introduction see Jasper Neel, "Reading and Writing: A Survey of the Questions about Texts," in *Research in Composition and Rhetoric: A Bibliographic Sourcebook*, ed. Ronald Lunsford and Michael Moran (Westport, Conn.: Greenwood Press, 1984), pp. 157–68. For a much fuller introduction see Anika Lemaire, *Jacques Lacan*, trans. David Macey (London: Routledge & Kegan Paul, 1977). See also Jacques Lacan, *The Four Fundamental Concepts of Psycho-Analysis*, ed. Jacques-Alain Miller, trans. Alan Sheridan (New York: Norton, 1978), and *Ecrits: A Selection*, trans. Alan Sheridan (New York: Norton, 1977).

19. The *OED* traces *character* back to two words, χαρακτήρ, meaning an instrument for marking or engraving, and χαράττ-ειν, meaning "to cut a furrow in" or "engrave."

20. The ideas in this paragraph and many of those in the remainder of the essay are taken from the writing of Jacques Derrida, especially *Writing and Difference*, trans. Alan Bass (Chicago: University of Chicago Press, 1978); "White Mythology: Metaphor in the Text of Philosophy," trans. F. C. T. Moore, *New Literary History* 6 (1974): 7–74; and "Living On: Border Lines," in *Deconstruction and Criticism* (New York: Seabury Press, 1979), pp. 75–176.

21. To explore the labyrinthine web constituting the scholarly edifice around *Lear* see Larry Champion's *"King Lear": An Annotated Bibliography*, 2 vols. (New York: Garland Publishing, 1980). For Barnet see "Some Limitations of a Christian Approach to Shakespeare," *ELH* 22 (1955): 81–92.

22. Bradley, *Shakespearean Tragedy*, pp. 285, 291, 324, 326–27. John Danby's argument is that the operative philosophy in *Lear* is Christian patience, not stoicism: see "King Lear and Christian Patience," *Cambridge Journal* 1 (1948): 305–20. Danby advances his Christian-redemptive reading in other places also: *Shakespeare's Doctrine of Nature* (London: Faber & Faber, 1949), and "The

Tragedies," in *The Living Shakespeare* (Greenwich, Conn.: Fawcett, 1960), pp. 120–33. L. C. Knights, *King Lear: Some Shakespeare Themes* (London: Chatto & Windus, 1959), pp. 74–109.

23. McFarland, "Image of the Family," pp. 91–118; Weiss, "As the Wind Sits," p. 85; Michael Goldman, *"King Lear*: Acting and Feeling," in *On "King Lear,"* p. 46.

24. Hardin Craig, "The Ethics of King Lear," *Philological Quarterly* 4 (1925): 97–109. In "The Great Trio: Hamlet, Othello, and King Lear," in *An Interpretation of Shakespeare* (New York: Dryden Press, 1948), pp. 178–219, Craig concludes that Lear is sane, wise, and "at peace with the world" (p. 215) when he dies. John Holloway, *The Story of the Night* (Lincoln: University of Nebraska Press, 1961), pp. 77–95.

25. Geoffrey L. Bickersteth, *The Golden World of King Lear*, Annual Shakespeare Lecture of the British Academy, 24 April 1946 (London, 1947), pp. 9, 26, 27; Bickersteth agrees with Chambers and Bradley, concluding that Cordelia's death causes Lear's heart to break "in an ecstasy of joy" because she no longer has to live.

26. Oscar J. Campbell, "The Salvation of King Lear," *ELH* 15 (1948): 93–109.

27. Robert B. Heilman, *This Great Stage* (Baton Rouge: Louisiana State University Press, 1948).

28. George I. Duthie, cited in Brooke, "Ending of *King Lear*," p. 74.

29. J. C. Maxwell, "The Technique of Invocation in *King Lear*," *Modern Language Review* 45 (1950): 142–47.

30. Whitaker, *Mirror up to Nature*, pp. 209–10.

31. Kirsch, *Shakespeare's Royal Self*, pp. 222, 293, 316.

32. Battenhouse, "King Lear," pp. 269–302, especially 301–2.

33. Algernon Charles Swinburne, *A Study of Shakespeare* (London, 1880), p. 172, cited in Myrick, "Christian Pessimism."

34. Hazelton Spencer, *The Art and Life of William Shakespeare* (New York: Harcourt Brace, 1940), pp. 324–33. Spencer is not so nihilistic as those who follow in this paragraph. He does, for example, see Lear dying in peace. Even so, he sees the play exploring the overwhelming forces of evil against which humans have no chance.

35. Prosser H. Frye, *Romance and Tragedy* (Boston, 1922), pp. 155 and 297.

36. Knight, *Wheel of Fire*, p. 168.

37. Muir, *Shakespeare's Tragic Sequence*, p. 141.

38. Harrison, *Shakespeare's Tragedies*, pp. 158–62.

39. Judah Stampfer, "The Catharsis of King Lear," *Shakespeare Survey* 13 (1960): 1–10.

40. Brooke, "Ending of *King Lear*," pp. 76–87.

41. Jan Kott, *Shakespeare Our Contemporary*, trans. Boleslaw Taborski (Garden City, N.Y.: Doubleday, 1964), pp. 87–105.

42. William R. Elton, *King Lear and the Gods* (San Marino, Calif.: Huntington Library, 1966), especially pp. 260–63.

43. Alvin B. Kernan, "King Lear and the Shakespearean Pageant of History," in *On "King Lear,"* pp. 7–24.

44. Compare chapters 8 and 9 in *The Wheel of Fire*; Barbara Everett, "The New *King Lear*," *Critical Quarterly* 2 (1960): 325–39; Mack, *"King Lear" in Our Time*, pp. 114–17; Snyder, *Comic Matrix*, especially pp. 179 and 161–68.

45. My ideas on case making and evidence are explained more fully by Stanley E. Fish, "Normal Circumstances . . . ," *Critical Inquiry* 4 (1978): 625–44.

46. The phrase is cited in J. Hillis Miller, "The Figure in the Carpet," *Poetics Today* 1 (1980): 107.

47. For ideal interpreters and the Schleiermacherian position upon which they are based see E. D. Hirsch, Jr., *Validity in Interpretation* (New Haven, Conn.: Yale University Press, 1967) and *The Aims of Interpretation* (Chicago: University of Chicago Press, 1976).

48. The *OED* traces *theme* back to the ancient Greek verb τιθέναι, meaning "to put," "set," "place," or "lay down."

49. P. W. K. Stone, in *The Textual History of "King Lear"* (London: Scolar Press, 1980), argues for the provenience of the quarto. For an introduction to the radical new idea that Shakespeare wrote two *Lears* see *The Division of the Kingdoms: Shakespeare's Two Versions of "King Lear,"* ed. Gary Taylor and Michael Warren (Oxford: Clarendon Press, 1983). The quotes are from pages 14 and 19 of Stanley Wells's Introduction to this collection of essays. I am deeply grateful to my colleague at Northern Illinois University, Professor William P. Williams, who introduced me to this book and told me about the revolution in textual studies of *Lear*.

50. One of the ideas that Derrida plays with most frequently is that of the margin of the text. Where does any text begin? With the first word? The title? The color and shape of the book? The location of the book? The idea of bookness? See *Dissemination*, trans. Barbara Johnson (Chicago: University of Chicago Press, 1981), pp. 1–59.

51. The ideas in this paragraph and the conception of this essay were suggested by Hillis Miller's "*Wuthering Heights* and the Ellipses of Interpretation," *Notre Dame English Journal* 12 (1980): 85–100.

52. This paragraph and many of my ideas about "reading" were suggested by Roland Barthes, *The Pleasure of the Text*, trans. Richard Miller (New York: Hill & Wang, 1975); and *S/Z*, trans. Richard Miller (New York: Hill & Wang, 1974).

53. Even this line carries another split—that between the Aristotelian, and therefore pagan, idea *ex nihilo nihil fit* and the orthodox Christian idea that God made creation from nothing.

54. For a different sort of reading of a letter/no letter see Barbara Johnson, "The Frame of Reference: Poe, Lacan, Derrida," *Yale French Studies* 55–56 (1977): 457–505.

55. Thomas McFarland gives a thorough explanation of how we cannot simply despise Edmund, Goneril, and Regan, pp. 97–106.

Contributors

NANCY R. COMLEY is associate professor of English and director of Freshman English at Queens College of the City University of New York. She is editor of the poetry section of *Elements of Literature* (Oxford University Press) and coauthor, with Robert Scholes, of *The Practice of Writing* (St. Martin's Press).

SHARON CROWLEY is associate professor of English at Northern Arizona University. She is the author of numerous articles on rhetorical theory and the teaching of composition and the editor of four volumes published by the National Council of Teachers of English, among them *The Teaching of Composition* and *English Teacher Preparation*.

ANDREW P. DEBICKI is University Distinguished Professor of Spanish and Portuguese at the University of Kansas. He is a winner of the Standard Oil Award for excellence in teaching. His most recent book is *Poetry of Discovery: The Spanish Generation of 1956–1971* (University Press of Kentucky).

GEOFFREY H. HARTMAN is Karl Young Professor of English and Comparative Literature at Yale University and also director of the School of Criticism and Theory. His most recent books are *Criticism in the Wilderness: The Study of Literature Today* (Yale University Press), *Saving the Text: Literature/Derrida/Philosophy* (Johns Hopkins University Press), and *Easy Pieces* (Columbia University Press).

BARBARA JOHNSON is professor of Romance Languages and Literatures at Harvard University. She is the translator of Jacques Derrida's *Dissemination* (University of Chicago Press), editor of *The Pedagogical Imperative: Teaching as a Literary Genre* (Yale University Press), and author of, among other books, *The Critical Difference: Essays in the Contemporary Rhetoric of Reading* (Johns Hopkins University Press).

DAVID KAUFER is associate professor of Rhetoric and English at Carnegie-Mellon University. He is the author of numerous articles on irony, argumentation, revision, composition theory, and computer-aided instruction.

VINCENT B. LEITCH is associate professor of English at Mercer University. Author of numerous scholarly articles, he has also written, among other books, *Deconstructive Criticism: An Advanced Introduction* (Columbia University Press).

J. HILLIS MILLER is Frederick W. Hilles Professor of English and Comparative Literature at Yale University. His most recent book is *Fiction and Repetition: Seven English Novels* (Harvard University Press). *The Linguistic Moment* is forthcoming from Princeton University Press. He will be president of the Modern Language Association in 1985/86.

JASPER NEEL is associate professor of English at Northern Illinois University. He was formerly chair of the Department of English at Francis Marion College, director of the Association of Departments of English, and editor of the *ADE Bulletin*. The author of numerous articles on composition theory and critical theory, he edited *Options for the Teaching of English: Freshman Composition* (National Council of Teachers of English).

PAUL NORTHAM is a graduate student in English at the University of Kansas and the recipient of a Graduate Honors Fellowship. His dissertation is to be entitled "The Narratological Imperative."

GAYATRI CHAKRAVORTY SPIVAK is professor of English at Emory University. She is the author of numerous articles on critical theory and is the editor and translator of Jacques Derrida's *Of Grammatology* (Johns Hopkins University Press).

GREGORY L. ULMER is associate professor of English at the University of Florida. He is the author of numerous articles on contemporary criticism and theory. *Applied Grammatology: Post(e)Pedagogy from Jacques Derrida to Joseph Beuys* has recently been published by Johns Hopkins University Press.

GARY WALLER is professor of Literary Studies and head of the Department of English at Carnegie-Mellon University. He is the author of numerous articles on Shakespeare, Renaissance poetry, and contemporary fiction.

G. DOUGLAS ATKINS is professor of English at the University of Kansas. A former fellow of the School of Criticism and Theory, he is the author of *The Faith of John Dryden* (University Press of Kentucky) and *Reading Deconstruction/Deconstructive Reading* (University Press of Kentucky), as well as numerous articles on eighteenth-century English literature and contemporary criticism.

MICHAEL L. JOHNSON is professor of English and chair of the Department of English at the University of Kansas, where he was formerly director of Freshman-Sophomore English. He is the author of *The New Journalism* (University Press of Kansas), numerous scholarly and critical articles, and several books of poetry and poetic translations.

Index

209